THE REAL FOUNDATIONS
Literature and Social Change

By the same Author

*

SCOTTISH LITERATURE AND
THE SCOTTISH PEOPLE
1680-1830

The
Real Foundations

LITERATURE AND SOCIAL CHANGE

By

DAVID CRAIG

1973

CHATTO & WINDUS

LONDON

Published by
Chatto & Windus Ltd
42 William IV Street
London W.C.2

*

Clarke, Irwin and Co. Ltd
Toronto

ISBN 0 7011 1981 0

© David Craig 1973

Printed in Great Britain by
T. & A. Constable Ltd
Edinburgh

For
Bill, Colin, Keith, Max, Mike, and Nigel
colleagues and comrades

Acknowledgements

I make the usual acknowledgements to the editors and publishers of the following books and periodicals in which some of the following chapters first appeared in a different form:—Arnold Kettle (Ed.), *Shakespeare in a Changing World* (Lawrence & Wishart); *Marxism Today*; *Essays in Criticism*; *The Critical Quarterly*; *New Left Review*; K. D. Duval (Ed.), *MacDiarmid. A Festschrift* (Duval, Edinburgh); and *Continuum* (Lancaster).

Acknowledgements are made for permission to quote as follows:
Extract from *Waiting for Godot* by permission of Faber & Faber and Grove Press, Inc., Copyright © 1954 by Grove Press.
Extracts from the poetry of T. S. Eliot are from his volume *Collected Poems 1909-1962* by permission of Faber & Faber and Harcourt Brace Jovanovich, Inc.; Copyright © 1963, 1964, by T. S. Eliot.
Extracts from *Collected Poems* of Hugh MacDiarmid, © Christopher Murray Grieve, 1948, 1962, by permission of Macmillan Publishing Co., Inc.
Extract from *Absolute Beginners* by Colin MacInnes, by permission of MacGibbon & Kee.

Upon the different forms of property, upon the social conditions of existence, rises an entire superstructure of distinct and peculiarly formed sentiments, illusions, modes of thought and views of life. The entire class creates and forms them out of its material foundations and out of the corresponding social relations. The single individual, who derives them through tradition and upbringing, may imagine that they form the real motives and the starting point of his activity. . . . And as in private life one differentiates between what a man thinks and says of himself and what he really is and does, so in historical struggles one must distinguish still more the phrases and fancies of parties from their real organism and their real interests, their conception of themselves from their reality.

KARL MARX (1852)
The Eighteenth Brumaire of Louis Bonaparte

. . . if research requires a division of forces, a humane education requires a synthesis, however provisional, of the results of their labours, and to encourage us, by seeing these results, not as isolated fragments, but as connected parts of a body of living tissue, to acquire a more synoptic and realistic view of the activities composing the life of society. The subject, as I interpret it, is concerned not merely or mainly with the iridescent surface of manners, fashions, social conventions and intercourse, but with the unseen foundations, which, till they shift or crumble, most men in most generations are wont to take for granted.

R. H. TAWNEY (1958)
'Social History and Literature'

Stupid people often accuse marxists of welcoming the intrusion of politics into art. On the contrary, we protest against the intrusion. The intrusion is most marked in times of crisis and great suffering. But it is pointless to deny such times. They must be understood so that they can be ended: art and men will then be freer. Such a time began in Europe in 1914 and continues still.

JOHN BERGER (1965)
The Success and Failure of Picasso

7

Contents

9

Introduction

I N arranging these studies of particular matters as a book, and in rewriting them so as to bring out the causal and other links between their themes, no sequence other than a historical one, by dates, even occurred to me. I cannot but think of each piece of literature (or each person, or house, or idea or institution or habit, or tree or cloud) as being what it is by reason of the particular place and time at which it grows into existence and has its day. Of course everything embodies elements of earlier existences, whether received genetically or by social evolution. But this reinforces the prime truth that to be alive is to be embroiled in an unending continuum of cause and effect whose special pressure on the artist is to situate him in the life of his species and so to reduce greatly the extent to which he can create at his own sweet will. Sartre puts this memorably in his pages on what it felt like to awaken into history during the Thirties:

> Each day we had lived revealed its true face; we had abandoned ourselves to it trustingly and it was leading us to a new war with secret rapidity, with a rigour hidden beneath its nonchalant airs. And our life as an individual which had seemed to depend upon our efforts, our virtues, and our faults, on our good and bad luck, on the good and bad will of a very small number of people, seemed governed down to its minutest details by obscure and collective forces, and its most private circumstances seemed to reflect the state of the whole world. All at once we felt ourselves abruptly *situated*.[1]

The writer comes to consciousness amidst particular conditions that include the things that the people of his age tend to do, the most powerful forces then felt to be acting in and on humanity, and the sorts of function his art has at that time. Living amongst all this, how could the writer, except by the most willed and improbable jump, shrug off his age and fail to make its particular scenes and

[1] *What is Literature?*, trans. Bernard Frechtman (1967 ed.), 157.

concerns the dominant ones in his art? If this seems unexceptionable and obvious, or if my air of rebuttal looks gratuitous, the reader should turn to the book that follows, especially chapter 8, where I cite examples of how common it is to try and magic away the links and overlaps between literature and history.

The dream of transcending the historical life around and in us may matter very much, may seem real, to a community or a person, he may ache to throw himself up and out of mundane life with its stresses, shortcomings, and humiliations. The danger for the artist is that in trying to stretch beyond experience he narrows his access to it. In 'closing his eyes on the world's evidence' (a phrase of Ted Hughes's) he drains his art of actual stuff. This shows in the careers of two great poets, Wordsworth and Eliot. They can still write remarkably at the moment of striving to transcend, in *The Prelude* and 'Ash Wednesday'. But the more they turn to God, the Church, the after-life, the more they lose the tang and activity of real experience, they begin to plod, to force their rhythms, while leaning heavily on phrasing that draws its charge from contexts outside the poetry. This is obviously a debatable judgement, and in being so it shows that to see literature as part of history is no less a literary-critical act than the kind of analysis and evaluation of literature as a work of art which is what most critics do.

By 'to see literature as part of history' I don't mean the paraphrasing of philosophies contemporary with such-and-such a writer in the name of studying his 'world-picture', or the writing of vignettes on 'Dickens's London' or 'the England of Jane Austen', which are the commoner ways of placing a work in its setting. The nature of the best literature doesn't lead me to think that formal philosophy is likely to be the next most important thing to a writer after his own experiences, and by the same token the literature whose philosophical counterpart can readily be named is not usually the best. If there are some rather obvious thoughts about Life in Pope's 'Essay on Man', it does little either for our thinking or our taste in poetry to trace the originals in Bolingbroke's pat and abstract philosophisings. So with the 'social background'–this metaphor, which is the bane of historical writing about literature, suggests a flat backdrop in front of which artists perform and not a complex organism in the midst of which they and their media have their being.

'Complex organism', 'unending continuum of cause and effect', and the like remain mere phrases until they have taken on meaning in the course of exploring whatever historical conditions turn out to be necessary to understand as fully as one can this novel or that poem. It is the particular critiques that follow, and not these simple opening remarks, that I look to for whatever convincing or persuasive effect this book may have. What I hope I am moving towards and readying myself to write, or help to write, is a social history of literature from the Renaissance to the present. It should be none the less scrupulous and sensitive in its analyses for being boldly explanatory in a historical way and none the less clear in its mapping of the contours of that history for being attentive to the special qualities of individual works and writers. The consciously historicist[1] approach to literature is still in its infancy, and critics still tend to work solo rather than in a team of like-minded intellectual workers. This being so, it isn't yet possible to organise into a comprehensive theory and method the principles on which the history of literature could be written or to apply them in a large-scale and sequential way. I also know from my experience that it is hard to move between literature and history, in one's teaching and thinking, without running foul of entrenched academic suspicions, misunderstandings, and *parti pris*. Yet are historians and critics not busy in different ways at one task—the clarifying and interpreting of recorded human experience, in the spirit of Isaac Babel's slogan, 'You must know everything'?

If, then, we are concerned to know what people have made of their situation, social history can give us the situation and 'straight' literary criticism can give us (an aspect of) what they have made of it. The aim of the approach attempted in this book is to treat them together, as they naturally are.

Lancaster, August 1972

---

[1] I use this word, in spite of Popper's efforts to discredit it, because there seems to be no other that epitomises the inseparably close union of historical and literary studies that I aim at. I do believe that we can 'discover the "rhythms" ... or the "trends" that underlie the evolution of history', but I do not believe we can use them, in the social sciences, for exact 'historical prediction'. My historicism, therefore, is what Popper calls an 'interpretation' and is not what he calls a 'theory'. (Karl R. Popper, *The Poverty of Historicism*, 1961 ed., 3, 150-1)

Section One

LOVE AND SOCIETY

CHAPTER 1

Shakespeare, Lawrence, and Sexual Freedom

CULTURAL change is bound to act upon our more intimate as well as our more social selves, yet the deeper the experience the more rooted it must be in the scarcely (or very slowly) changing human organism. Presumably, therefore, the view we take of our passions changes more in the course of history than do the passions themselves, and one of the richest cases of this that we have in the literary record is the likeness between Shakespeare's *Measure for Measure* and many a tale of D. H. Lawrence's. The play approaches its theme-problems in so free and open a spirit that I find I need make little adjustment in passing from it to such major short fictions of Lawrence's as 'Daughters of the Vicar', 'The Virgin and the Gypsy', 'The Captain's Doll', and 'St Mawr'. All five are broadly alike in that they analyse, by dramatic means, values that reach to the core of our living—love and fulfilment, integrity, personal freedom. They do so with a piercing or cleansing effect that comes from their remarkable avoidance of the loose ardour, uplift, overt sermonising, or moral prompting that are the likely failings of such work. Both writers are masters at affirming 'humanity' and at sensing, and rising triumphant over, whatever is 'anti-life'. 'Humanity' and 'life', however, are by themselves so abstract—so prone to do little more than boost or dignify the particular view-point of whoever uses them—that it is best to consider right away the specific likenesses between that group of works.

The gap bound to exist between writers widely separated in time is remarkably narrow in this case because Shakespeare is here concerned so much with core-values, so little with surface manners. The hero, Claudio, though nominally a gentleman of Vienna, has few particular traits or turns of phrase to mark him as such—little of the courtliness that appears as burlesque in Sir Andrew Aguecheek and seriously in those superb compliments paid to Perdita by Florizel in *A Winter's Tale*. Claudio is sheerly human, above all in

17

his speech affirming life itself that opens, 'Ay, but to die, and go we know not where'. It might be said that the tragedies are no less concerned with such core-values as love and integrity. But the tragic method is to expose humanity to the most extraordinary and terrifying forces conceivable, whereas *Measure for Measure* is like the best modern fiction in dealing directly with the kind of experience that comes to us all, exceptional or not, and with the sort of integration we must bring to personal living if we are to live it through happily.

The very personal nature of the play starts from its subject – the young man who has committed the crime and sin of having intercourse with his loved one before they are married, the temptation to similar behaviour on the part of the governor who sits in judgement over them. The treatment this subject demanded, the sort of truth to intimate experience, comes out in the many likenesses (unique for a supreme Shakespeare play) to his own most personal work, the sonnets. When Claudio says, in helpless disgust at his own fall –

> So every scope by the immoderate use
> Turns to restraint. Our natures do pursue,
> Like rats that ravin down their proper bane,
> A thirsty evil; and when we drink, we die   (I.2.121-4)

– he is not far from the more extreme state of mind presented in the sonnet on lust (No. 129) –

> Enjoyed no sooner but despised straight;
> Past reason hunted, and no sooner had,
> Past reason hated, as a swallowed bait,
> On purpose laid to make the taker mad.

The Duke's lofty pretended tribute to Angelo –

> O, your desert speaks loud; and I should wrong it
> To lock it in the wards of covert bosom,
> When it deserves, with characters of brass,
> A forted residence 'gainst the tooth of time
> And razure of oblivion   (V.1.9-13)

– echoes thoughts and images common in the sonnets, especially the middle group on time and transience: 'brass eternal slave to mortal rage', 'brass, nor stone, nor earth, nor boundless sea/But sad mortality o'ersways their power' (Nos. 64, 65). Indeed, the consonance between the sonnets and the play is such that No. 94

almost attaches itself to the play as a condensed characterisation of
the Angelo type–the man who tries to be right by keeping himself
rigidly intact from experience. As the sonnet puts it–

> They that have power to hurt and will do none,
> That do not do the thing they most do show,
> Who, moving others, are themselves as stone,
> Unmoved, cold, and to temptation slow–
> They rightly do inherit heaven's graces,
> And husband nature's riches from expense. . . .

The profound ironies to which the poem then moves are precisely
those dramatised in *Measure for Measure*. The imagery the poet needs
is close to what is regularly used by other characters about Angelo–

> Lord Angelo is precise;
> Stands at a guard with envy; scarce confesses
> That his blood flows, or that his appetite
> Is more to bread than stone. . . .   (I.3.50-3)
>
> . . . he, a marble to her tears, is washed with them,
> but relents not. . . .   (III.2.238)

The quite strong likelihood of a seventeenth-century date for the
later and more subtle sonnets[1] makes it possible that these poems
belong to the same point in the growth of Shakespeare's interests
as does the play, which was probably first produced at Christmas,
1604.

This Angelo imagery leads us to the heart of the play and also of
its kinship with the Lawrence tales. The freedom Claudio has
enjoyed with the girl he is engaged to, Juliet, is by no means
approved by the dramatist in the spirit we now call permissive. Yet
Claudio, who has followed his impulse, is made to confront Angelo,
who tries to guard against just that, as a champion of life against
whatever thwarts or deadens it. The speech in which Claudio over-
flows into his affirmation of life must be quoted in full, for there are
few passages in English that express with such deep-reaching power
what it is to be a human being alive in the world. Claudio is meant
to be pleading with his sister not to value her own chastity above
his life, but the speech is not an argument: it bursts out of him,
without logical calculation, as an expression of that sheer cleaving
to bodily breathing consciousness without which we could not go
on living:

---

[1] The arguments for and against this dating are reviewed by Ivor Brown in
his Introduction to the Nonesuch *Complete Works of Shakespeare* (1953), I, xxvi.

CLAUDIO: Death is a fearful thing.
ISABELLA: And shamed life a hateful.
CLAUDIO: Ay, but to die, and go we know not where;
          To lie in cold obstruction, and to rot;
          This sensible warm motion to become
          A kneaded clod; and the delighted spirit
          To bathe in fiery floods or to reside
          In thrilling regions of thick-ribbed ice;
          To be imprisoned in the viewless winds,
          And blown with restless violence round about
          The pendent world; or to be worse than worst
          Of those that lawless and incertain thought
          Imagine howling—'tis too horrible.
          The weariest and most loathed worldly life
          That age, ache, penury, and imprisonment
          Can lay on nature is a paradise
          To what we fear of death.   (III.1.117-33)

One would not have believed that things literally beyond experiencing could have been imagined with this physical intensity that strikes right home to our senses.[1] The meaning that arises from the scene is not that Claudio is 'right' in what he has done. It is that, as his imagery shows, he is, in his own being—in the way he takes life and can express its essence—the antithesis of Angelo with his deathly wish to ignore and repress real impulses.

Before we consider how this conflict is resolved inside the quite strict morality of the play, some of the likenesses to Lawrence should be pointed out. He too is intent on showing what makes for fullness of experience and what ties it down to a narrow, deadening habit by contrasting pairs of people through the imagery that establishes the opposed types. In 'Daughters of the Vicar' there are the two girls, one of whom acts, thinks, and marries as is expected of someone 'in her position', the other of whom breaks passionately out of the Victorian class taboos. Mary with her 'white brow and grey eyes' contrasts in every way with Louisa, 'short and plump and rather flushed'. Mary accepts the curate, Massey, who 'lacked the full range of human feelings, but had rather a strong, philosophical mind, from which he lived. . . . There was no spontaneous exclamation, no violent assertion or expression of personal conviction, but all cold, reasonable assertion.' 'Cold' is the Angelo

---

[1] The only remotely comparable thing I know of is Tolstoy's tale 'The Death of Iván Ilých'—the dying man's sense of being thrust into a black sack.

word, 'warmth' is Claudio's; and Louisa is attracted by the young miner Alfred – 'she wanted to see his face more distinctly in her mind, ruddy with the sun' (he has been in the Navy), 'his golden-brown eyes, kind and careless, strained now with a natural fear' (at his mother's illness), 'the fine nose tanned hard by the sun, the mouth that could not help smiling at her.'[1] The perfectly lifelike fullness of the description at every point rules out any lapse into too glib or foregone a contrast, yet we cannot mistake the clear opposition between the lifeful and the deathly – the curate so worried about his child's health that he cannot relax into his fatherhood, the vicar's family virtually disowning the young couple who have followed their impulse across the class barrier.

This basic polarity figures in Lawrence's fiction again and again; with the fertility of genius he is able to show us under the aspect of the large guiding idea the utmost variety of particular situations. In *The Rainbow* the idea is vested in the couple Skrebensky and Ursula, the girl warm-hearted, outspoken, the man a cavalry officer in the heyday of imperialism and the invasion of Africa, so rigid in his adherence to the military code ('"It's about the most serious business there is, fighting. . . . It matters whether we settle the Mahdi or not"') that Ursula comes up against him on every essential issue until their very love-making, to which finally they have to will themselves, reaches a dead-end, expressed in images of hardness and sterility that recall the Angelo language: 'She was puzzled, hurt by some hopeless fixity in him, that terrified her with a cold feeling of despair. . . . He felt as if the knife were being pushed into his already dead body. With head strained back, he watched, drawn tense, for some minutes, watched the unaltering, rigid face like metal in the moonlight, the fixed, unseeing eyes . . . all within her was cold, dead, inert. Skrebensky appeared at breakfast. He was white and obliterated.'[2]

In 'The Virgin and the Gypsy' a like polarity is created, through imagery still closer to Shakespeare's poetry. The urbane rector, deserted by his wife for Another Man, defends his pride by shutting his imagination against this woman who must still exist somewhere. He takes refuge in an idealised image of the pure young bride that by itself suggests the shrinking from experience that will have dissatisfied her in him:

[1] *The Tales of D. H. Lawrence* (1948 ed.), 53, 55, 59-60.
[2] *The Rainbow* (1949 ed.), 313-4, 448, 486-7.

For in the pure loftiness of the rector's heart still bloomed the pure white snow-flower of his young bride. This white snow-flower did not wither. That other creature, who had gone off with that despicable young man, was none of his affair. . . . Yes, the white snow-flower was forgiven. He even had made provision in his will for her, when that other scoundrel–but hush! Don't even *think* too near to that horrid nettle in the rank outer world! She-who-was-Cynthia. Let the white snow-flower bloom inaccessible on the heights of the past. The present is another story.[1]

The imagery here–and the passage is virtually poetic–is from the vein repeatedly drawn on to characterise Angelo–

> A man whose blood
> Is very snow-broth   (I.4.57-8)

–or as the gossip of the town puts it:

> Some report a sea-maid spawned him; some, that he was begot between two stock-fishes. But it is certain that when he makes water his urine is congealed ice; that I know to be true. . . .
> (III.2.100-3)

This is also the vein of imagery that Lawrence uses in 'The Captain's Doll' when he wants to suggest by contrast the inner vitality of the seemingly indifferent Captain Hepburn. Hepburn, in Austria just after the Great War, is contemptuous of the nostalgic escapism (as he sees it) that makes a cult of bare mountains. His trip to the glacier with Hannele, the woman he will marry, shows how he turns towards whatever makes for relationship and humanity. Reacting against the ardently open-air young people whose cult of the physical helped pave the way for the triumph of Nazi racism, he says to Hannele: ' "Their loftiness and their uplift. I hate their uplift. I hate people prancing on mountain-tops and feeling exalted. I'd like to make them all stop up there, on their mountain-tops, and chew ice to fill their stomachs." ' And on the glacier itself–among veritable 'snow-flowers'–we arrive at metaphors that directly recall the ones Claudio uses to figure his sense of the deathly nothingness beyond the grave, the 'thrilling regions of thick-ribbed ice'. So Hepburn glimpses and gladly turns his back on

> A world, a terrible place of hills and valleys and slopes, all motionless, all of ice. Away above the grey mist-cloud was

[1] *Tales*, 1026-7.

looming bigger. And near at hand were long huge cracks, side by side, like gills in the ice. It would seem as if the ice breathed through these great ridged gills. One could look down into the series of gulfs, fearful depths, and the colour burning that acid, intense blue, intenser as the crack went deeper. And the crests of the open gills ridged and grouped pale blue above the crevices. It seemed as if the ice breathed there.

The wonder, the terror, and the bitterness of it. Never a warm leaf to unfold, never a gesture of life to give off. A world sufficient unto itself in lifelessness, all this ice.[1]

It is 'The Virgin and the Gypsy' that shows most fully the Shakespearean quality of Lawrence's treatment of love and freedom, or the Lawrencian quality of Shakespeare's. When we read in the tale that the rector's ex-wife had been, as a mother, 'glamorous but not very dependable . . . a great glow, a flow of life, like a swift and dangerous sun in the home, forever coming and going' and that the rector's falsely hallowing memory of her 'like a porcelain wreath, froze on its grave', we are reminded—obliquely but distinctly—of the image that closes Shakespeare's 'Angelo' sonnet: it gives us another, related way of regarding the unnatural stagnancy that comes of repression—

> For sweetest things turn sourest by their deeds,
> Lilies that fester smell far worse than weeds.

Compare Lawrence's image for the obsessive suspicions that the rector and his doting mother project onto his former wife: 'out of the squalid world sometimes would come a rank, evil smell of selfishness and degraded lust, the smell of the awful nettle, She-who-was-Cynthia.' This readiness to scent depravity, the potential of hidden nastiness that it implies, comes out in the drama of the tale when Yvette is challenged by her father over her friendship with the 'immoral' Eastwoods—the Major living with a married woman until her divorce comes through and they can marry:

> When his conservatism and his abject sort of fear were uppermost, he always lifted his lip and bared his teeth a little, in a dog-like sneer.
> 'I hear your latest friends are the half-divorced Mrs Fawcett and the *maquereau* Eastwood,' he said to Yvette.
> She didn't know what a *maquereau* was, but she felt the poison in the rector's fangs.

[1] *Tales*, 540, 545-6.

'I just know them,' she said. 'They're awfully nice, really. And they'll be married in about a month's time.'

 ... He looked at her in hate, as if he could kill her. And he backed away from her, against the window-curtains of his study, like a rat at bay. Somewhere in his mind he was thinking unspeakable depravities about his daughter, as he had thought them of She-who-was-Cynthia. He was powerless against the lowest insinuations of his own mind.[1]

Angelo enjoys an absolute power not possessed by the Rector, and will use it to the limit of blackmail, seduction, and execution. But there is little to choose between their inner selves. In *Measure for Measure*, too, the man is surprised and undermined by his own impulses (after his first interview with Isabella, come to plead for her brother's life):

> What's this, what's this? Is this her fault or mine?
> The tempter or the tempted, who sins most? Ha,
> Not she; nor doth she tempt; but it is I
> That, lying by the violet in the sun,
> Do as the carrion does, not as the flower,
> Corrupt with virtuous season. . . .
>   Oh fie, fie, fie!
> What dost thou, or what art thou, Angelo? (II.2.162-73)

And a little later, on the verge of the second interview:

>   . . . Oh heavens!
> Why does my blood thus muster to my heart,
> Making both it unable for itself
> And dispossessing all my other parts
> Of necessary fitness?   (II.4.19-23)

The Rector and Angelo do not know themselves.[2] There is a gross discrepancy between their 'perfect' public fronts and the inner suggestibility by the repression of which their dignified fronts (the law, the Church) have been maintained. These two master writers are supreme in their ability to trace their way through this swarm of impulses that goes to make us what we are, and it is this that

---

[1] *ibid.*, 1079-80.

[2] 'Knowing oneself'—an essential theme of the play. In one of her strongest appeals to Angelo, Isabella speaks of
>   . . . man, proud man,
> Dressed in a little brief authority,
> Most ignorant of what he's most assured,
> His glassy essence. . . .   (II.2.117-20)

and Escalus' highest praise for the duke is that he was 'One, that above all other strifes contended especially to know himself.' (III.2.219)

gives the depth to their analyses of the more public values such as justice, righteousness, discipline, authority.

So far the discussion may have suggested a simple opposition, in the play and the tales, between the 'artificial' surface of social living and the real life of personal feelings; or a too-easy satirical viewpoint that works by suggesting that principles and public attitudes are mere shams that crumble at the test. This would have been so if Shakespeare had set Claudio free without any ordeal of judgement and imminent execution or if Lawrence had made Yvette take the 'easy' road into a fool's paradise of 'free love' with the gypsy. In fact there is no primitivist or anarchic opposition, in these works, between control and freedom. In both, pure freedom is radically tested. Lucio the womaniser asks Claudio when he is in jail:

LUCIO: Why, how now, Claudio, whence comes this restraint?
CLAUDIO: From too much liberty, my Lucio, liberty;
          As surfeit is the father of much fast,
          So every scope by the immoderate use
          Turns to restraint.   (I.2.118-22)

The reader of Lawrence is at once reminded of the opening of 'St Mawr': 'Lou Witt had had her own way so long, that by the age of twenty-five she didn't know where she was. Having one's own way landed one completely at sea.' The same idea–a basic one of Lawrence's–is used in 'The Virgin and the Gypsy' to define the rather aimless pleasure-seeking in which Yvette and her sister have virtually been encouraged by the Rector's falsely easy-going, would-be man-of-the-world broadmindedness. The girls and their friends are Bright Young Things of the Twenties: 'they had nothing really to rebel against, any of them. They were left so very free in their movements. Their parents let them do entirely as they liked. . . . The keys of their lives were in their own hands. And there they dangled inert.'[1]

Some such critique of 'pure freedom' is, I should say, indispensable for an understanding of man in society. As Maxim Gorky once put it: 'I'm against freedom beyond that line at which freedom becomes abandon, and this conversion is known to begin where man, no longer aware of his actual social-cultural value, gives free rein to the ancient Philistine individualism concealed in him' (the

[1] *Tales*, 556, 1037.

Rector's 'conservative anarchism') 'and cries out, "I'm so charming, original, unique, but I am not allowed to live as I please."'[1] What is so difficult is the drawing of the line in the right place. This is a problem of government (including self-government) in any community, and particularly in the Vienna of *Measure for Measure*. The play, it has been said, 'analyses the inherent difficulty of practical government to a sensitive mind'. This critic, Wilson Knight, goes on to argue that the play unfolds a 'deeply Shakespearean sexual ethic, close alike to Gospel teaching and modern psychology . . . pharisaic righteousness is shown as superficial and natural instinct treated with sympathy.'[2] How are Christian teaching and modern psychology unified in the play? It is Isabella who has the agonising dilemma of trying for such a reconciliation. Shall she, a virgin, about to take the nun's vow of chastity, give herself sexually to Angelo to win a reprieve for her brother who has behaved unchastely with his betrothed? The question for the modern person is: does Shakespeare *approve* of Isabella's fiercely uncompromising chastity?

In one of the best-known studies of the play the Christian answer to this problem is pushed as far as it could well go, and perhaps further: 'Isabel decides without hesitation [not to defile herself to save Claudio]. Now whatever we think of that instant decision, it is certainly not un-Christian. Christianity could never have lived through its first three hundred years of persecution, if its ranks had not been stiffened by men and women who never hesitated in the choice between righteousness and the ties to their kinsfolk.'[3] All that remains to do is to equate this with 'modern psychology'. The most modern psychologists I know of who have discussed this matter are G. M. Carstairs (the professor of Mental Health in the University of Edinburgh), in his 1962 Reith Lectures, and some members of the committee who recently published *Towards a Quaker View of Sex*. In his third lecture Carstairs suggested that the old, Pauline notion of chastity appeared to have been left behind by young people, more and more of whom have intercourse before marriage and don't mind if their eventual marriage partners

---

[1] Quoted by L. F. Ilyichov at a meeting between Party & Government Leaders and Writers & Artists in Moscow, December 17 1962: see Supplement to *Soviet Literature* (Moscow), 1963, No. 2, 12.

[2] G. Wilson Knight, 'The Shakespearean Integrity', in *Shakespeare Criticism, 1935-1960*, ed. Anne Ridler (1963), 187.

[3] R. W. Chambers, *'Measure for Measure'*, in Ridler, 9.

have done so too: 'It seems to me that our young people are rapidly turning our own society [like the Trobriand, the Samoan, etc] into one in which sexual experience, with precautions against conception, is becoming accepted as a sensible preliminary to marriage; a preliminary which makes it more likely that marriage, when it comes, will be a mutually considerate and mutually satisfying partnership.'[1] The Christian ministers who commented on this were opposed, in a proportion of two to one, to Carstairs's permissive ideas, and so were the responsible Church bodies, for example the Temperance and Morals Committee of the Church of Scotland. The present-day Christian view appears to be (in the words of the Moderator of the Scottish Church's General Assembly) that 'the Christian emphasis on chastity is absolutely essential.'[2]

Here something of the distance inevitable between seventeenth and twentieth century outlooks begins to appear. For I think it is true, as is said in the best study of the play, that 'A Claudio who took an advanced twentieth-century line in these matters might have made a more "interesting" "character"; but such an emancipated Claudio was no part of Shakespeare's conception of his theme. Nor . . . are there any grounds for supposing that Shakespeare himself tended to feel that the prescription of premarital chastity might well be dispensed with.'[3] This is useful because it makes clear the definite view of conduct that the play presents. But the hint of a sneer in 'advanced' and 'emancipated' is not acceptable. For Shakespeare achieves that necessary, and difficult, compromise between principle and our natural behaviour by showing how chastity can be maintained only *at a cost*. In that second interview with Angelo, Isabella says, in one of her most vehement protestations:

> . . . were I under the terms of death,
> The impression of keen whips I'd wear as rubies,
> And strip myself to death as to a bed
> That longing have been sick for, ere I'd yield
> My body up to shame. (II.4.100-4)

The impression this makes is erotic—this sense cannot be shaken off. And the effect is to move Isabella a little nearer to Angelo as one

---

[1] *The Listener*, November 29 1962, 892-3; cf. *Towards a Quaker View of Sex* (1963) 6, 15, 17-18.

[2] *The Observer*, December 9 1962; *The Scotsman*, December 24, 1962.

[3] F. R. Leavis, 'The Greatness of *Measure for Measure*, in *The Common Pursuit* (1952), 162.

of those whose rigorous principles serve, unconsciously, as a defence against the unacknowledged strength of their own passions. As Carstairs puts it in his lecture, 'It has always been those whose sexual impulses have been precariously repressed who have raised the loudest cries of alarm over other people's immorality.' In Isabella's speech, it seems, some unfulfilled sensuality is seizing the chance offered by the threat of violation to flow out and satisfy itself by imaginary indulgence in the pangs of martyrdom.

The Christian critic handles this issue by a simple appeal to history:

> We may call this fanaticism: but it was well understood in Shakespeare's day. Foxe's *Martyrs* was read by all; old people could still remember seeing the Smithfield fires; year after year saw the martyrdoms of Catholic men (and sometimes of Catholic women like the Ven. Margaret Clitherow). It was a stern age—an age such as the founder of Christianity had foreseen when he uttered his stern warnings. . . . 'If any man come to me, and hate not his father, and mother, and brethren and sisters, he cannot be my disciple.'

Merely to state facts from history surely evades just those issues of real impulse, real moral dilemma, that *Measure for Measure* was framed to explore. Martyrdom will have been familiar to Shakespeare's fellow-citizens, yes, but why are we to conclude from this that Shakespeare will have uncritically taken over the familiar unthinking and accepting attitudes to it? The Christian critic has to comment that 'For all her silence and modesty, Isabel has the *ferocity* of the martyr.'[1] (my italics). No analyst of human experience as deep as we have seen Shakespeare to be could have missed the peculiar strain or flaw of integration expressed in such a tension between submissiveness and ferocity. It is this sort of tension that the old master writers could show by sheer insight and the modern psychologist has been able to explain, by his theories and findings on how we develop and maintain our selves.

Beside such insights a literal adherence to Church tenets appears naive. It is as naive to argue that Claudio is subdued into accepting death by the sheer goodness and rightness of Isabella's Christian arguments. 'We find,' says Chambers, 'that Claudio, who before Isabel's outburst'–'Wilt thou be made a man out of my vice'–'had been gripped by the mortal fear of death, is now again master of his soul:

[1] Chambers, *op. cit.*, 9, 15.

> Let me ask my sister pardon. I am so out of love with life that
> I will sue to be rid of it.'

In fact Claudio's turn into submission follows, not on this, but on
the disguised Duke's pretence that Angelo had only been testing
Isabella's virtue: Claudio must die anyway, according to the
original sentence. It is crucial for the whole drift of the play to see
that it is this, not Isabella's appeal, that has made Claudio submit,
for this is the scene (III.1) in which the great speech for life is
uttered. *After* this speech comes Isabella's outburst:

> Is't not a kind of incest to take life
> From thine own sister's shame? What should I think?
> Heaven shield my mother played my father fair!
> For such a warped slip of wilderness
> Ne'er issued from his blood.

Even after all this Claudio still reacts by broken-off, agonised
pleading: 'Nay, hear me, Isabel. . . . Oh hear me, Isabella. . . .'
The force of living impulse in him is not, and could not be, damped
down by his sister's invoking of sacred chastity. If it had been, the
play would have been a far less vital thing than it is, for that speech
of Claudio's, clinging to the 'warm motion' of the 'delighted spirit',
is one of the play's deep centres, and to suppose it negated or out-
weighed by lofty 'principles' would be to suppose Shakespeare
setting his face against what we must call *life*.

Lawrence's criticism of the Isabella type is much more drastic
than Shakespeare's—he is that much further from the old moral
authority of the Church. The authors of *Towards a Quaker View of
Sex* quote and approve a suggestion of John MacMurray's that
nowadays we must think of 'chastity' not as abstinence but as
'emotional sincerity'.[1] This idea is Lawrencian: it might almost
have come from, say, the passage on what a critic must be from his
essay on Galsworthy: 'A critic must be emotionally alive in every
fibre, intellectually capable and skilful in essential logic, and then
morally very honest.'[2] As one who led the revolt against the long
Victorian regime of strict taboo on the discussion of intimate
experience, Lawrence was bitterly against the cults of innocence,
'purity', and self-sacrifice at the expense of passional fulfilment.
His attitude to love outside marriage is given in the terse,

---

[1] *Op. cit.*, 47 (the phrase is from MacMurray's *Reason and Emotion*).
[2] 'John Galsworthy', in *Phoenix*, ed. Edward D. MacDonald (1936), 539.

unanswerable comment on the adultery in *Anna Karénina*: 'Nobody in the world is anything but delighted when Vronsky gets Anna Karénina.'[1]

This insistence on passional realities belongs closely with Lawrence's many criticisms of the 'purity' that the so-spiritual Victorian ethos had exalted: together, these two ideas form one of his main touchstones for genuineness in literature. In that same essay, for example, he says of Tolstoy's *Resurrection* (and it is also true, implicitly, of much other nineteenth-century fiction), 'The convict train is quick and alive. But that would-be-expiatory Prince is as dead as lumber.' The following passage, inspired by Hawthorne's *Scarlet Letter*, could almost be a gloss on *Measure for Measure* (as well as on his own tales):

> Oh, Hester, you are a demon. A man *must* be pure, just that you can seduce him to a fall.
> His [Arthur Dimmesdale's] spiritual love was a lie. And prostituting the woman to his spiritual love, as popular clergymen do, in his preachings and loftiness, was a tall white lie. Which came flop.
> We are so pure in spirit. Hi-tiddly-i-ty!
> Till she tickled him in the right place, and he fell.
> Flop.
> Flop goes spiritual love.
> But keep up the game. Keep up appearances. Pure are the pure. To the pure all things, etc.

In *The Scarlet Letter*, Dimmesdale, who has 'fallen'—who has made love, does what Isabella's words only hint at: he flogs himself, punishing himself for his fleshly love for Hester Prynne:

> Previously, he had governed his body, ruling it, in the interests of his spirit. Now he has a good time all by himself torturing his body. . . . He wants to get a mental grip on his body. And since he can't quite manage it with the mind, witness his fall—he will give it what for, with whips. His will shall *lash* his body. And he enjoys his pains. Wallows in them. To the pure all things are pure.[2]

The relevance to Angelo is plain. Lawrence is criticising what he terms 'spirituality', the goodness that can keep itself pure only by backing away from experience. Isabella is nearer this than the

---

[1] 'The Novel', in *Reflections on the Death of a Porcupine* (1934 ed.), 104.
[2] *Studies in Classic American Literature* (1953 ed., New York), 99-100.

Christian critic will admit. Lucio, the rake, who yet speaks for
fertility and naturalness, is allowed to say to her:

> . . . though 'tis my familiar sin
> With maids to seem the lapwing, and to jest,
> Tongue far from heart—play with all virgins so:
> I hold you as a thing enskied and sainted,
> By your renouncement an immortal spirit,
> And to be talked with in sincerity,
> As with a saint. (I.4.31-7)

It matters considerably for the interpretation of the play whether
Lucio says (and the dramatist means) this straight. Isabella answers
at once, 'You do blaspheme the good in mocking me.' So Lucio's
vocal tone has been cynically bantering. Is this because he, the
womaniser, can't speak otherwise? or because her inexperienced
modesty is only too quick to suspect such a man of being insincere?
Once again, it seems to me, the truth is mixed. Lucio does mean
that she is 'out of this world' in the perfection of her virtue, his
compliment is paid sincerely, yet he is himself so eloquent a spokesman for full life (his next speech marvellously evokes fertility—in
tribute to Juliet's pregnancy) that the compliment to Isabella turns
double-edged: there is so much richness in this world that to be
'above it' is an impoverishment.

Words such as 'saint' or 'righteous' or 'purity' thus cannot be
used simply in the context of works such as these. Yet again it must
be said that the 'opposite pole' to piety—a fleering at religion or
automatic debunking of all hallowed values, is not in them either.
Both writers hold a fine balance. In Lawrence, who spoke out so
directly on problems of modern living, the difficulty sometimes led
to confusion and self-contradiction. Within the same four years he
can write, first this—

> You will play with sex, will you! You will tickle yourself as
> with an ice-cold drink from a soda-fountain! You will pet
> your best girl, will you, and spoon with her, and titillate your-
> self and her, and do as you like with your sex?

—and then this:

> The late British Home Secretary, who prides himself on
> being a very sincere Puritan, grey, grey in every fibre, said
> with indignant sorrow in one of his outbursts on improper
> books: '—and these two young people, who had been perfectly
> pure up till that time, after reading this book went and had

sexual intercourse together!!!' *One up to them!* is all we can answer.[1]

Certainly the weight of that moral authority that he won for himself by the candid sensitivity of his writing about love went to the support of 'emotional sincerity', whether or not this clashed with the respectable code. Yet he, naturally, could not win quite free of a bad past: he is typical of the 'romantic love' ethos in tending to present couples living out their experiences together on a kind of super-social plane of their own, mercifully (if that is the word) freed from those necessities, the childbearing and rearing, the earning and home-making, that are in fact inseparable from stable love relations as we know them and that have helped to build up our norms of sexual behaviour. It seems to me, indeed, that Lawrence was able to vest so much of his hope for humanity, for a human way forward, in the lives of couples cut off from any community (Birkin and Ursula at the end of *Women in Love*) only because he had stripped them of all those commitments that would inevitably lead them back into fully social living.[2]

Here we have reached the point past which the likeness between the Elizabethan writer and the modern cannot be taken. The two could arrive at insights so akin because of the continuity, through changing social epochs, of the human organism with its characteristic feelings. But successive epochs are bound to put the stress on rather different fibres in the organism. The historically typical thing about *Measure for Measure* is that it could envisage *a necessary relation between the most intimate experiences and a social code*. It analyses 'the inherent difficulty of practical government to a sensitive mind' and the specific thing to be governed is our passional experience. Not that Shakespeare was writing a tract to influence marriage legislation; the form of the play is, as Leavis puts it, 'a controlled experiment', an acting-out of a situation as though to test what degree of personal freedom is right for society. But the society, though not historical, is realistically there, with its state apparatus of ruler and deputy, constable, prison, and executioner, laws and penalties.

---

[1] *Reflections on the Death of a Porcupine*, 122; 'Pornography and Obscenity', in *Phoenix*, 174.

[2] In the opening chapter of his *D. H. Lawrence: Novelist*, Leavis firmly defines the shortcoming that childlessness made for in Lawrence's base in life but he loses sight of it in his critiques of the fiction itself: on *Women in Love*, see below, ch. 7, 163-4.

That point has only to be stated for us to feel how unthinkable it is for a modern writer to make intimate experience the subject of a presentation so taken up with the public and the organised. Shakespeare must have been able to feel status, role, function, the whole of the more communal side of life as continuous with the most private experience. In the 'Angelo' sonnet he can use imagery from business to figure the deeper levels of character:

> They rightly do inherit heaven's graces,
> And husband nature's riches from expense;
> They are the lords and owners of their faces,
> Others, but stewards of their excellence.[1]

This is also the way of Shakespeare's contemporary, Donne. By drawing imagery from public life in poems such as 'The Anniversarie' and 'The Canonization', Donne doesn't at all detract from their passionate intensity–he strengthens it by figuring it as part of the word at large:

> Here upon earth, we'are Kings, and none but wee
> Can be such Kings, nor of such subjects bee.
> Who is so safe as wee? where none can doe
> Treason to us, except one of us two? . . . .

> . . . And thus invoke us; You whom reverend love
>   Made one anothers hermitage;
> You, to whom love was peace, that now is rage;
>   Who did the whole worlds soule contract, and drove
>   Into the glasses of your eyes
>   (So made such mirrors, and such spies,
> That they did all to you epitomize,)
> Countries, Townes, Courts: Beg from above
> A pattern of your love!

I think it is true to say (though hard to verify) that public imagery would have been felt an intruder in almost all poetry of personal experience from the middle seventeenth century down to our own time. Until the Restoration, personal poetry had been mainly that of an aristocracy accustomed to warfare (or at least arms-bearing), statecraft, and the ceremonies of the Court. The social supremacy and unified outlook of so exclusive a class made possible an assured habit of expression that could draw on their whole way of life when materials were needed for the idioms, metaphors, allusions that are the stuff of poetic language. To

---

[1] See also Sonnet 124, 'If my dear love were but the child of state'.

mention a single example: this nobility was skilled in arms and there is almost no experience in the lyric range of the later Tudor and early Stuart period for which arms-bearing cannot supply an image. This is true of work as different as the love-poetry of Wyatt or the Irish Pierce Ferriter, a piece in high style like Chapman's wedding hymn from *Hero and Leander*, Bishop King's grave and tender exequy for his wife, Marvell's most graceful poetry on the splendours of the country house and even his metaphysical dialogues that balance against each other, as though in chivalric contest, the abstractions of philosophers and theologians.

The nobility and gentry could say anything, without worrying about being thought 'low' or censured by genteel opinion for failing to *keep up appearances*. No later school of writers enjoyed quite such immunity. One or another genteel taboo (or its opposite, the deliberately scandalous *pour épater le bourgeois*) has deformed our literature ever since. It is not only that the love poetry of the generations after the Commonwealth had lost the art of grafting public references onto the more intimate veins of writing. For a long time, at least outside the folk tradition, there was very little passionate expression at all. In one of his 'Lives' Aubrey prints a poem in the pastoral manner, probably written early in the seventeenth century by one of the court or playhouse gallants to 'the greatest Beautie of her time in England', the wife of John Overall:

> Face she had of Filberd hue
>   and bosom'd like a Swan
> Back she had of bended Ewe,
>   and wasted by a span.
> Haire she had as black as Crowe
>   from the head unto the toe
> Downe downe all over her
>   hye nonny nonny noe . . . .
>
> To sport it on the merry downe
>   to daunce the Lively Haye;
> To wrastle for a green gowne
>   in heate of all the day
> Never would she saye me no
>   yet me thought I had tho
> Never enough of her
>   hye nonny nonny noe.[1]

[1] *Aubrey's Brief Lives*, ed. O. L. Dick (1962 ed.), 293-5.

This poetry is totally open to experience in the flesh. To catch it in
its full flow and pitch of ecstasy–to enact the quiver, thrill, and
spring of it–the poet has needed a verse that moves with the
unfettered ease of song. Presently (for historical reasons too complex
to detail here) rifts deepen in the culture, art poetry seals off its
relations with the popular modes and thereby congeals, in rhythm
and content alike. What remarkable literature of tenderness or
desire can we remember from after the Cavaliers until the close of
the eighteenth century? Only Rochester's ruthlessly frank lyrics;
and the only thing at all like them (apart from folk songs) is the
love poetry of Burns, who came from another culture. The squalid
manoeuvres of the Restoration drama hardly deserve to count; and
the great Augustans (Dryden, Pope, and Johnson) were much
more concerned with politics, business, the literary life, and abstract
morals than in what touches us most intimately.

The age before the Victorian saw the Romantic movement,
which is usually thought of for its rediscovery of emotion. But it is
remarkable how rarely the passions expressed are those dealt with
in *Measure for Measure*. Byron–again the exception is an aristocrat–
can describe a love affair with uninhibited fullness (in *Don Juan*),
but the other Romantics tended to treat love as a kind of specialised
experience to be cultivated in a hot-house, artificially disentangled
from the rest of our living. In Keats's last sonnet, steeped though
it is in passion in a way the eighteenth century had found impossible,
it still feels as though the poet is enclosed in his *own* emotions, in
what his own imagination is making of his love–

> Pillow'd upon my fair love's ripening breast,
> To feel for ever its soft fall and swell,
>   Awake for ever in a sweet unrest,
> Still, still to hear her tender-taken breath,
> And so live ever–or else swoon to death.

This typically Romantic way with passion has almost nothing of
Donne's sense of his sweetheart as a distinct other person, so close
to him yet existing in her own right with a reality as intense as his
feelings for her–

> Then since that I may know;
> As liberally, as to a Midwife, shew
> Thy self: cast all, yea, this white lynnen hence,
> There is no pennance due to innocence.

> To teach thee, I am naked first, why then
> What needst thou have more covering than a man.[1]

In Shelley, as in Keats, the loved one tends to disappear into the
overweening glamour of the poet's own imaginings—

> Rose leaves, when the rose is dead,
> Are heaped for the beloved's bed;
> And so thy thoughts, when thou art gone,
> Love itself shall slumber on.

The watery poetry of the Victorians could not recover for
literature the full image of love; by that time, too, folk song had
been nearly cut through at the root;[2] and the Victorian novel, great
in almost every area it touched, is wanting precisely in a candid
treatment of love, although it deals in every sort of substitute or
sublimation, particularly that rather hectic spirituality which is
common to the best writers and the feeblest.[3] The deepest kind of
encounter between men and women, after dawning again in
Hardy's last novels, re-emerged into the light of a full artistic
presentation in Lawrence—above all, I would say, in the passages
on young love in *The Rainbow* and in those superb scenes of love-
making in *Lady Chatterley's Lover*, both beautiful and intensely actual,
that have been blown upon lately with every kind of smoking-room
horse laugh and literary sneer. Lawrence, however, hardly recovered
the wholeness of a Donne or Shakespeare, for he could not reunite
the public and the intimate at the level of *Measure for Measure* or
Donne's *Songs and Sonets*. Although he was a profound interpreter
of societies and adept at seizing on the essentials of a community or
an age, yet *organised society* is usually felt in his work to jeopardise,
rather than support or order, the private life. In his most ambitious
effort to present a whole society with its collective habits and
traditions, *Women in Love*, the trend is away, away from the
communally organised, out onto a limb where at least the unique
individual can 'be himself'. In this novel the working people are
seen (from a distance) as barbaric and aboriginal; the organised
workers are judged to be selfish, destructive, anarchic; and domestic
middle-class life is a dreary dead-end: '"the world all in couples,

---

[1] Elegie XIX, 'To his Mistris Going to Bed'.
[2] See below, ch. 3, 89-92.
[3] See below, ch. 2, 45-7.

each couple in its own little house, watching its own little interests, and stewing in its own little privacy—it's the most repulsive thing on earth . . . .'''.[1] This is the gist of every passage on homes and the common habits of people; it is what the hero, Birkin, says at the points where he is most plainly carrying the author's message;[2] and towards the end, in the chapter 'Flitting', the two main women, Ursula and Gudrun, are made to explicitly repudiate as 'unthinkable' the 'ordinary' life with a man 'in the social world'. Although Lawrence did with another part of himself greatly value the societal impulse in man, in practice his attitude was more often contemptuous: 'Men clotting together into social masses in order to limit their individual liabilities: this is humanity.'[3] And he viewed social organisation as only minimally relevant to our deeper experience—his long essay 'Democracy' is at one on this with the letter already cited: 'I think the state is a vulgar institution. But life itself is an affair of aristocrats. In my soul, I'd be as proud as hell. . . . The state is an arrangement for myriads of peoples' living together. And one doesn't have brothers by arrangement.'[4]

It is of little use to blame Lawrence's particular temperament for the extremity of his position. This extreme kind of individualism will probably go on rising in successive waves for as long as we are domineered over by enormous units of various kinds and the very surroundings in which we have our community—i.e. the pattern of our towns—are shaped almost exclusively by convenience for the making of profits. In such conditions one of the hardest things is for a sensitive person to feel social organisation either as a source of values or as continuous with his own living. No doubt this couldn't be taken for granted by Shakespeare either. It has been suggested that *Measure for Measure* comes at a point when he was increasingly concerned 'with the shortcomings of authority' (Angelo embodies this). 'Shakespeare was still fully conscious of the dangers of disorder, but he was now more concerned with the evils of power' and less inclined to rest in 'order' as an indubitable value.[5] Yet the very

---

[1] Ch. 25, 'Marriage or Not'; see below, Ch. 7, 163-4.

[2] E.g. compare Birkin on 'liberty, equality, fraternity' in ch. 8 with Lawrence's letter of January 3, 1915 to Lady Ottoline Morrell: *Letters*, ed. Aldous Huxley (1932), 213.

[3] 'The Novel', in *Reflections on the Death of a Porcupine*, 112.

[4] With *Letters*, 213, compare 'Democracy' in *Phoenix*, 701-4.

[5] Kenneth Muir, '*Timon of Athens* and the Cash Nexus', in *Modern Quarterly Miscellany*, No. 1 (1947), 62-6.

fact that he could conceive of a problem of passionate love as able to be presented inside a framework of social organisation shows how it still came much more naturally for him to acknowledge man's fundamental dependence on community that it does for Western writers at the present time.

CHAPTER 2

Adam Blair and the Literature of Repression

THERE is a Scottish novel, largely forgotten now, which shows up very fully the moral-emotional pressures at work during the years that saw the coming of age of the novel in Britain. It does so all the more fully because it mixes acute consciousness of self with an unwitting deference to those taboos that prevented such consciousness from growing up in people in a whole or natural way. The novel is *Some Passages in the Life of Mr Adam Blair* (1822[1]), the first imaginative work by J. G. Lockhart, Scott's son-in-law and biographer. In writing it Lockhart did undoubtedly mean with a large part of himself to tell a sober tale of a sin and its due punishment, as a piece of life typical of the Scotland that had barely passed away. His father, the minister of a Lanarkshire parish, used to tell his son the true story of a minister deposed from his charge as punishment for 'fornication'. This was the nucleus of the novel. Many a case of the kind can be found in the records of the General Assembly of the Church of Scotland during the eighteenth century. They take us into that world of severe moral sanctions against which Burns was rebelling in most of his very finest poems–in 'The Twa Herds', 'The Ordination', 'The Holy Fair', and 'Holy Willie's Prayer'.

So the source of Lockhart's material was that pre-industrial Scotland in which almost every value, belief, and social drive took a religious form and operated inside the framework of the Kirk. But Lockhart, the quick-minded young lawyer, at home in the literary circles of Regency Edinburgh, no longer himself partook of that Presbyterian ethos. When he wrote *Adam Blair* he had behind him a career at Oxford as an Exhibitioner in Classics. Probably his father (like the father of Reginald Dalton in the novel that followed *Adam Blair*) had given him *The Pilgrim's Progress* and

[1] Reissued by the Edinburgh University Press: Scottish Reprints No. 1, 1963.

other Christian classics to read when he was a boy; but at Balliol he had been reading the works of Boccaccio and Machiavelli, and he was one of the first literary men to admire Wordsworth and Byron.[1] During his early days in Edinburgh, around 1815, the quickening movement of masses of people into the towns, to a life of crammed streets and tenements, factory work, and political agitation, was transforming life and literature. Change permeated art in the form of romanticism—the sensibility that feels experience as a flux of emotions. *Adam Blair*, for all its dutiful references to the old framework, nevertheless makes us feel the stir of the new sense of life. We don't mainly remember from it a scene with solidly real surroundings, a variety of people distinct in all their traits, a wider society visible, so to speak, close at hand. Rather we remember the distinctive emotional *timbre*—anguished bereavement dulled into quiet submissiveness, passion distraught at the fight with its own inhibitions, the sentiments of reverence, desire, remorse: all given in the eloquent abstractions of early-Romantic prose, rather than in precise evocation of behaviour itself. Over this whole a colouring is thrown in the form of 'atmosphere': dark nights, which lend themselves to strange suggestions, are more typical of the book than daylight.

This atmosphere is shared with many a Victorian classic—*Jane Eyre* and *Wuthering Heights*, passage after passage in Dickens, the side of Disraeli's *Sybil* typified by 'the fair Religious' (Sybil herself)— and also, unfortunately, with the fake Ossianic poetry published by MacPherson sixty years before, although Lockhart's talent was fine enough to get a certain reality of emotional portrayal even from MacPherson's headlong verbiage. *Adam Blair* is thus one of the first pieces of Scottish literature (since the end of the Middle Ages) in which the author seems as much at home in the general British cultural climate as in the Scottish. Nevertheless the book does belong, though in a new form, to the main Scottish tradition, for it shows a minister as the centre of gravity in his community. To John Maxwell, old crofter, senior elder, and Adam Blair's staunch stand-by in the parish, Adam is 'his Minister'—as we should say nowadays 'my doctor', or in America 'my analyst'. It was the minister above all who had to live the values and fight the moral bugbears of his society. This is what accounts for the psychological

[1] Andrew Lang, *The Life and Letters of John Gibson Lockhart* (1897), I, 19, 51, 71.

core of the novel and the matters that modern readers must find hardest to enter into imaginatively – the appalling consequences that follow on Adam's adultery, the fatal and near-fatal illness, the total ostracism that falls on Adam and ruins his daughter's life.

The doubt we may well feel about the plausibility, and the justice, of this upshot was anticipated by the old *doyen* of Scottish literature, Henry Mackenzie, author of *The Man of Feeling* (1771), in the review of *Adam Blair* that he published in *Blackwood's Magazine* for March 1822. He knows that readers outside Scotland may hardly believe in 'that utter prostration of mind, and that long remorse, which are here so ably depicted'. But for him it is explained by 'the sanctity of the clerical character' which in Scotland is 'a part of the national belief and feeling'. Such a sin committed by a minister would, he says, give 'a shock to the whole moral and religious associations of every mind in the country' – if English readers thought Adam's penalties too severe, Scottish ones might well consider them too light. This is probably exaggerated. Scottish piety can hardly have been so unanimous, or so highly strung. Throughout the eighteenth century a goodly section of the people in Scotland had leant to an anti-clericalism, passionately expressed by Burns, that would have found in a minister's downfall a chance for derision and scathing propaganda. But Mackenzie's view is true in essence. It is certainly the case that devotion to religious belief, Kirk, and minister was still the backbone of morality for great sections of the people. The fanaticism remembered from Knox's Reformation and from the Killing Time when the troops of the Anglo-Catholic monarchy had hunted the Covenanters over the moors of the south-west had lasted on as a solemn and severe sense of Christian duty. *Adam Blair* is set in the 1750s. People could still retail first-hand memories of the heroic Covenanting ministers, as Jeanie Deans's father does in Scott's *Heart of Midlothian*, and the new generation of ministers, milder and more genteel by far, actually had to warn their congregations against yearning for the more stirring time when their faith had been persecuted.[1] It has been said that the Covenanting ministers were 'more conspicuous as prophets than as pastors'[2] – more given to preaching fiery sermons than to supervising the morals of their parishioners. By the middle eighteenth century it was very much

---

[1] W. L. Mathieson, *The Awakening of Scotland* (Glasgow, 1910), 235.
[2] Mathieson, *Church and Reform in Scotland* (Glasgow, 1916), 314.

into the supervision of morals that religious zeal was flowing. The suspicious vigilance and fanatical suppression that went into it were something we can now barely imagine. In Edinburgh (let alone the outlying towns and villages) the town Presbytery enacted and the Town Council enforced that no social visits could be paid on Sundays, for these were 'useless communications' on a day meant for higher things. 'Scizers' patrolled the streets to arrest people found there during Church service, and there was also a ban on 'idly gazing out of windows' which exposed you to the risk of 'beholding vanities abroad'.[1] The iron fingers of the clergy had their grip on everything. Village girls could be physically examined by the local Kirk Session to find out which of them could be feeding a bastard child that had been abandoned in the street. The Session could also punish people for 'fornication' or slander, and offenders could be made to sit on a stool for weeks in Church, wearing a coarse gown, in full view of the congregation. In *The Heart of Midlothian* Scott makes Jeanie Deans tell the Queen that women were so terrified of this public shaming that they often took refuge in the very concealment of their pregnancy which counted as a capital crime if the baby died.

The minister had to be in his own person the exemplar of this severe moral code, and in *The Wealth of Nations* Adam Smith says that the ministers' influence on the people was based on the real leadership they gave by their behaviour.[2] In time the code began to relax, and during a general Assembly of the Church held at about the time in which *Adam Blair* is set we find a minister of the Moderate (or liberal) party congratulating his colleagues on having escaped from the rigour of the days when 'religion was so far driven, especially in ministers, that it was a principle they should not be conversible and should only be taken up upon serious things in common conversation.'[3] But the struggle between intolerance and broadmindedness was to carry on for some time yet. One of the most famous of the new liberal clergy was Alexander Carlyle, minister of Inveresk just east of Edinburgh, and he described in passages from his memoirs that apply to 1747 how his parishioners mistrusted him because he was 'too young, too full of levity, and too much addicted to the company of my superiors', because he

---

[1] Hugo Arnot, *The History of Edinburgh* (1779), 192, 204 and n. 2.
[2] Bk. V, ch. 1, Part III, article 3 (1904 ed., 295).
[3] Mathieson, *Awakening of Scotland*, 192.

'danced frequently in a manner prohibited by the laws of the Church . . . wore my hat agee; and had been seen galloping through the Links one day between one and two o'clock.'[1] This does not leave much that the minister *could* do or be, and Adam Blair's offence was no small fault of manners but the sin of adultery.

Such was the social experience that Lockhart had behind him in writing *Adam Blair*. But he did not deal with it through painstaking description of 'manners' as had been the method of his immediate forerunners, Scott and John Galt. Ten years before he had been planning a novel that would use 'an immense quantity of anecdotes and observations I have made concerning the state of the Scotch, chiefly their clergy and elders.' But *Waverley* came out in 1814, Galt's *Annals of the Parish* in 1821, and by then it looked, especially to a young writer anxious to make his own mark, as though the vein of fiction-as-social history was worked out.[2] By the 1820s, too, the Romantic poetry had sunk into his sensibility, with the result that he told his old Scottish story in a manner vibrant with emotion. The reader today is bound to feel that the manner from Chapters 13 to 19 is hectically melodramatic, and these are the chapters in which Adam sleeps with Charlotte, his dead wife's cousin. No sooner have they done this than Lockhart plunges them into a nightmare train of sufferings. Devils creep round them, they hesitate on the brink of suicide, hector each other in the manner of grand opera ('torment me not. . . . Shall the curse cling to me forever?'), and finally fall into the inevitable Romantic prostration—fever, coma, and for one of them death. If Lockhart's readers did not query the plausibility of all this, it was because they were so attuned to the code which regarded the least 'irregularity', or extra-marital passion, as an unspeakable crime. Indeed, some readers were scandalised that adultery should have been dealt with in a novel at all.[3] The real trouble is that the adultery remains literally unspeakable in the novel—Adam and Charlotte's love is never shown or acknowledged—their 'fall' is followed by a couplet of poetry ('The moon hid her light/From *his* heaven that night') and a quadruple row of asterisks. Lockhart has even had to make

[1] *The Autobiography of Dr Alexander Carlyle of Inveresk (1722-1805)* (1910 ed.), 216-7 and n.
[2] *Life and Letters*, I, 71-6.
[3] *Life and Letters*, I, 302.

the pair drunk, as though to avoid facing the possibility that an unmarried couple might in all sanity have intercourse. But here he is perhaps realistic: it seems that in that epoch of maximum repression young brides, who had been completely blinkered and chaperoned until the last minute, only got through the ordeal of their wedding night by taking alcohol.

My suggestion is not that a novelist from such a culture should, or could, have presented love-making in the open modern way, or even with the brutal candour of the eighteenth century. What one expects is that the novelist should be perfectly clear-sighted, as much about what convention obliges him to skirt round as about his main material. Lockhart brings his couple to the point of consummated passion while scarcely suggesting one step in the growth of this strong feeling. When Adam is thinking over all Charlotte has meant to him—'long pleasant walks . . . interesting conversations . . . restoration of his own mental serenity . . . the charming, kind looks of Charlotte . . . her heroic resolution' (in putting up with her own impossible husband)—there is no word of anything verging on acknowledged passion. This, it might be argued, is to present a man without enough self-knowledge to realise the feelings gathering force inside himself. But, as we read through the novel, it affects us rather as a sheer gap—a withholding of essentials on the part of the author. After the months of Platonic intimacy during which, evidently with no consciousness on their part, Charlotte has become virtually a wife-figure for Adam, the first of the clearly inevitable outbursts of passion between the two occurs, after Charlotte has rescued Adam and his little girl Sarah from drowning. Her clothes are half torn off by the struggle in the water. Adam 'fell upon his knee close beside Charlotte and his child, and throwing one arm round each, he drew them both towards his bosom, and began to kiss them alternately, cheek, and brow, and lip, hastily and passionately, as if ignorant or careless that he was within sight of anyone.' Here we are bound to wonder: is the scene credible? could the man, however distraught, conceivably have been so oblivious of bystanders and of all normal restraints as to kiss the woman like that? Is the obliviousness not the author's? is he not, in spite of himself, coming out with such a moment as a kind of unconscious substitute for the acknowledged, though perhaps guilty, love that the reader today will all along have regarded as crying out to be presented?

Several pages later Lockhart might seem to be aware enough of the emotions involved: Adam's sleep on the night after the rescue is full of nightmares, dreams of exotic languor and heat, and also directly erotic images: 'Beautiful women's shapes, smiling eyes and burning blushes, darted in glimpses here and there from amidst the thickest of tumults.' Yet a little later again, as we have seen, Adam still does not say to himself, 'I love her', and we can't even sense any strain of repression on his part. His nightmares, like the kissing after the rescue, are a flickering into sight of something which for the most part has been allowed—by the novelist—to stay buried.

If there is evasion here, it has its counterpart in the direct suppression that follows Adam's confession and penance. He is utterly humbled, 'silent, laborious, penitent, devout. . . . Seldom, except on the Sabbath day, did he for many months quit the narrow precincts of the field to which he had returned' (as a labourer). His former friends never come near him, Sarah never marries although she has 'ripened into womanhood' and become 'the most beautiful girl in that part of the country'. It is not that such an outcome is inconceivable in itself. The trouble is that Lockhart presents this outcome, in all confidence that his readers will approve, as the perfection of goodness and a supremely just moral consummation.

This kind of morals—setting the highest value on self-abnegation, repression, and self-sacrifice—is at the core of work after work as the nineteenth century goes on: think of *Jane Eyre* (1847), Hawthorne's *Scarlet Letter* (1850), and George Eliot's 'Janet's Repentance' (from *Scenes of Clerical Life*, 1857). In *Jane Eyre* Rochester is married to a lunatic—we cannot but feel that it is no marriage and that he, as a natural man, must look for another woman. But Charlotte Brontë cannot face this: Jane and Rochester will come together, yes, but not until he has been blinded in the very fire that rids him of his ghastly incubus. Like Lockhart, Charlotte Brontë has a flickering awareness of what she is suppressing: the couple do acknowledge their strong feelings for each other, and the blinded Rochester can even challenge Jane by saying she now wants to marry him only because she 'delights in sacrifice'. But Jane's reply, made to carry the moral of the book, is: '"I love you better now, when I can be really useful to you, than I did in your state of proud independence."' So the meeting of equals in a marriage that could fulfil their whole natural selves is thwarted and side-tracked, and a maimed and repressed life is given the highest value.

George Eliot wrote in a letter about *Jane Eyre*: 'All self-sacrifice is good, but one would like it to be in a somewhat nobler cause than that of a diabolical law which chains a man soul and body to a putrefying carcase.'[1] Yet she herself, for all the courage of her private life, was not immune to that morbid side of contemporary morality. Her *Scenes of Clerical Life* first appeared in *Blackwood's Magazine*, which was careful to give the middle-class Victorians what they liked and what was good for them. (Lockhart was its leading contributor in the 1820s.) In the third *Scene* the heroine, Janet, is married, like Rochester, to a monster—her husband is drunkard, bully, sadist. But just when it looks as though the desperately needed divorce may come about, the man is stricken with *delirium tremens*, and his sufferings so renew Janet's devotion to him that she nurses him selflessly until his death. Her whole situation and capacity for emotion, like Adam and Charlotte's in *Adam Blair*, cry out for a partner, and, like them, she gets one only for the author to keep the relationship either buried or else sublimated into a thin substitute for the real thing. Janet's real love is the curate Tryon. But he is tuberculous. In so many nineteenth-century works, if you are good you are 'not long for this world'—the more virtuous, the more sickly. The pair acknowledge their love once, after the husband's death and shortly before the curate's, and Janet then faces the rest of her life as 'a solemn service of gratitude and patient effort.' It is as though George Eliot, like Lockhart and Charlotte Brontë, wants us to feel that such resignation and such thankfulness for small mercies is somehow *supremely good*, that this kind of martyred saintliness raises human moral capacities to their highest level.

This notion has been strong in Christian belief for centuries.[2] It is the morals of the downtrodden—mankind despairing of justice in this life and helpless against a Nature he could control so little. All these novelists stress Christian values: Adam with his minister's duties; Rochester 'bending his sightless eyes to the earth' and praying to '" my Redeemer to give me strength to lead henceforth a purer life than I have done hitherto"'; Tryon telling Janet that

---

[1] *George Eliot's Life*, ed. J. W. Cross (n.d.), 104.
[2] See above, ch. 1, esp. 26-8.

when he himself had been wicked in his student days, a friend had
'"made it clear to me that the only preparation for coming to
Christ and partaking of his salvation, was that very sense of guilt
and helplessness which was weighing me down."' We are readier
nowadays to ask why a life repressed, curtailed, or trodden into
submissiveness should be a better life than one that is fulfilled and
thriving in itself.

In her most searching analysis of this strange ethos Q. D. Leavis
points out that Victorian fiction, masterpieces and potboilers alike,
was steeped in 'the attitudes formed round the words "noble" and
"pure", and the idea of self-sacrifice for its own sake,' and she
analyses a case from the old best-seller Florence Barclay (whose
novel *The Rosary* I can remember seeing on the bedside tables of
old-fashioned boarding houses) in which a man regards it as
'sacrilege' for a daughter to criticise her mother even if she has
deserved it. 'An ideal that directly conflicts with experience,' writes
Mrs Leavis, 'is none the less quite gratuitously given moral support.'[1]
Such was the popular literary atmosphere that still tinged the
emotions of millions early this century. It shows the real perplexities
involved that the greatest successor of the nineteenth-century
tradition in fiction, D. H. Lawrence, should have done–should
have been forced to do–more than any other writer to free morals
from the old cowering negatives and self-denials. In Lawrence, the
deepest kind of encounter between men and women re-emerges
into the light of a full artistic presentation. It had been shunned
by the writers, with scarcely an exception, for over a century.
Lawrence disliked Lockhart for the censorious righteousness of his
attitude to Burns, in the *Life* of him he wrote in 1828,[2] and he
repeatedly criticised the line of fiction that has just been traced:
'I'm sure poor Charlotte Brontë, or the authoress of *The Sheik*, did
not have any deliberate intention to stimulate sex feelings in the
reader. Yet I find *Jane Eyre* verging on pornography and Boccaccio
seems to me always fresh and wholesome.' In 'The Novel' he
develops the idea that 'nearly all great novelists have a didactic
purpose, otherwise a philosophy, directly opposite to their passional
inspiration,' and his key case is a novel that, like *Adam Blair*,

---

[1] *Fiction and the Reading Public* (1932), 245, 326.
[2] 'Those damned middle-class Lockharts grew lilies of the valley up their ----,
to hear them talk. . . . Don't, for God's sake, be mealy-mouthed like them. . . .
No, my boy, don't be on the side of the angels, it's too lowering.' (*Letters*, 694-5)

concerns adultery–Tolstoy's *Anna Karénina*. In a few straight
sentences we have the nub of the matter:

> Vronsky sinned, did he? But also the sinning was a consum-
> mation devoutly to be wished. The novel makes that obvious:
> in spite of old Leo Tolstoy. . . . There you have the greatness
> of the novel itself. It won't *let* you tell didactic lies, and put
> them over. Nobody in the world is anything but delighted
> when Vronsky gets Anna Karénina.[1]

What Lawrence opposes above all is submission to a principle that
we have to will ourselves to believe–that does not emerge from the
real needs of our natures. This is a key problem in *Adam Blair*.
Adam, raised again to the ministry after his penitential spell as a
labourer on the land, has to rebuke sinners from the pulpit–'but
he never failed to commence his address to the penitent before him,
by reminding him, and all present, of his own sin and its consequences.' One is driven to wonder how such self-mortification was
humanly possible. Could a man be so subdued as to act as a living
object-lesson his whole life long, meek and uncomplaining? would
the ego not revolt at all, through some sort of self-hatred or hatred
of his fellows?

It may be that in those communities the religious code was so
unquestioned by many that sheer dutifulness was all-powerful and
wholly permeated the man. The Kirk had the extraordinary
authority described already. Unfortunately, the contemporary
records are not insightful enough to reveal what kind of psychological toll was taken. Burns and his friend Gavin Hamilton in their
Ayrshire village loathed the machinery of spying, admonishing, and
public shaming, and many of Burns's poems are the retaliations of
a generous mind against the squashing of the self that the code
entailed. Some stories by the Glasgow town crier, Dougal Graham,
give us a vivid record of life at the period of *Adam Blair* and there
we see an old woman raging at repenting stools and sackcloth
gowns as 'papist rites an' rotten ceremonies'.[2] But these are cases of
simple war between the Kirk Session and those who will not
knuckle under. It would have taken a writer of subtler insight than
any then available to show the complexities of repression and self-

---

[1] 'Pornography and Obscenity', in *Phœnix*, 174, 176-7; *Reflections on the Death
of a Porcupine*, 104-5.
[2] *The Collected Writings of Dougal Graham*, ed. George MacGregor (Glasgow,
1883), II, 21-2.

deception that must actually have occurred in the minds of those who submitted.

What those novelists as a group seem to represent in the collective consciousness of their class at that time is moral conscience that has hypertrophied and become so over-susceptible that it is forced compulsively into the most harrowing ordeals. This seems to be what was happening. Conscience was the strongest element surviving from the older religious culture, now that the less tenable things–Calvinist predestination, the literal truth of the Bible, the unquestioned authority of minister and Kirk Session, superstitions that had acted as moral deterrents–were losing their power over the freer minds. In Presbyterian Scotland, or the Nonconformist England that produced George Eliot, conscience emerged as an overweening faculty operating more and more on the individual's more private experiences as people grew less part of a closed church community, less aware of a Power 'up there' to worship, less interested in technical problems of theology, and more taken up with the real life of which theology had been the fantastic projection.

Lockhart's own generation was notable for a drift away from formal religion. In Scotland, James and John Stuart Mill, Thomas Carlyle, and earlier the great surgeon and anatomist William Hunter had all paused at the brink of the ministry and then turned away. Their counterparts in England were such men as Matthew Arnold, the poet Clough, and Leslie Stephen. But the mental habit of anxiously weighing and testing one's actions in the light of an 'ultimate' or 'transcendent' value long outlived the religious cult it had been bound up with. The peculiar quality of *Adam Blair*–its raw material rooted in old Presbyterian Scotland but the doing of it steeped in the rather hectic emotionality of the Romantic frame of mind–is due to its position at this stage in the re-absorption of religious feelings and ideas into the general atmosphere of our culture.

We have still to explain why such a consciousness prevailed, and even re-intensified itself, at just this time. Where Fielding had been able to deal with a seduction, elopement, or rape with crude lightheartedness, or else as a vehicle for a perfunctory moral, for the Victorian or an immediate predecessor like Lockhart it must all be veiled–less definite, less straightforward, more felt. We say 'Victorian' or 'Regency'. But why did this deep change occur when it did? It can hardly have been spontaneous–occurring in the human psyche on its own.

The major changes in material and social life during the period that went to form that first nineteenth-century generation included the swelling affluence of people engaged in trade and the rapidly growing numbers of them. This class had also become, as is attested by many of the eighteenth-century records of periodicals, lending libraries, etc, the dominant section of the public for fiction. And the life of this class was more and more one in which 'appearances had to be kept up'–the material means for keeping them up (linens and cottons, china and glassware for the table, capital to build imposing houses and meeting places) were multiplying year by year.[1] Suburbs grew up round the towns, at a decent distance from the working-class slums, and tradesmen ceased to live above their work or to share tenements with either workers or noblemen.[2] Lockhart himself has left us, in *Peter's Letters to his Kinsfolk* (1819), some of the very best contemporary descriptions of that middle class, for example the counting-house blood, the counting-house dandy, and the counting-house 'bear' whom he saw in action in Glasgow, and their womenfolk who confided in visitors that they wouldn't dream of living in so disagreeable a city were it not for their husbands' business there. . . .[3] A very large number, he says, meant to spend their profits on land and then take 'their place in the great body of British gentry, with as much propriety as any that elevate themselves to that most enviable of all human conditions.' These were the Glaswegians most akin to the Edinburgh middle class in their mindfulness of aristocracy and close ties with the land (the type of Bailie Nicol Jarvie in Scott's *Rob Roy*). It was Edinburgh that had been the cradle of Scottish literature since the start of the eighteenth century, and Edinburgh was at this time deliberately building a *polite* society–clean markets, capital punishment executed in decent privacy, merchants doing their business in a dignified Exchange instead of in pubs or on the streets, and a proper segregation of the classes both in hostelries and in the city sections where they lived.[4]

[1] George S. Pryde, *Scotland from 1603 to the Present Day* (1962), 143-4.
[2] David Craig, *Scottish Literature and the Scottish People, 1680-1830* (1961), 29-30, 37-8.
[3] *Op. cit.*, III, 169-71.
[4] Craig, *Scottish Literature*, 38-9.

Such a transformation in the social conditions couldn't but affect people in their intimate living. Courting quite changed. Before, young people, poor or well-off, had sauntered together in the meadows, parks, and fields that fringed the town. But as the half-wild grassland was built over, as the New Town laid out its formal parks, as more and more folk from the middle and upper classes felt that 'in their position' their behaviour must at least appear irreproachable, courting was transformed. Now only 'artizans and serving-girls' went together in the town meadows.[1] This writer dates the change from thirty years before–that is, the time when the ideal of civic dignity, a studious expunging of all that could be thought uncouth, had become dominant.

Such changes were at work in Boston and London as well as Edinburgh and Glasgow.[2] It may seem a far cry from the growth of business to the shrinking yet intense sensibilities of Charlotte Brontë and the rest. Yet history shows that bourgeoisification was the root change from which most else in the culture flowed. Dickens, with his piercing social insight, saw the connection perfectly well and fixed it in one of his best symbols, Podsnappery, the sacred principle of never 'bringing a blush to the cheek of the young person'. This attitude spread outwards, as *Our Mutual Friend* shows, from the newly-rich above all. The novelists I have discussed are typical of those who were at least emotionally honest enough to feel, and record, the pangs of repression that resulted.

[1] *The Scottish Songs*, ed. Robert Chambers (Edinburgh, 1829), 179 n.
[2] The parallel English development is richly detailed by Edward Thompson, who concludes by endorsing the view that 'the period of decisive moral change was not at the time of Victoria's accession, or even in the nineteenth century at all, but . . . during the decade 1790-1800.' (*The Making of the English Working Class*, 1963, 401-3 and 402 n. 2)

Section Two

INDUSTRIAL CULTURE

CHAPTER 3

Songs of the Bleak Age[1]

Those put into golden chairs to write
will be asked about those who
wove their coats.
Not for elevated thoughts
will their books be searched, but
a passing sentence which helps to establish
some particular feature of men who wove coats
will be read with interest, for it may describe
famous forebears.

Brecht, 'Literature will be Searched'

LITERATURE and song are a main part of the living memory of
our country, and one might think it would be taken for granted that
the acts, feelings, and living conditions of the majority–those who
live by their work–would be searched out and recreated most
keenly. Yet it is not long since the idea of culture as the expression
of a whole people was overlaid by partial and élitist views. Eric
Hobsbawm has written that just before the War it was still looked
on as eccentric or not the thing to bother writing the history of a
trade union, such as Raymond Postgate's history of the builders.
Since then many of the histories which have not only amassed more
data but changed our way of understanding the past (and the
present) have been written by people (e.g. Cole and Postgate,
Christopher Hill, Edward Thompson, and Hobsbawm) who have
given a prime place to the 'labouring men' of society; and many
of the growing-points in literary studies (e.g. the approaches of
Richard Hoggart and Raymond Williams) are as they are because
these men have developed their special ways of thinking and
working in the Workers' Educational Association and kindred
movements.

When poems, fiction, songs, and other sorts of expression are
discussed among working-people, time and again they come out

---

[1] 'The Bleak Age' is applied in this chapter to a wider period than in the book
that started the phrase, J. L. and Barbara Hammond's *The Bleak Age* (1934;
rev. ed., 1947). This necessarily concentrated on the 1830s and '40s. Much of the
bleakness outlasted that worst time, and the songs reflect this.

with the phrase 'down to earth'. This is *the* valued quality – the touchstone of truth and relevance. The idea isn't necessarily reductive, intolerant of subtlety, reducing everything to simple statements, or grudgingly suspicious of the complex or unusual (though it can be). In the people's songs[1] the down-to-earth comes out as an unfailing concreteness, an effect of a nail solidly hit. This is natural to the utterance of those who live by hard work with things[2] – at least when they are talking about what they know; but in the by-turns manic and self-pitying lyrics of the songs most popular for generations now, such utterance can't be heard. If it comes out at all, it is in the music, most especially in the hard-driving beat which has at last, since skiffle and rock came in, challenged the characterless and sugary music of the crooners.

In the parts of the country where the industrial culture has the longest tradition, for example the coalfield of Durham and Northumberland, this sense of grip on familiar facts continues to come out in songs about working life:

For ma-ny long years the pit's done its best, And sets have rolled oot the flats, north, east and west. And

---

[1] I use this phrase instead of 'folksongs', which is too oldtime and rural in connotation to sound right in the industrial age. Yet recent writers (e.g. A. L. Lloyd, *Folk Song in England*, 1967, 1969; Frank Howes, *Folk Music of Britain – And Beyond*, 1969) are misleading when they argue that industrial songs are not the equal artistically of the pre-industrial and are therefore not true folk songs but 'workers' songs'. Questions of quality should not be mixed up with questions of social origin and function. What we are all discussing is the lyric material that circulated with the least intervention of centralised media and the cash nexus and the most creative participation of people in the ordinary walks of life. Obviously, after the industrial revolution the centralised media encroached more and more on what people made for themselves. But there was no absolute cultural break. Howes writes that industrial songs 'have not been subject to the refining process of oral transmission' (p. 173). How does he think a family of singing miners like the Elliotts of Birtley got their repertoire? Again, if the unknown singers who made up the canal-boat version of Ewan MacColl's 'Champion at Keepin' 'Em Rollin' got the original from a disc, this differed little from the common folk practice of adapting songs from printed sources such as song-sheets and song-books.

[2] The detailed theory behind this point is discussed more fully below: ch. 12, pp. 262-3; ch. 14, pp. 298-9.

all   of the   ru - mours that clos - ing was   due   Have

all   been put   down,   for at last·   it   is   true.

Wey, Aa've filled in the Fan Pit, Aa've cut in the seam
In the Newbiggin Beaumont since Aa was fifteen.
Aa've worked in the sections and in the main coal,
Man, it's hot doon the Monty, she's a dusty aald hole.
So farewell te ye, Monty, Aa knaa yer roads well.
Yor work has been good an yor work has been hell.
Ne mair te yor dorty aald heap will Aa come,
For yor coal is aal finished an yor life it is done.[1]

The last verse particularly shows how the downright idiom need
not mean obvious emotions or a simple hard bash. The mixed
feelings put as an antithesis in 'Yor work has been good an yor
work has been hell' carry on into the seeming contempt of 'dorty
aald heap', and the whole is tinged with affectionate familiarity—
hence the warmth with which the mine is personified in the final
line. This play of feelings in the seemingly blunt language is the
counterpart of that straightfaced speech—jokes said like bare facts
with no glimmer of a grin—along with a dislike of overt sentiment
('gush'), that are familiar to me among working-people in the
north-east of Scotland and the north of England and are probably
common everywhere. Akin to this is that perfect downrightness
which might seem aggressive but is only direct, as in the first line
of a linen weavers' song—

> Oh do you know her or do you not,
> This new doffing mistress we have got?
> Elsie Thompson it is her name,
> And she helps her doffers at every frame.[2]

Such directness has been misunderstood, patronised, or ignored
ever since genteel taste imposed itself in the rise of the town middle-
class in the later seventeenth century. Among songsters whose

---

[1] Johnny Handle and Lou Killen, 'Farewell to the Monty': *Songs for the Sixties*,
ed. Peggy Seeger and Ewan MacColl (1961), 19; sung by Killen on *The Iron Muse*
(Topic 12T86, 1963), side 2, band 9.
[2] Sung by Anne Briggs on *The Iron Muse*, side 2, band 5.

names are known, Burns is supreme, yet the urbane critics objected
to the 'want of respectfulness in the general tone of his gallantry'
and to his 'approaching his mistress on a footing of equality'.[1] It
was during Burns's lifetime and just after his death that the folk
tradition began to change as more and more people went to work
in factories in the black cities of the Midlands and North and the
Scottish Lowlands. When such social change occurs, it is often the
case that the new forms of culture which people need to organise
themselves and their thoughts are evolved by adapting existing
forms rather than by throwing up brand-new ones, and so it is
with the songs. For example, the culture of the industrial villages
remained traditional in its feasts and fairs and rites and emblems
for generations after the factory system had got under way. That
is why some of the great Reform and Chartist demonstrations have
so much the air of community revels.[2] In Lancashire, Derbyshire,
and elsewhere there were the wakes or annual fairs, and the songs
sung along with the shows included such favourite routines as a
kind of stylised quarrel between husband and wife–evidently a
form of the ritual, traditional in the north of England, for exor-
cising the demon of ill-temper from a quarrelsome marriage.[3] At
Droylsden, north-east of Manchester, where Robertson's jam
factory now is, two men on a cart played the married couple. They
drove through the streets spinning flax and singing a quarrel dialogue. In the usual versions there is no phrase that couldn't have
been sung at any time in the seventeenth or eighteenth century:

> It's Dreighlsdin wakes, un' wey're comin' to teawn,
> To tell yo o' somethin' o' greet reneawn;
> Un' if this owd jade ull lem'mi begin,
> Aw'l show yo heaw hard un how fast au con spin.
>
> (Chorus) So it's threedywheel, threedywheel, dan, don,
>   dill, doe.[4]

These versions end with the usual pious moral:

> So let us unite, un' live free fro' o' sin,
> Un' then we shall have nowt to think on but spin.

[1] Francis Jeffrey, *Contributions to the Edinburgh Review* (1846 ed.), II, 147.
[2] See below, ch. 5, pp. 128-9.
[3] A Swaledale version is given in Edmund Cooper, *Muker: The Story of a
Yorkshire Parish* (Clapham, Yorkshire, 1948), 84.
[4] John Harland (ed.), *Ballads and Songs of Lancashire* (1882 ed.), 147-9 (the
chorus is presumably a vestige of a spinners' worksong).

At some point the 'unite' motif has come to stand for the new political solidarity, and the couplet becomes

> Let all spinners unite an' let's live as one,
> An' we'll feight for our reights 'stead o' feightin' at home.[1]

It is a world of difference, between a trade carrying on in the old unquestioning way, with little awareness of itself as a force for change in a social world, and one that has awakened to its potential in a competitive society.

The frequency of such changes in the songs shows how fully and acutely they register the quakes in society. 'The Collier Laddie', a favourite of Burns's, must be one of the oldest industrial songs extant, from the days when mining was a country industry. The prolonged narrative and leisurely tune with ample scope for vocal ornaments are no different from such classic ballads as 'Lord Randal'. Yet the content and some of the phrases anticipate the kind of society in which relationships are made and valued *via* money and the classes face each other in conscious conflict.[2] A laird as he rides by tries to entice a miner's girl. She stays true to the man from her own class, and when she answers him back, she uses her wage to stand for her self-reliance:

> I can win my five pennies in a day,
> And spen't at nicht fu brawlie;
> And mak my bed in the collier's neuk,
> And lie doun wi my collier's laddie.

The laird has tempted the girl by offering his property:

> See ye not yon hills and dales,
> The sun shines on sae brawlie?
> They a' are mine, and they shall be thine,
> Gin ye'll leave your collier laddie.[3]

---

[1] Sung by Ewan MacColl on *Second Shift* (Topic 10T25, 1958), side 1, band 2.

[2] It would be a help if this ballad could be exactly dated. The version we have must surely come from after 1775 when the first Act was passed freeing Scottish colliers from the semi-slavery whereby they were 'astricted' or tied to their place of work. The wage the girl mentions is not conclusive since we don't know her trade. The average female wage in Cumberland, a region akin to south-west Scotland, was 4d a day in 1797, and this is perhaps a clue: if the girl had been in the mines like her sweetheart, her wage would have been included in that of the man, probably her father, to whom she acted as 'bearer', and she could not have quoted it to the laird as a sum on its own. (George S. Pryde, *Scotland from 1603 to the Present Day*, 134; F. M. Eden, *The State of the Poor*, 1797, II, 84; Tom Johnston, *History of the Working Classes in Scotland*, Glasgow, 1920, 330-8).

[3] Robert Chambers, *The Scottish Songs*, 531 n.; a longer version is in *Come All Ye Bold Miners*, ed. A. L. Lloyd (1952), 44-6.

This verse is in fact an adaptation of one from 'The Demon Lover':

> 'O what hills are yon, yon pleasant hills,
> That the sun shines sweetly on?'
> 'O yon are the hills of heaven,' he said,
> 'Where you will never win.'[1]

This ballad (in which the devil tempts a carpenter's girl) is one of those that embody elements from furthest off in the realm of medieval fantasy. In the imagination of the industrial age, the heavenly hills become real–indeed, real-estate. Presumably the link between the two songs was that the devil was a natural forerunner of the landlord.

Another of the transitional songs suggests further aspects of the change. This is 'The Waggoner', from the community of keelmen on Tyneside:

> Saw ye owt o my lad
> Gannin doon the waggon-way
> Wi his pocket full o siller
> And his bag full o hay?
>
> O–my lad's a bonny lad,
> The bonniest I see,
> Tho' he's sair frowsy-freckled
> And he's blind iv an ee.[2]

The jaunty swing of it, the sheerly happy wording, the occasional high crowing note in the tune, especially the drawn-out 'O', are the very soul of blitheness, and as such they suggest the older country singing, for example the waggoners' own songs made to be sung on long slow journeys,[3] rather than the later, industrial type. Indeed that first verse owes its form to a Scottish country bairn-rhyme–

> Saw ye ocht o my luv
> Comin frae the market,
> A peck o meal upon her back,
> A baby in her basket?[4]

---

[1] *English and Scottish Popular Ballads*, ed. F. J. Child (1904 ed.), 546 (my quotation is from Child No. 243, version F).

[2] Sung by Johnny Handle on *The Collier's Rant* (Topic TOP74, 1962), side 2, band 3; calling the one-eyed lad handsome must be a very old popular joke: a fairy-tale in verse from fifteenth-century Scotland, 'King Berdok', calls the cuckoo (one of the lovers in the poem) 'Ane bony bird, and had bot ane e'.

[3] See A. L. Lloyd, *The Singing Englishman* (n.d.), 59.

[4] 'The Waggoner' also returned to the bairn-rhyme tradition: Mrs F. Horner of Richmond, Yorkshire, recalls her Newcastle grandmother singing the following to a clapping game–

'The Waggoner' is blithe and at the same time close to the realities of wage-earning – a blend less and less common as the nineteenth century wore on. Where did the blitheness spring from? There is the girl's natural happiness; but that inseparable mingling of love, money, and trade in her image of her sweetheart makes the cheerfulness sounds integral to his work and economic position. This seems to me a distinctively early-proletarian kind of thing. In all the songs of Burns, which are the biggest single body of peasant songs that we have, there is only one that mingles love, money, and trade like that, namely 'The Dusty Miller', and the songs from Burns's own peasant point of view (the miller was of course a businessman) mention money almost exclusively in the form of the dowry (or tocher) and never as a wage. It would seem, therefore, as though the long-standing economic independence of the colliery workers lived on to colour 'The Waggoner'. The miner who cut and raised the coal might also cart it for sale to customers. The team of miners thought of themselves as self-employed artisans and were entitled to fix their own rates. This will have been, often, a desperately hard life; it was also literally more free, more mobile, than that of the factory hand who clocks in and clocks out at the one job year after year. Direct-contract work and the multiple job were already on the way out by 1800, and earlier in the north of England than elsewhere because the deeper workings called for specialisation, full-time work, and big capital. This was the beginning of the end for what has been called 'the traditions of the "free" miner' which 'coloured responses until the 19th century'. 'The Waggoner' was first printed in a book in 1808, and in 1792 the waggoners along with the pitmen, keelmen, and seamen of the north-east were starting to agitate in crowds for liberty, equality, and a republic.[1] This is not the old heedless life. The traditional devil-may-carelessness of the keelmen – voiced in songs such as 'The

---

Clap hands my bonny lad,
Your daddy's comin doon the waggon way,
With his pocket full of money
And his cart full of hay.

A garbled vestige of the same rhyme is also sung by Mary Barton to her little boy at the end of Elizabeth Gaskell's novel.

[1] T. S. Ashton, *The Industrial Revolution* (1948), 52; Thompson, *Making of the English Working Class*, 63, 103; David Ogg, *England in the Reign of Charles II* (1963 ed.), 78.

Keel Row' and 'The Sandgate Lass on the Ropery Banks'[1]—was
beginning to seethe along the channel of political struggle. But we
may assume that a song usually circulated by word of mouth for
some time before it got into print and in that case 'The Waggoner'
could well be reaching back from its own time to an earlier kind of
freedom.

Verve and high spirits are not unknown in the songs of the bleak
age itself. But unalloyed cheerfulness is never felt to be integral to
the job. A Rhondda miners' song, 'The Best Little Door-boy' (sung
to one of the commonest of folk-tunes, which turns up in the village
mummers' plays and also in the Victorian music-hall), is spirited
all right yet each of the cheery details is palpably ironic:

The work-men in the Rhon-dda are won-der-ful boys, They
get to their work with-out a-ny noise; They say thro the
Rhon-dda you nev-er will see A mer-ri-er lot than in
Tip-pe-ra-ry. Too-ra-loo, too-ra-lay,
The best lit-tle door-boy that's un-der Jim Grey.

and again:

> Two girls from Treorchy pull out a full tram,
> They've holes in their stockings, they don't care a damn!

and again:

> Oh talk about hauling—it's nothing but fun,
> To do her on the level, as well as on the run,
> To hook her and sprag her and holler 'Gee-way!'
> I'm the best little doorboy that's under Jim Grey.[2]

[1] *Come All Ye Bold Miners*, 47-9.
[2] *The Shuttle and Cage*, ed. Ewan MacColl (1954), 25.

This is double-edged merriment: you only have to sing it and feel on which words the bite comes to realise that satisfaction in the doing of the job is tempered by a wry awareness of how hard a grind it is. This is typical of the songs made in the bleak age, and typical of the ordinary humour of the miners.[1] It seems that as the working people became fully industrialised–doing one job only, under intensively disciplined conditions, and living off this alone[2]– the iron entered into their souls (for all that material standards of living often improved) and it could not be got out again without a struggle, both grim and invigorating, which itself became a potent influence on their song-making.

The best songs of the more social kind from the onset of this phase are all from the handloom weavers, which agrees with Thompson's suggestion that the experience of the handloom weavers 'seems most to colour the social consciousness of the working class in the first half of the century'.[3] The inventions that headed the break-through to machine industry came thronging in the 1760s, '70s, and '80s– the water-frame, spinning jenny, mule, and self-acting mule, plus Watt's steam engine, shortly to be harnessed to cotton manufacture. The workmen who had to learn to use the new machines were unusually self-reliant artisans with a long tradition of organisation: by the first quarter of the eighteenth century there were weavers' unions (really 'friendly societies') in Devon, Wiltshire, Somerset, and Gloucestershire, by the 1730s a woolcombers' union in the Yorkshire worsted industry, and by mid-century laws against 'trade clubs' in the silk and flax manufacture.[4] Artisans who orga- nised so early must have had amongst them an unusually high proportion of men with minds able to seize upon and see through to the marrow of any vital new matter. The first result of mechanisa- tion was a wave of affluence:

> . . . old barns, cart-houses, out-buildings of all descriptions were repaired, windows broke through the old blank walls,

---

[1] E.g. Roger Dataller, *From a Pitman's Note Book* (1925): 'All our humour is two-edged. . . . "This is our birthday"–when the roof comes in. "I've got a champion little present," said a trammer today as the blood trickled down his chin. "The loveliest pit I've ever seen in my life."' (161).

[2] See also below, ch. 5, pp. 114-5.

[3] *Making of the English Working Class*, 212 n.

[4] Sidney and Beatrice Webb, *The History of Trade Unionism, 1660-1920* (1920 ed.), 31-41; G. N. Clark, *The Wealth of England, 1496-1760* (1946), 175-6; John Clapham, *A Concise Economic History of Britain (to 1750)* (1951 ed.), 261.

and all fitted up for loom-shops; new weavers' cottages with loom-shops arose in every direction, every family bringing home weekly from 40 to 120 shillings.

This was after the mule but before the steam-driven loom – before the terrible slump, the cutting of wages by as much as two-thirds, the beginning of the end for the outworker in his cottage, when the end of the wars with France coincided with the sweeping introduction of the power-loom: 2400 in use by 1813, then 14,150 by 1820 and over 100,000 by 1833, a fifty-fold increase in twenty years.[1]

It was at some point in this process that an unremarkable song from Yorkshire, 'The Yorkshire Weaver', appeared as a broadside from Manchester – greatly vitalised, full of intimate passion and its imagery rich in the stuff of social living, and all as a result of stretching itself to take in the industrial experience. The original goes like this:

am a weav-er to my trade And I am a cour-ting a
pret-ty fair maid, If I but could her fa-vour gain I'd
nev-er re-turn to my loom a-gain.

She's the finest lass in Morley Town,
She always walks out in a fine silk gown,
At weaver lads she looks in scorn,
I wish that a weaver I'd ne'er been born![2]

---

[1] Arnold J. Toynbee, *The Industrial Revolution*, 1884 (Boston, 1956), 63 (quoting Baines's *History of the Cotton Manufacture*, 1835); *ib.* 134, n. 14; Harland, *Ballads and Songs of Lancashire*, 169.

[2] Frank Kidson (ed.), *English Peasant Songs* (1929), 36-7.

By the 1820s it has become this:

I am a hand weav - er to my trade. I fell in love with a fac - tory maid. And if I could but her fa - vour wi - n I'd stand be - side her and weave by steam.

My father to me scornful said:
How could you fancy a factory maid
When you could have girls fine and gay
And dressed like to the Queen of May?

As for your fine girls, I don't care,
And could I but enjoy my dear
I'd stand in the factory all the day
And she and I'd keep our shuttles in play.

I went to my love's bedroom door
Where oftentimes I had been before,
But I could not speak nor yet get in
To the pleasant bed my love layed in.

How can you say it's a pleasant bed
When nowt lies there but a factory maid?
A factory lass although she be,
Blest is the man that enjoys she.

Oh, pleasant thoughts come to my mind
As I turned down the sheets so fine
And I seen her two breasts standing so
Like two white hills all covered with snow.

Where are the girls? I'll tell you plain,
The girls have gone to weave by steam,
And if you'd find 'em you must rise at dawn
And trudge to the mill in the early morn.[1]

[1] Sung (unaccompanied) by A. L. Lloyd on *The Iron Muse*, side 2, band 2.
Mr Lloyd has the song on four broadsides from different Manchester publishers
and considers them to be about the 1820s. The song must certainly have originated
some time after 1785 when the steam-powered loom was first patented.

C

The difference is as great as could be. The earlier songster's attitude of abasement before a 'superior' class goes with an inability to catch more than a few items from the surface of his situation, whereas the industrial songster is alert to his situation and able to make it over completely into artistic terms. The imagery is fresh and heartfelt, unabashedly sensual, and able to use craft terms for erotic implications. At the close it rises to the stark dignity of Villon, and the tune with its effect of a single pipe playing is the perfect music for these words. It is the acme of folk poetry in that it is both down-to-earth and tender. The much greater all-round percipience of the later song bears out what contemporaries used to say about the higher intelligence of townspeople: for example, Marx and Engels's arrogant yet suggestive comment (in the *Communist Manifesto* of 1848) on 'the idiocy of the village'. The experience of being industrialised must have jolted the faculties into wakefulness. Of course urbanisation also stunned and deformed various faculties. What 'The Weaver and the Factory Maid' has in common with the country songs is its unabashed sensuality. From about 1800 onwards the erotic is forced underground – onto the walls of the 'public conveniences' – or way up into the air in the sublimations of the Romantic poets and novelists.[1] During the century after the date of that song it was not possible for an artist to move with ease across the gamut of his experience, and it seems to me that popular song has not recovered this ability yet.

As the bleak age set in, the songs harnessed themselves to the hard graft of protest and industrial struggle. The whole human embroilment, the values that were jeopardised and those that were confirmed, are expressed wonderfully in two songs, one from the Lancashire cotton country and the other from the linen-making in the eastern lowlands of Scotland. Both songs are doubly revealing in that they evolve markedly as they pass down from generation to generation. The first classic in this vein is 'Jone o' Grinfilt [John of Greenfield] Junior', which Harland collected at Droylsden from an old handloom weaver. The prototype of the song had been made up on the road between Oldham and Manchester, and this is the place to point out that if one lists the names of places occurring in industrial songs plus sources of songs plus sites of customs on which songs were based, one area far outdoes any other: the cluster of industrial communities which by now have mostly been swallowed

---

[1] See above, ch. 1, 35-6; ch. 2, 44-7.

up in north-east Manchester. Woodhouses, Failsworth, Greenfield, Greenside, Shaw, Droylsden, Hyde, Dukinfield, as far north-east as Delph and as far down as Gorton–there is the first heartland of industrial song. It was there also that the first brunt of mechanisation was felt. Lancashire before Yorkshire, cottons before woollens. And the men who felt and expressed the stresses of that time were repeatedly the artisans. The militant crowd in Paris in 1789 were mainly from the small workshops. In London the Corresponding Society was supported mainly by tradesmen, shopkeepers, 'mechanics'. The Sheffield cutlers passed round Tom Paine's *Rights of Man* and in Scotland the Dundee weavers. In the Chartist Forties the scheme for helping needy workpeople to settle on the land appealed first in cotton (not coal-and-iron) districts, and in Lancashire more than anywhere, and by occupations to cotton overseers, spinners, stockingers, lace-weavers, tailors.[1] If one moves in closer, one can see how in both singing and speaking the handloom weaver had been able to act as the mind and voice of his class. It is recorded of one of the last of them at Haslingden near Blackburn that 'The old man would chat away to me. When not talking he would be humming or singing snatches of some old ballad'. In the same district a man born in 1820 wrote from Accrington in 1890 that 'The handloom weavers were generally very sedate and sage and thought deeply over the questions which engaged the public mind; and when they spoke, their utterances were given in all earnestness and in a manner calculated to set those around them thinking.' Again, in Dent Town in the western dales of Yorkshire there was a complete system of spinning galleries which

> formed a highway of communication to a dense and industrious rural population which lived on flats and floors. . . . [They] were at all seasons places of free air. . . . For there might be heard the buzz of the spinning-wheel, and the hum and the songs of those who were carrying on the labours of the day; and the merry jests and greetings sent down to those who were passing through the streets.[2]

In such a place the conditions of work did not curb the minds and tongues of people. For a time they remained able to express in song the closing-in of the forces that presently drove them through into

---

[1] *Chartist Studies*, ed. Asa Briggs (1960), 317, 330-1. See also below, 99.
[2] C. Aspin, *Haslingden 1800-1900* (Haslingden, 1962), 33; Adam Sedgwick, *A Memorial by the Trustees of Cowgill Chapel* (Cambridge, 1868), viii-ix.

a different type of culture in which poetry of a fine quality would no longer spring up from sources of a local-communal kind. 'Jone o' Grinfilt Junior' strikes me as a piece of life expressed in its entirety with its flow and ebb of feeling, its crucial details, and its own idiomatic nuance. It was sung (according to Chapter 5 of *Mary Barton*, in which it is called 'The Oldham Weaver') in 'a kind of droning recitative' and it goes like this:

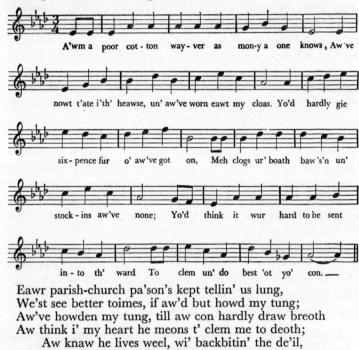

Eawr parish-church pa'son's kept tellin' us lung,
We'st see better toimes, if aw'd but howd my tung;
Aw've howden my tung, till aw con hardly draw breoth
Aw think i' my heart he meons t' clem me to deoth;
    Aw knaw he lives weel, wi' backbitin' the de'il,
    But he never *pick'd o'er* in his loife.

Wey tooart on six week, thinkin' aich day wur th' last,
Wey tarried un' shifted, till neaw wey're quite fast;
Wey liv't upo' nettles, whoile nettles were good,
Un' Wayterloo porritch wur' th' best o' us food;
    Aw'm tellin' yo' true, aw con foind foak enoo,
    Thot're livin' no better nur me.

Neaw, owd Bill o' Dan's sent bailies one day,
Fur t' shop scoar aw'd ow'd him, 'ot aw' couldn't pay;
Bur her're just to lat, fur owd Bill o' Bent,
Had sent tit un' cart, un' ta'en t' goods fur t' rent;
    They laft nowt bur a stoo' 'ot're seeots for two;
    Un' on it keawrt Marget un' me.

The bailies sceawlt reawnd os sly os a meawse,
When they seedn o' th' things wur ta'en eawt o' th' heawse;
Un t' one says to th' tother, 'O's gone, theaw may see.'
Aw said, 'Never fret lads, you're welcome ta'e me.'
    They made no moor ado, bur nipt up th' owd stoo',
    Un' wey booath leeten swack upo' th' flags. . . .

My piece wur cheeont off, un' aw took it him back;
Aw hardly durst spake, mester looked so black;
He said, 'Yo're o'erpaid last toime 'ot yo coom.'
Aw said, 'If aw wur', 'twur wi' wayving beawt loom;
    Un i' t' moind 'ot aw'm in, aw'st ne'er pick o'er again,
    For aw've wooven mysel' to th' fur end.'

So aw coom eawt o' th' wareheawse, un' laft him chew that,
When aw thowt 'ot o' things, aw're so vext that aw swat;
Fur to think aw mun warch, to keep him un' o' th' set,
O' th' days o' my loife, un' then dee i' the'r debt:
    But aw'll give o'er this trade, un work wi' a spade,
    Or goo un' break stone upo' th' road.

Eawr Marget declares, if hoo'd clooas to put on,
Hoo'd go up to Lunnon to see the great mon;
Un' if things did no' awter, when theere hoo had been,
Hoo says hoo'd begin, un' feight blood up to th' e'en,
    Hoo's nout agen th' king, bur hoo loikes a fair thing,
    Un' hoo says hoo con tell when hoo's hurt.[1]

    clem, *starve*: pick'd o'er, *threw the shuttle*: tooart, *held on*: tit, *donkey*:
    keawrt, *sat*: beawt, *without*: hoo'd, *she had*.

Once again it had taken industrial pressures to raise popular
expression to this level. The model for the song was 'Jone o'
Grinfilt's Ramble', a comic piece made up for beer-money by two
mill workers, which is in the common vein of consciously provincial
farce: a yokel from the village ventures out into the wide world
where he gets by on a mixture of dopeyness and cunning:

When aw went for a soger, aw ment for to ride,
Soa they brought meh a tit, un aw gat on at wrang side,
Aw geet on at wrang side, boh aw soon tumbled oer;
Meh officer said aw should niver ride more.
    Aw thowt, that's quite reet, aw con goo o meh feet
    As fur as aw wish for to goo.[2]

---

[1] Harland, *Ballads and Songs*, 169-72: the elaborately phonetic spelling is
presumably to catch as precisely as possible the accent of the man from whom he
got it (and is repeated by Mrs Gaskell, who says in the text of her novel that she
is 'copying' the song for the reader unfamiliar with Lancashire). The broadside
versions, e.g. the 1860 Manchester version quoted by Lloyd (*Folk Song in England*,
325-7), are much nearer Standard English.
[2] Harland, *Ballads and Songs*, 162-4.

During the French wars this had been the most popular song in Lancashire. The slump immediately the war was over, when the end of army contracts for woven and knitted cloth coincided with the first undercutting of prices by factory goods, turned the old heedless farce into a classic of social poetry in which every word seems precisely weighted with hard experience. The keeping between tune and words is perfect: for example, the way in which the peaks in the tune come on the words that most need stressing and the grip and distinctness with which the words fit into the short line that clinches each verse. The protest being voiced is dogged and bitter without one note of shrill self-pity. The whole is steadied by resilient humour in the teeth of the worst deprivation, by the man's decent, straight conviction of rights deserved but denied, and by the honesty of his determination not to speak up about his own hardships until he has made sure that they are *shared*: 'Aw'm tellin' yo true, aw con foind foak enoo,/Thot're livin' no better nur me.' The business with the stool and phrases like 'He're just to lat' make a kind of cool joke as the weaver watches the dismantling of his home, but by the end of that verse we have been brought with perfect naturalness to an image of deprivation which could hardly be bettered in its utter bleakness, pointed up by the three laboured stresses, 'Un' ón it keawrt Márget un' mé'.

This condition of being not only hard up against it but also wholly aware of this predicament was now the nerve of working-people's experience. Francis Place the Radicals' backroom organiser, who had himself worked at making up cloth for a master tailor in London, brings this out in passage after passage of priceless evidence. He and his wife had lived and worked in a single room in which they had had to see their son die of smallpox:

> A neat clean room, though it be as small as a closet, and however few the articles of furniture, is of more importance in its moral consequences than anybody seems hitherto to have supposed.

And again:

> The working-man must have no relaxation; he who drudges constantly against his will, must have no such propensities as are allowed and cherished in his superior . . . there are times when he is unable to bring himself to the conclusion that he must continue working. I know not how to describe the sickening aversion which at times steals over the working-man, and utterly disables him, for a longer or shorter period, from following his usual occupation. . . .

And again:

> . . . a very considerable number of our skilled labourers, are
> in poverty, if not in actual misery; a large portion of them have
> been in a state of poverty and great privation all their lives.
> They are neither ignorant of their condition nor reconciled to
> it. . . . To escape from this state is with them of paramount
> importance. Among a vast multitude of these people not a
> day, scarcely an hour, can be said [*sc.* to pass] without some
> circumstance, some matter exciting reflection, occurring to
> remind them of their condition, which (notwithstanding they
> have been poor and distressed from their infancy, and however
> much they may *at times* be cheerful) they scarcely ever cease,
> and never for a long period cease, to feel and to acknowledge
> to themselves with deep sensations of anguish. . . .[1]

'Jone o' Grinfilt' so hit the centre of this experience that the last
three lines became proverbial. Version after version appeared,
hitting off the Jacobins, then Chartism, the New Poor Law, and
finally the Crimean War;[2] and only twenty years ago a form of it
could still be got from a man in the village of Delph, not far from
the Manchester conurbation but just over the border into the West
Riding. But by now it has been worn down into three verses and a
chorus made out of the hardest of the hardship elements, the
humour has gone, and so has the defying of the middleman. It now
goes like this:

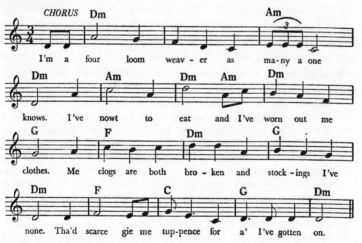

CHORUS Dm — Am

I'm a four loom weav-er as ma-ny a one
knows. I've nowt to eat and I've worn out me
clothes. Me clogs are both bro-ken and stock-ings I've
none. Tha'd scarce gie me tup-pence for a' I've gotten on.

---

[1] Graham Wallas, *The Life of Francis Place, 1771-1854* (1925 ed.), 10, 14-15, 162-3, 382.

[2] Harland, *Ballads and Songs*, 164-5, 173-5.

VERSE Dm   C   G   Dm

Owd_ Bil - ly o't Bent he kept tel - ling me long, We

Am   Dm   G

might have bet-ter times if__ I'd nob but howd me tongue. Well I've

F   Dm   G   Dm

how - den me tongue till__ I near lost me breath, And I

C   G   Dm

feel in my heart that I'll soon clem to death.

The tune is different: it needs the slow tempo and the dragging
instead of running rhythm that MacColl gives it when he sings it
unaccompanied.[1] The experience is now felt to be lonely, not
shared, and the refrain ends the song on a downbeat instead of a
note of dogged resistance. Since this is the version that has lived
on through and past the end of the trade it sprang from, we may
assume that the erosion of the song went on abreast of and amidst
the erosion of the way of life. Finally it was collected in an old
cottage-industry village on the moor edge, too far from a cotton
centre to be absorbed into the factory conurbation, doomed therefore to stagnate, to lose its young people and see its able-bodied
men commuting or emigrating for work. In the words of a witness
before the Select Committee on Emigration which met in 1826-
1827:

> There are two distinct classes of hand-loom weavers in
> Lancashire, those who are living in large towns and those in
> the country places among the hills ... they are at this moment
> by far the most distressed class of persons in Lancashire, for it
> has been their custom to take small tracts of land at high rents,
> which the husband and his sons cultivate, while the woman
> and her daughters have two, three or four handlooms ... from
> the profits of which they ... pay their rents ... at the same
> time that their loom-work fails them, their poor-rates are
> increased for the relief of other weavers who have no land.[2]

[1] *The Shuttle and Cage*, 4-5; sung on *Shuttle and Cage* (Topic 10T13, n.d.), side 1,
band 6.
[2] Quoted from John Clapham, *Economic History of Modern Britain*, The Early
Railway Age 1820-1850 (1926), 180 and n.

The other classic song from that phase, which is 'The Wark o' the Weavers' from Angus in Scotland, is much more ambiguous as evidence of morale. It is by one of Scotland's many weaver poets, David Shaw, and was written for an Annual General Meeting of the Forfar Weavers' Friendly Society. It goes like this:

This song is outstanding not only for its level-paced, driving rhythm but also for its lyric. It doesn't tell a story or find a symbol for a mood or a personal situation; it is an exposition. Verse 2 is a riposte to the middlemen who mock at the weavers as 'thin-faced,

[1] *The Shuttle and Cage*, 10-11; sung on *Shuttle and Cage*, side 1, band 1.

bleached-like cloots'. Verse 3 names various trades and callings all of which depend on textiles (not forgetting the export market). Verse 4 argues that woven cloth is indispensable throughout society. Verse 5 shows that the same is true even of the most independent ('The women need nae barbers and the dykers need nae clerk'). The sixth and last verse is an optimistic peroration:

> The weaving is a trade that never can fail,
> As lang's we need ae cloot to keep anither hale;
> So let us aye be merry ower a bicker o' guid ale,
> And drink tae the health o' the weavers.

This is a considered approach, an educated approach, and as such it is new in the workers' songs. It presumably dates from the decades after the French wars–Shaw lived from 1786-1856; and it was then that the workers in Lowland Scotland were founding adult education in Britain.[1] It was a dogged, practical, enquiring kind of mind that went into this new cultural initiative–this will to analyse the system that employed and exploited people. Intellect rooted in labour–that is what we feel to be the core of the almost pugnacious good-humour in 'The Wark o' the Weavers'. Although the song originated in Angus, it was collected most recently in Fife, and early in the nineteenth century the linen weavers in those counties had their own infant schools, libraries, bank, Scientific Club, drawing academy, and literary magazines and they shared actively in a tradition of free-thinking, Jacobinism, and republicanism.[2]

This suggests a community in good heart; but if trade was flourishing, why did it need to protest its indispensability? The men in the song must have been handloom weavers who got materials from the middleman for working-up, made the piece in their own time, and brought it for sale themselves ('oor wark upon oor back'). This is freedom of a kind; but the weaver poets are full of resentment at the whiphand the dealers had over them. In Lancashire: 'My piece wur cheeont off, un' aw took it him back;/Aw hardly durst spake, mester looked so black'. In Scotland the Paisley weaver poet, Alexander Wilson, mimics the slimy tones of the buyer who spoils the piece he is offered and then blames the workmanship so that he can cut the price:

> Dear man!–that wark'll never do;
> See that: ye'll no tak telling' . . .

---

[1] For details see below, ch. 4, 93.
[2] E. J. Hobsbawm, *The Age of Revolution* (1962), 214.

He denounces corruption:

> What town can thrive wi sic a crew
> Within its entrails crawlin' . . .

and he appeals to decent opinion:

> Wha cou'd believe a chiel sae trig
> Wad cheat us o' a bodle?
> Or that sae fair a gowden wig
> Contained sae black a noddle?[1]

The weavers' position was in fact precarious, and though linen held its own, the cottons and woollens of the more central and southern parts of the Lowlands also felt the remorseless squeeze of the factory with its power-looms. By 1839 there were still 37,000 weavers in Scotland who worked up the merchants' raw materials, and they were now at the mercy of the market. In one public appeal the weavers from Kirkcaldy in Fife gave the cost of a week's necessaries for a family of five as 11/5, and since the post-war slump they had had in their worst times to work a 96-hour week for 3/6.[2] From this it would seem that the vitality of 'The Wark o' the Weavers' gets its assertive note from the Angus men's awareness that their fellows not far away had their backs to the wall.

The tune quoted above and the singing style suited to it are remarkable for keeping to a level with little rise and fall and for the incessant beat, as though a thick forefinger were being thumped into the palm to enforce an argument in the public bar. There is a different version which goes like this:

¹ *The Poems and Literary Prose of Alexander Wilson*, ed. A. B. Grosart (Paisley, 1876), II, 59–69 (Wilson was fined for libel, ordered to burn his poems at the town cross, and imprisoned because he couldn't pay the fine: see Craig, *Scottish Literature*, 90).

² Pryde, *Scotland from 1603*, 235–6; Mathieson, *Church and Reform in Scotland*, 144, 148, 152.

was-na for the wark o' the weav - ers. If it

was - na for the weav - ers what wad they do? They

wad-na hae claith made oor o' oor woo', They

wad - na hae a coat neith-er black nor blue, Gin it

was-na for the wark o' the weav - ers.

This has a marked rise and fall, and as sung its tempo is easy-going compared with the hard-driving version discussed already. It is taken from Ford's *Vagabond Songs* of 1890 (*via* a recent song book[1]), and that is prior to MacColl's collecting of the other version from his Fife source. Yet I suspect it, for at the end of last century Scotland was suffering from a bad attack of bogus folk culture: it was the time of the Celtic Twilight, the Hebridean fishermen's songs were being soulfully arranged for the drawing-room piano, the Lowland villages were being presented by the Kailyard novelists as a cosy mini-paradise full of ministers and homely old women. The very word 'vagabond' sorts oddly with the self-employed artisan who walked to market or to the dealer's to sell what he had made. And the particular singer who records this more easy-going version is from a different region (Aberdeenshire) and is a perfect adept at the debased folk style popularised by Harry Lauder: his vocal tone hovers on the edge of a couthy chuckle, and he takes advantage of those rises and falls in the tune to put in a kind of unctuous scoop. The most likely history for the song would

---

[1] *101 Scottish Songs*, ed. Norman Buchan (1962), 54; this version is recorded by John Mearns on *Five Scottish Folk-songs* (SR 4512 EP, Aberdeen, n.d.), side 1, band 2.

therefore seem to be this: Originally it had a strikingly four-square tune and ongoing tempo suited to the dogged intellect that is in the words and which sprang from the weavers' culture in its best days. It was written, however, to make the best of a threatened way of life, and the imminent victory of the city and its industry–a victory both economic and cultural–first crushed out the self-sufficient country worker and then turned his art into a schmaltzy travesty.

The other remarkable songs of this transitional time bring out how the modes of thought or sensibility that still came naturally to the workman singer were being forced into obsolescence by the changes in which he was caught up. One named singer stands out from Harland's collection: John Grimshaw of Gorton. His nickname was 'John Common', which is closely akin to the legendary wage-earning hero in Scottish lore, 'Iohne the common-weil', from the sixteenth-century *Satyre of the Thrie Estaits*. The best of Grimshaw's surviving pieces both take the part of the handloom weaver. 'Handloom *v.* Power-loom' is not a classic of the transition, but every phrase in it is meaty. Its rough swing seems to embody, not the old heedless heartiness, but a rather desperate sense of being carried along in a breakneck process:

> Come all you cotton-weavers, your looms you may pull down;
> You must get employ'd in factories, in country or in town;
> For our cotton-masters have found out a wonderful new scheme,
> These calico goods now wove by hand they're going to weave by
> steam . . .
>
> In comes the surly winder, her cops they are all marr'd;
> 'They are all snarls, and soft, bad ends; for I've roved off many
> a yard;
> I'm sure I'll tell the master, or the joss, when he comes in;'
> They'll daub you down, and you must pay;–so money comes
> rolling in.[1]

cops *cones (of thread)*

So many weaving terms are used that the song–like the most remarkable of the erotic songs from the same culture, 'The Bury New Loom'[2]–must have been meant for a close community who were at one in their habits, feelings, and grievances: it is noteworthy that the three most detailed verses are all against shop fines,

[1] Harland, *Ballads and Songs*, 188-9.
[2] Lloyd, *Folk Song in England*, 321-2.

that special bugbear of people coming under factory discipline for the first time.[1] Grimshaw's companion piece, 'The Hand-loom Weavers' Lament', is much less sure in its fitting of idiom into the lyric verse-form, and this is typical of a cultural dilemma to be discussed later—the inevitable difficulty people had in adapting traditional utterance to quite new kinds of struggle and controversy. The 'Lament' is most trenchant and imaginative when it is off-setting Biblical imagery against the facts of inequality:

> When we look on our poor children, it grieves our hearts full
>   sore,
> Their clothing it is worn to rags, while we can get no more,
> With little in their bellies, they to their work must go,
> Whilst yours do dress as manky as monkeys in a show.
>
> You go to church on Sundays, I'm sure it's nought but pride,
> There can be no religion where humanity's thrown aside;
> If there be a place in heaven, as there is in the Exchange,
> Our poor souls must not come near there; like lost sheep they
>   must range.
>
> With the choicest of strong dainties your tables overspread,
> With good ale and strong brandy, to make your faces red;
> You call'd a set of visitors—it is your whole delight—
> And you lay your heads together to make our faces white.[2]

Thus the language of the ancient Hebrew laments and protests still rose to the lips: the Luddites hanged in 1813 sang hymns on the scaffold, the most free-thinking Lancashire workers nevertheless knew the Bible thoroughly.[3] More often than not, the humble mien, the wishful language, and even the very verse-forms of the hymn or metrical psalm were used by unemployed men at their most abject, when they begged submissively for charity.[4] It took time to burn through long-standing illusions and arrive at a non-utopian view of life. Just as the labour movement first adopted the language and some of the forms of religion on the way to a fully

---

[1] See Engels on power-loom weavers' fines in Marx and Engels, *On Britain* (Moscow, 1953), 212-5.

[2] Harland, *Ballads and Songs*, 194-5.

[3] Edward Thompson, 'Homage to Tom Maguire', in *Essays in Labour History*, ed. Asa Briggs and John Saville (1960), 290, n. 1; Thompson, *English Working Class*, 428.

[4] E.g. the framework-knitters' 'Lamentation' and 'Petition' from Sutton in Nottinghamshire: *The Common Muse*, ed. V. de Sola Pinto and A. E. Rodway (1957), 118-9; 'The Mechanic's Appeal to the Public': *Modern Street Ballads*, ed. John Ashton (1885), 21-3.

political style of work–for example, 'communist churches' and 'Chartist churches', the Owenite agitators known as 'social missionaries', the general strike planned for 1838 under the name of a 'sacred month'[1]–so presently the unions themselves emerged as a source of song and left behind the old appeal to some higher power.

From about the middle of the nineteenth century, the great bulk of the songs that communicate industrial experience are from the coalfields; and after the end of the century such pieces virtually cease being created. The former point agrees with Thompson's view of what 'colours the experience of the working class': he goes on to say that 'The miners and metal-workers do not make their influence felt until later in the century'–that is to say, their potential as a force in the culture was not released until the 'second Industrial Revolution' with its demand for coal and iron for the railways and the making of heavy machinery. From about 1844 onwards we have a sequence of sustained, original, and forceful pieces, including pre-eminently 'The Coal-owner and the Pitman's Wife' from Shotton Moor in County Durham, 'The Blackleg Miners' probably from the Bishop Auckland area in the 'Eighties, 'The Durham Lock-out' from Stanley in County Durham in 1892, and a whole run of very fine pit disaster ballads in which the always latent tragedy of the miner's life rises up in a poetry of special dignity. (The peaks of this line are from north Lanarkshire in 1877, east Durham in 1882, and west Fife in 1901.[2]) This body of work makes a *tradition* and one that images contemporary life more effectively than the main art poetry of the same phase.[3] It is the lyric expression of the movement defined in Engels's classic passage on the wave of strikes in 1844 where he says that they 'had torn the miners of the North of England forever from the intellectual death in which they had hitherto lain; they have left their sleep, are alert to defend their interests, and have entered the movement of civilisation'.[4]

---

[1] G. D. H. Cole and Raymond Postgate, *The Common People* (1956 ed.), 321; Wallas, *Life of Place*, 378; E. Frow, 'Robert Owen', in *Marxism Today* (October 1958), 298-9; A. L. Morton, *A People's History of England* (1956 ed.), 434.

[2] These songs are: 'The Blantyre Explosion', 'The Trimdon Grange Explosion', and 'The Donibristle Moss Moran Disaster' (see *Come All Ye Bold Miners*, 78-80); they are sung on *Shuttle and Cage*, *The Collier's Rant*, and *The Iron Muse*.

[3] This summary judgement is worked out more fully below: see ch. 8, 179-81.

[4] Marx and Engels, *On Britain*, 293.

So far as verbal expression went, this was a hard thing to do. Most of these songs are poetry in the vernacular flawed with cliché. For example, 'The Coal-owner and the Pitman's Wife' is quite in the vein of Langland with its semi-allegorical story of the poor woman confronting the rich man, dubbed 'Lord Firedamp', and threatening him with the pains of hell where the devil, 'like a mad bull with a ring through his nose', is busy tormenting the rich.

> 'Aye, the way I got out, the truth I will tell.
> They're turning the poor folk all out of hell.
> This is to make room for the rich wicked race,
> For there is a great number of them in that place.
> Derry down, down, down derry down.'[1]

This piece has been got only in fragments in the county of its origin, Durham, and the full version is from a Lancashire miner who lives near St Helens, which may well reflect the spread of miners' militancy in the middle 'Forties away down through the West Riding and south Lancashire into Derbyshire and the east Midlands.[2] Unfortunately the song is clumsily done: the verses are repetitive, the lines are padded out with inexpressive stock tags, and the words lollop so awkwardly to the tune that a singer is forced to stress words against the grain of idiomatic utterance. From about this time onwards, various kinds of hack-work, from the commercial routines of disabled miners singing in the workmen's halls to the churning out of broadsides for mass publication by the like of James Catnach and John Pitts of Seven Dials,[3] intrude on the accustomed ease and resource of a song tradition which had flowed from the unforced needs of particular communities.

It is also noticeable that such failures of keeping between lyric and tune occur very commonly where the subject is *the system*. The following are among the weakest verses in 'The Coal-owner':

> 'If you be a coal-owner, sir, take my advice,
> Agree with your men and give them a full price.
> For if and you do not, I know very well,
> You'll be in great danger of going to hell.
> Derry down, etc.

---

[1] *Come All Ye Bold Miners*, 94.
[2] Marx and Engels, *On Britain*, 288-90.
[3] Lloyd, *Folk Song in England*, 353-5; Pinto and Rodway, *The Common Muse*, 3-4, 26-7.

'For all you coal-owners great fortunes has made,
By those jovial men that works in the coal trade.
Now, how can you think for to prosper and thrive
By wanting to starve your poor workmen alive?'
    Derry down, etc.

Or again, from a broadside ballad on the weavers' strikes of 1853:

Though the masters find they lose a deal, the tide must soon be
  turning,
They find the men won't, quietly, be robbed of half their earning.

(Chorus) It's high time that working men should have it their
  own way,
    And for a fair day's labour, receive a fair day's pay.

This is not singable: there is no rhythmic spring from one word to
another, and the words are so much blunt assertion, devoid of
specificity. The same is true of one of the farm-workers' union
songs of the 1870s whose sales attest its popularity:

Says the master to me, 'A word or two more;
We never have quarrelled on matters before;
If you stick to the Union, ere long, I'll be bound,
You will come and ask me for more wages all round.

'Now I cannot afford more than two bob a-day
When I look at the taxes and rent that I pay,
And the crops are so injured by game, as you see,
If it is hard for you it's hard also for me.'

And this was to be sung to 'Bonny Dundee', an even more jaw-
breaking feat than singing the 'Hand-loom Weavers' Lament' to
'A-Hunting We Will Go' . . .[1] In America a little later they were
undergoing the same struggle with intractable material, for example a miners' song by one 'Red Ore' Donaldson which even
the finest banjo-player in the world cannot make run with enough
momentum:

Come all you hardy miners and help us sing this song,
Sung by some union men, four hundred thousand strong.
With John White, our general, we'll fight without a gun,
He'll lead us on to victory and sixty cents a ton.

[1] Ashton, *Modern Street Ballads*, 18-19; Reg Groves, *Sharpen the Sickle!* (1949),
251, and for the sales of this song, 'My Master and I', see *British Working Class
Movements*: Selected Documents 1789-1875, ed. G. D. H. Cole and A. W. Filson
(1951), 606; Harland, *Ballads and Songs*, 195.

Come all you hardy miners and help us sing this song,
On the 21st day of April we struck for sixty cents a ton;
The operators laughed at us and said we'd never come
All out in one body and demand that sixty cents a ton.[1]

Even the classic of this kind, the song of greatest stature from the
period of the Great Unrest, Tommy Armstrong's 'The Durham
Strike', sags when it seeks to versify *the system*. The tune is this:

The one very bad verse goes like this:

With tyranny and capital they never seem content,
Unless they are endeavouring to take from us per cent;
If it was due what they request, we willingly would grant;
We know it's not therefore we cannot give them what they
    want.[2]

The fact is that people were not only having to sing about something they had never before thought through; it was also something
that could of its nature not be known wholly at first hand. Profit-
and-loss, 'redundancy', rate of exploitation, surplus value—these
cannot be touched or felt, they are themselves abstractions from
experience; and they had not had generations in which to take on
an accustomed symbolism, as had fertility, mortality, or other of
the country themes. This was a stumbling block for the whole of the
oral culture. For example, London had its hundreds of 'street
patterers' who called out the riddles, rhymes, and 'true life stories'

[1] Sung by Pete Seeger on *American Industrial Ballads* (New York, 1956), side 1,
band 9.

[2] *Song Book . . . of the late Thomas Armstrong*, ed. W. H. Armstrong, 1909,
(Chester-le-Street, 1953 ed.), 4.

that they had for sale. All the leading coster-mongers are said to have been Chartists; Feargus O'Connor the Chartist leader was their 'trump' (hero); and many risked their freedom to sell the left-wing *Poor Man's Guardian*. But politics was just what they found it hardest to make their own:

> To 'work a litany' [extemporise a commentary on politics] is considered one of the higher exercises of professional skill on the part of the patterer. In working this, a clever patterer . . . is very particular in his choice of a mate, frequently changing his ordinary partner, who may be good 'at a noise', or a ballad, but not have sufficient acuteness or intelligence to patter politics as if he understood what he was speaking about . . .

And less than a dozen in London were up to it.[1] Yet here was some of the prime stuff of modern life.

Nevertheless the staying-power of the song tradition was such, especially in areas where both the older culture and labour militancy were strong and could supplement each other, that it remained able to convey the gist and the detail of ordinary life as could no other medium at that time. Poetry had become almost wholly escapist; workmen's attempts at art poetry were commonly an indigestible amalgam of the Old Testament, Milton, and Shelley;[2] and although the novel often bravely tried to take on the new ways of life, its place in the culture as the main medium, the *family* medium, put curbs on the experiences it could present and the social perspectives it could hold out. A major case of this is studied below (in chapter 5); here it need only be said that so far as the life of working-people was concerned, the novel regularly collapsed into soft-headed visions of 'salvation' or betterment as something that might spring up quasi-miraculously from outside their own movements.

> . . . the social critique, though still remaining strong, becomes more and more a by-product of the formal plot. So, artistically, the latter sections of Dickens's novels (for that matter it seems to me the last sections of the vast majority of eighteenth and nineteenth century English novels) tend to fall considerably short of the rest of the book.

[1] *Mayhew's London*, ed. Peter Quennell (n.d.), 55-6, 65, 149.
[2] For a large and varied sample, see *An Anthology of Chartist Literature*, ed. Y. V. Kovalev (*Moscow*, 1956).

And again:

> ... there can be no question yet of the worker-writer producing
> a novel from a 'spontaneous', positive aesthetic *need*–the need
> to express the life of the workers as, despite all alienation and
> misery, a positive, valid *life*.[1]

The songs did spring from such a need. They were steeped in the
daily living of the industrial communities, they were often called
forth by life-or-death issues, and they had a variety of practical
functions.[2]

The final phase of industrial song is typified by the work of
Tommy Armstrong from Tanfield, between Stanley and Gateshead
in north Durham. The range of his work is wide. He could make
songs portraying the domestic upheavals of a strike as pungent
farce, with a touch (in the refrain) of the old village talent at
creating a figure of fun:

> There they went fre hoose te hoose te put things on the road,
> But mind, they didn't hort thersels wi liftin heavy loads,
> Some wid carry the poker oot, the fender or the rake,
> If they lifted two at once, it was a great mistake.
>
> O what wid aw dee
> If aw'd the pooer mesel?
> Aw wid hang the twenty candymen
> And Johnny that carried the bell.[3]

He could make a pit disaster song that turns clichés from the
hymnal style into heartfelt myth, partly by grafting familiar local
facts onto the rhetoric and partly by means of a steady and dignified
tune:

---

[1] See two essays of John B. Mitchell's, on Tressell's *The Ragged Trousered
Philanthropists* and on 'Problems of the Development of the Proletarian-
Revolutionary Novel in 19th-century Britain', in *Zeitschrift für Anglistik und
Amerikanistik* (Berlin), I (1962), 50-1; III (1963), 253-8.

[2] Not only raising money for strike pay and disaster funds but also by way of
daily interchange; one miner is on record as saying (of about 1900): 'Making
rhymes and songs used to run through the pit like a fever. Some of 'em seemed to
go daft thinking up verses. Even us young lads used to answer back in rhyme.'
(Lloyd, *Folk Song in England*, 364).

[3] 'The Oakey Strike Evictions', 1885, on *Tommy Armstrong of Tyneside* (Topic
10T112, 1965), side 2, band 1 (the candymen or bailiff's labourers were rag-
collectors from the slums, the only men the owners could get to carry out evictions
of strikers: Thompson, *English Working Class*, 429).

Oh, let's not think of to‑mor‑row lest we dis‑ap‑poin‑ted be.___

Our joys may turn to sor‑row as___ we all may dai‑ly see.___

To‑day we may be strong and heal‑thy but soon there comes a change,___

As we may see from th'ex‑plo‑sion that has been at Trim‑dom Grange.___

Men and boys left home that morning for to earn their daily
  bread,
Nor thought before that evening they'd be numbered with the
  dead.
Let's think of Mrs Burnett, once had sons but now has none –
By the Trimdon Grange explosion, Joseph, George and James
  are gone.
. . . Death will pay us all a visit, they have only gone before.
We'll meet the Trimdon victims where explosions are no more.[1]

Above all, in 'The Durham Lock‑out' (the author called it 'The
Durham Strike', but the dispute was started by a *cut* in wages)
Armstrong was able to turn the basic stuff of labour struggle into a
song whose stature and fullness approaches that of the classic or
'big' ballads. The tune (quoted already) is again dignified and well
suited either to the accordion with its swelling cadences or the
unaccompanied voice with plenty of room to shape a cadence.[2]
The wording has the rooted restraint we saw in 'Jone o' Grinfilt':

I need not state the reason why we have been brought so low,
The masters have behaved unkind, which everyone will know;
Because we won't lie down and let them treat us as they like,
To punish us they've stopt their pits and caused the present
  strike.

[1] *Come All Ye Bold Miners*, 78‑9, 129; sung by Lou Killen on *The Colliers' Rant*,
side 1, band 2.
[2] It is recorded on *Second Shift, The Iron Muse*, and *Tommy Armstrong of Tyneside*
but always abridged of several verses, good as well as bad, and of the chorus.

The chorus that follows brings in an effect of militant anger lashing out: the plagues of Job are called down on the bosses in a flare of rage typical of this vein in working-class sensibility as we know it from Burns and Lewis Grassic Gibbon, Robert Tressell and Alan Sillitoe:

> May every Durham colliery owner that is in the fault,
> Receive nine lashes with the rod, then be rubbed with salt;
> May his back end be thick with boils, so that he cannot sit,
> And never burst until the wheels go round at every pit.

Again this modulates, into lines rich in positive feeling for the pit (although Armstrong as a lad of nine, his legs crippled with rickets, had had to be carried to work on his brother's back):

> The pulley wheels have ceased to move, which went so swift around,
> The horses and the ponies too are brought from underground;
> Our work is taken from us now, they care not if we die,
> For they can eat the best of food, and drink the best when dry.

By means of those last lines with their perfectly ordinary vernacular diction even the owners have been brought into the circle of mankind with its basic needs. Amidst his militancy Armstrong does not forget the human cost of militancy:

> The flour barrel is empty now, their true and faithful friend,
> Which makes the thousands wish to-day the strike was at an end.

Protest is reaffirmed with restrained trenchancy:

> Let them stand, or let them lie, to do with them as they choose,
> To give them thirteen and a half, we ever shall refuse.
> They're always willing to receive, but not inclined to give,
> Very soon they won't allow a working man to live.

And the song then ends with thanks to comrades in other counties,[1] reminding us that this was a song meant to go round with the hat—an art that sprang from practical needs and made poetry of them.

Such work indeed sees industrial living as 'a positive, valid *life*', and the culture's need of this was clamant. In 1856 George Eliot had written severely on the 'unreality' of the social novels

---

[1] *Song Book of . . . Armstrong*, 3-4.

that professed 'to represent the people as they are'.[1] But even in this classic and pioneering essay it is plain that she cannot conceive of working life as able to be absorbed into the artistic media:

> Opera peasants, whose unreality excites Mr Ruskin's indignation, are surely too frank an idealisation to be misleading; and since popular chorus is one of the most effective elements of opera, we can hardly object to lyric rustics in elegant laced bodices and picturesque motley, unless we are prepared to advocate a chorus of colliers in their pit costume, or a ballet of charwomen and stocking-weavers.[2]

Contemporary life was felt to be growing less and less amenable to art; the waste-land complex had overtaken the intelligentsia. Matthew Arnold, to whom 'modern life' was a 'strange disease', used a news item about Nottingham to discredit the current complacency at affluence: 'what an element of grimness, bareness and hideousness mixes with it and blurs it; the workhouse, the dismal Mapperly Hills,–how dismal those who have seen them will remember;–the gloom, the smoke, the cold, the strangled illegitimate child!' To the sensitive literary man, this *was* industrialised England, and this was true whatever his political alignment. Lenin remarks in his essay of 1895 on Engels that 'nearly all the Socialists of that time and the friends of the working class generally regarded the proletariat only as an *ulcer*, and observed with horror how this ulcer grew with the growth of industry.'[3] Thus William Morris, touring Tyneside to speak at socialist meetings in 1887, grieved over the mining village of Seghill: 'most woful looking dwellings of man . . . the whole district is just a miserable backyard to the collieries . . . we plodded on through the dreary (O so dreary) villages, & that terrible waste of endless back-yard'.[4] As it happens

[1] 'The Natural History of German Life: Riehl', in 'Essays': *George Eliot's Works*, XII (Warwick ed., 1920), 490.

[2] Over a century later something like this was at last achieved, in Unity Theatre's musical about the Bryant and May workers, *The Matchgirls*, and the Sunderland Theatre's show about the miners, *Close the Coalhouse Door*.

[3] Lenin, 'Frederick Engels': *Reminiscences of Marx and Engels* (Moscow, n.d.), 59.

[4] E. P. Thompson, *William Morris: Romantic to Revolutionary* (1955), 520. I am not implying that Morris did not see much deeper into the positive living of the working-class than most contemporaries. But as Thompson later puts it, analysing Morris's *Chants for Socialists*: 'Morris rarely expresses any sense of *vitality* in the working class, but only in the Cause itself, the *hope* of the future. The hatred of industrialism as such is never absent for long.' (775).

there came out of this woefulness one of the most buoyant of
protest songs, in which untamed animal energies can be felt:

It's in the   eve - nin'   af - ter   dark That the black leg

min - er   creeps to   work With his mole skin   pants an' 'is

dir - ty   shirt. There goes the   black leg   mi - ner.

> They take their picks and down they go,
> To hew the coal that lies below,
> And there's not a woman in this town row
>   Will look at a blackleg miner.
>
> Oh Seghill is a terrible place,
> They rub wet clay in the blackleg's face,
> And round the heaps they run a foot-race
>   With the dorty blackleg miners.
>
> So divven't gan near the Delaval mine,
> Across the way they stretch a line
> To catch the throot and break the spine
>   Of the dorty blackleg miner.
>
> They'll take yer duds an' tools as well
> An hoy them doon the pit o hell,
> Doon ye go an fare ye well,
>   Ye dorty blackleg miner.
>
> So jine the union while ye may,
> Don't wait till yer dyin day–
> Forthat may not be far away
>   Ye dorty blackleg miner.[1]

Of course such fierce zest didn't have behind it a carefree social
life: the most hilarious poems and songs have often sprung, as a
release, from brutally hard conditions.[2] But the point here is that
in the workman singer's mouth, 'Seghill is a terrible place' is
ironical. Implicitly he is flinging a riposte at the genteel outsider's
view of himself and his people as 'terrible and savage pitmen', in

---

[1] Sung by Lou Killen on *The Iron Muse*, side 1, band 8.
[2] E.g. see Craig, *Scottish Literature*, 97-8.

the words of a Newcastle shopkeeper, or 'black animals', in the words of a mineowner's wife from Tyneside.[1] Treatment of blacklegs could be savage (like the occasional vitriol throwing earlier in the century). But the songmaker could realise, as nearly all outsiders failed to do, that *within* this 'savagery' lay a will to surmount it, that civilised values, social and personal, held steady in the blackest passages of the struggle: 'There's not a woman in this town row/ Will look at a blackleg miner', or again: 'So jine the Union while ye may'. The crisp, nimble rhythms of the song, the exact consonance between the high notes and the punchy emphases, voice its essential confidence in the human future to be won by the industrial means themselves.[2]

From about 1900, at least according to what has been found so far (and the collecting of songs in the coalfields has been particularly thorough), the creativity of people at large ceased to channel itself through song. No longer (until the recent upsurge of the pop groups) was any good work in this mode initiated by 'the folk': that is, by the cultural network other than the centralised media in which art is a commodity. It has been usual to say that 'labour songs have been silenced by the hum of machinery',[3] but this telescopes a process whose stages are not self-evident. It is true that in a society where most people worked in factories, songs died out or went underground partly through the bloody-minded policing of the authorities. This was true of the Lancashire mills[4] and also of many another trade. Throughout the second half of the nineteenth century in the upper Thames valley, for example, singing in pubs was crushed by a 'harsh and strict supervision of the police'. 'The houses at which it was held, *i.e.* those at which the poor labourers commonly gathered, were marked as disorderly places; the police looked upon song-singing as a species of rowdyism. Their frequent complaints and threats to the landlords filled them with misgivings; the result was that they were forced, as a means of self-protection, to request their customers not to sing on the premises, or, at any rate, *not to allow themselves to be heard.*' Just after 1900 housepainters in Hastings were sacked for singing hymns at work;

---

[1] Thompson, *English Working Class*, 429; *Come All Ye Bold Miners*, 13 (this woman's husband owned the pit whose elegy was quoted at the start of this chapter).

[2] The civilising force inherent in militancy is documented below, ch. 6, 139-40.

[3] George Thomson, *The Prehistoric Aegean* (1954 ed.), 446.

[4] See below, ch. 5, 116.

and at the same time one rule of a Welsh railway company was 'Not an instance of intoxication, singing, whistling, or hilarity while on duty will be overlooked, and besides being dismissed, the offender will be liable to punishment.'[1]

Yet can it be doubted that even without suppression the people's own songs would have withered? A potent two-fold tendency was at work. People became shamefaced about the old culture; and things that had been done by the songs came to be done in other media. For example, Alf Williams found in the upper Thames that if a farm worker left the farm for some other job, he 'felt ashamed of his songs'—although they included many matchless gems of love lyrics and celebrations of fertility—and if he joined a choir or band, he of course 'showed a preference for classical, or, at any rate, for standard pieces'. Fairs were restricted, which is the policing again, but often the trouble was straight cultural competition: the new church organs discountenanced the old village bands, teachers trained in the towns had little feeling for the village culture, and they also imported music from urban sources (which presently included bowdlerised folk songs kindly supplied by the great collector Cecil Sharp). We have a close-up of the process as it reached the dale of Dent, whose knitting galleries were described above. At one time, 'Men, women and children all knit. . . . They have knitting schools, where the children are taught; and where they sing in chorus knitting songs . . . all of them bear some reference to their employment and mode of life . . . they often get so excited that they say, "Neighbours, we'll not part tonight", that is, till after twelve o'clock.' But 'Formerly you might have met the waggoners knitting as they went along with their teams; but this is now [1838] rare; for the greater influx of visitors, and their wonder expressed at this and other practices, has made them rather ashamed of them, and shy of strangers observing them.'[2] So centralisation becomes a barely resistible force. Whatever has the metropolitan appeal, the *cachet* associated with the centres of national affluence, carries success with it. Whatever has the taint, even merely by association, of the old poverty and the supplanted social system is doomed to go under.

[1] *Folk-songs of the Upper Thames*, ed. Alfred Williams (1923), 24; Tressell, *The Ragged Trousered Philanthropists* (1955 ed.), 175; P. S. Bagwell, *The Railwaymen* (1963), 26.

[2] *Folk Songs of the Upper Thames*, 21, 23; William Howitt, *Rural Life of England* (1838), I, 307-9.

Secondly, functions filled by the songs were taken over by new media. These lines from a miners' song known in Nova Scotia and South Wales –

> Watch the rocks, they're falling daily,
> Careless miners always fail;
> Keep your hands upon your wages,
> And your eyes upon the scale[1] –

would be bound to lose their interest and usefulness in the face of safety regulations, trade-union leaflets and courses, and successful struggles over conditions. The final verse of 'The Durham Strike'

> The miners of Northumberland we shall for ever praise,
> For being so kind in helping us those tyrannising days;
> We thank the other counties, too, that have been doing the same,
> For every man who reads will know that we are not to blame –

would similarly be bound to lose out to the regular district conferences, the union journals, the rounds of branches by full-time officials. The working-people had been driven to face the propertied class on its level of organisation and centralised control. The whole lively drama of relations between particular people living in particular places – the natural stuff of song – drops out of currency as the workers come onto the stage of national affairs, national papers, parliaments, leaders, groupings. And this took effect particularly during the Great War (which must also have killed off thousands of local songsters) and its aftermath of economic crisis, in 1919, when the unions were accorded a '*locus standi* in the determination of essentially national issues that was undreamt of in previous times'.[2] The result was social gain of many kinds, with this social loss, that the quality of expression, the palpable concreteness of the realism with which people at large had given voice to their own experiences, lost out to gobbledygook. I have a song-sheet of the North Norfolk Divisional Labour Party, published in Cromer about that time, and it is all abstract rhetoric and well-meaning, windy pomposity. They are decidedly 'classical or, at any rate, standard pieces', by Morris, Edward Carpenter, Jim Connell, and others; they are to be sung to such tunes as 'Stand up, Stand up or Morning

---

[1] 'Miner's Life is Like a Sailor's', in *Come All Ye Bold Miners*, 104 (the tune of this song is the one used for the CND 'anthem', 'The H-Bomb's Thunder').

[2] Webbs, *History of Trade Unionism*, 645.

Light' and 'O Happy Band of Pilgrims'; and not one single phrase in them hits off the flavour and detail of the lives of those on whose behalf they were written.

The importance of such a cultural shift is hard to estimate. By itself it is not, in my view, a sufficient indicator of what is usually called 'quality of experience'. What would really matter would be if the decay in the more formal popular expression meant that people were more bored, at a loss, irked, sickened, or discontented by how they were living. So far, no investigator of cultures seems to have found how to validate such correlations between what a society says it feels and how it is really getting on.

NOTE:

This chapter had been drafted many times (and delivered in many places) before A. L. Lloyd's invaluable chapter on 'The Industrial Songs' was published. I had already, of course, drawn heavily on his research, which strikes me as one of the most important pieces of work in the whole of British cultural studies, and some of our analyses and conclusions overlap. But it seems to me that enough is different to make both essays necessary, in particular the closeness of the dovetailing which I attempt between analysis of song and of social history and my effort to see the overall curve of development of this family of songs.

CHAPTER 4

Militant Culture

THERE are several phases in our history in which we can see more clearly than usual how culture can expand through the struggle between class and class. At such times men can make a more or less permanent contribution to human understanding as a result of throwing themselves into the many-sided effort to better the lot of, and ultimately to set free, the sections of the people that bear the brunt of hardship, toil, and inequality. In this chapter three such periods are surveyed – the ones known to social and political history as the Reform period, the Chartist period, and the Great Unrest.

It is well known how the growth of the factory system and of towns, and the slump and acute hardship after the Napoleonic War, gave rise to the first sustained mass-political movement in our history since the Civil War, namely the Radical and Reform movements of the 1820s and 1830s. Towns that had begun to boom on the basis of a single industry (often cotton), centres of old handicrafts that were being undercut by factory goods, were alike filled with people who both suffered dire insecurity in their livelihoods and had the means at hand to begin to grapple with their situation. Men gathered in masses could co-operate, and multiply each other's forces. That characteristic modern type of knowledge, economics, was growing up, and facts were available as never before: in 1801 the first Census was taken – people need no longer be in doubt (as Cobbett was) about trends so basic as whether the population was rising or falling. There arose a new awareness of what the national income was and how unequally it was distributed.

The working people were driven to combine, not only in strikes and embryo unions and parties, but also to enquire in a systematic way into the system by which they were exploited. By the early 1820s Glasgow workers had set up an institute and engaged their own teachers of science and technology. In October 1823 Thomas Hodgskin was campaigning in London for the same kind of

93

institute, to teach (as well as chemistry and mechanics) 'the science of the production and distribution of wealth'.[1]

For generations the middle-class had been anxiously supervising efforts by working-people to expand their culture. Early in the eighteenth century cheap lending-libraries were frowned on, supposedly on moral grounds that probably cloaked a dislike of the people as a whole getting to know too much.[2] By the 1800s this had intensified, partly because learning and the new philosophy in particular were felt to have helped kindle the French Revolution. The attitude shows at its most invidious in Hannah More, the enormously popular reactionary publicist, who said that she believed in teaching poor children 'such coarse work as may fit them for servants. I allow of no writing for the poor.'[3] Once the workers' institutes were gaining a foothold, the opposition had to become subtler. Huskisson the politician–the only Tory to support the London Mechanics' Institute from the start–argued that teaching should be limited to bettering workmen in their trades. In short, they were to be encouraged to 'do their duty in that state of life to which God had called them'–as Charles Kingsley was to say a generation later when he was founding co-operative workshops for the declared purpose of inculcating 'industrial peace'.[4]

When the London Institute started, the middle-class at once moved in with their patronage and subscriptions. But Hodgskin's ideas were irreconcilably opposed to those of the propertied. Two years later he published his *Labour Defended Against the Claims of Capital*, a book from which Marx learned much, in which he argued that as working people produced everything, their whole product should come back to them, instead of being raked off as profit and rent. He was repeatedly stopped from giving lectures on these lines. Finally four were allowed, then he was stopped and forced to stay in future courses on the safe ground of psychology and the philosophy of history.[5] In the end he was replaced by a lecturer who even expounded a scheme for the emigration of 'surplus'

---

[1] Elie Halévy, *Thomas Hodgskin* (1956 ed.), 86-7.

[2] Ian Watt, *The Rise of the Novel* (1957), 43.

[3] Lionel Munby, 'On Culture and Socialism', in *Marxism Today* (September 1960), 283.

[4] Thomas Kelley, *George Birkbeck* (Liverpool, 1957), 105; John Saville, 'The Christian Socialists of 1848', in Saville (ed.), *Democracy and the Labour Movement* (1954), 151.

[5] Halévy, *Thomas Hodgskin*, 91; Kelly, *George Birkbeck*, 99, 116.

working people to an audience of workers. And the middle-class
and their Press rejoiced at the sight of 'clean, respectable-looking
mechanics' listening attentively to lectures on chemistry.[1]

However, Hodgskin's Institute was able to work in with a cluster
of activities which were both militant and educational at a high
level. It was supported by Cobbett and let on Sundays to followers
of Robert Owen, Cobbett, the leading Radical agitator Henry
Hunt, and the remarkable atheist Richard Carlile, one of the heroes
in England's struggle for a free press. The Institute thus became a
training ground for some of the most talented Chartists—Henry
Hetherington the fearless publisher of radical newspapers, William
Lovett who drafted the People's Charter itself.[2] In London especially, in the discussion groups, the middle-class economists were
staging what one of them, John Stuart Mill, called a 'fight to the
death' with those who took the side of the mass of the people.
Weekly public discussions were held at the Owenite Co-operation
Society in Chancery Lane. Here Mill came up against William
Thompson, the Irish Owenite, who in his *Labour Rewarded* (1827)
took Hodgskin's case a vital step further by showing how the return
of the whole product to the workers necessitated social ownership
of property.[3]

Thus Hodgskin had helped to found the line of working-class and
socialist thinkers in which later generations have been so rich—the
people who have *developed systematic thought through their active work for
the labour movement*. For such people as Robert Owen, Hodgskin and
Thompson, Bronterre O'Brien, William Morris, and the Webbs,
much of their inspiration, their subject-matter, and their clinching
determination to explain the world drew directly on their work in
the co-operative and socialist movements and in turn clarified
people's sense of what most needed to be done.

The next phase leads on continuously, both in the political
struggle and in the growth of culture. The workers had been per-
suaded to supply the mass force for a reform of Parliament which
in the short run benefited only the better-off householders. But
almost at once after the 1832 Reform Acts the workers were taking

---

[1] Brian Simon, *Studies in the History of Education, 1780-1870* (1960), 155, 157.

[2] Mabel Tylecote, *The Mechanics' Institutes of Lancashire and Yorkshire Before 1851*
(Manchester, 1957), 279 and n. 3; Kelly, *George Birkbeck*, 102-3.

[3] Mill, *Autobiography* (1924 ed.), 104-5; Max Morris (ed.), *From Cobbett to the
Chartists* (1948), 81.

the initiative, setting up their own organisations for further reform, bringing out the first labour paper that appeared regularly for many years running—Hetherington's *Poor Man's Guardian*, edited by Bronterre O'Brien.

Here, the industrial, political, and intellectual movements are scarcely separable. In 1829 the British Association for Promoting Co-operative Knowledge turned into the National Union of the Working Classes. By 1831 there were 500 regular paying members, 1000 irregulars, and at their meeting-house, the Rotunda in Blackfriars Bridge Road, they regularly had 1000 at their meetings with hundreds more turned away. Francis Place, the back-room manager of the Reform movement, bitterly describes their ideas:

> Some of these men were remarkably ignorant, but fluent speakers, filled with bitter notions of animosity against everybody who did not concur in the absurd notions they entertained, that everything which was produced belonged to those who, by their labour, produced it, and ought to be shared among them; that there ought to be no accumulation of capital in the hands of anyone to enable him to employ others as labourers, and thus by becoming a *master* make slaves of others under the name of workmen. . . .

By 1838, Place himself, who had wangled the middle-class infiltration of the London Institute in 1825, was having to admit that the independent workers' movement was 'a *new* feature in society produced by the increased intelligence of the working people. This is the first time that the desire for reform has been moved by them and carried upwards. Until now it has always proceeded downwards, and expired when abandoned, as it always has been, by their gentlemen leaders.'[1]

The working-class ideas mentioned so far have all been those indispensable in the struggle to understand and master their economic situation, and naturally these were the spearhead of their intellectual movement. But they were advancing on a broad front. It is striking to learn that in 1833 the working men's clubs were discussing the 'descent of man from the animal kingdom', or what was then called the Simian Theory—a forerunner of Darwin and Wallace's full-fledged theory, a generation later, of how man evolved from a species of ape.[2] There was no hard frontier between

---

[1] Graham Wallas, *Life of Francis Place*, 273, 271-3, 368.
[2] Max Beer, *A History of British Socialism* (1929 ed.), I, 287.

immediately useful labour thinking and culture of a less directly
militant kind. Mark Rutherford shows us, in that valuable piece of
social history his novel *The Revolution in Tanner's Lane* (1887), how
a Dissenter who was starting to move away from the old religious
culture could develop in several ways at once. The devout Zachariah
Coleman at the same time gets drawn into Radical demonstrations
(at the time of Peterloo) and begins to find in Byron's poetry a
stirring and kindling delight that he cannot explain in terms of his
old humbly pious values. Again and again when unruly emotions
flare up in him he finds himself authenticating or confirming them
to himself by recalling lines of Byron.[1] In the 1840s it was noticed
that Shelley and Byron were finding most of their readers among the
city workers: 'the bourgeoisie owns only castrated editions, family
editions, cut down in accordance with the hypocritical morality of
today'. The same is true of Burns. The core of his work – his best
satires on religion – were not in the more expensive Victorian
editions. It was the working people, handing round their tattered re-
sewn copies in stackyard and smithy, who were reading him whole.[2]

Why should working men have been in the forefront of such new
culture? Because they were not tied to any body of 'respectable',
safe, conformist ideas. Official religion would not tolerate scientific
explanations of how man originated, or poetry that was 'sensual
and worldly', and the workers would not tolerate official religion.
From his observations in Manchester in 1843-4 Engels concluded
that the worker 'does not understand religious questions, does not
trouble himself about them, knows nothing of the fanaticism that
holds the bourgeoisie bound; and if he chances to have any religion,
he has it only in name, not even in theory. Practically he lives for
this world, and strives to make himself at home in it. All the writers
of the bourgeoisie are unanimous on this point, that the workers are
not religious, and do not attend church.'[3] This exaggerates a bit.
The Census of 1851 recorded over half a million Methodists alone,
excluding Welsh Calvinistic Methodists, and religion in industrial
areas was in effect chapel religion; attendance at *church* was no
longer a measure of religiousness.[4] A Census, however, has to use

---

[1] 4th ed. (n.d.), 23-6, 109, 131.
[2] Engels, *Condition of the Working Class*, in *On Britain*, 275; Craig, *Scottish
Literature*, 112-4.
[3] *On Britain*, 158-9.
[4] For details of working people's church-going, see Dickens's *Hard Times*, ed.
David Craig (1969), Notes, 321.

D

minimum standards, e.g. literacy tested by the bare ability to write
one's name, which is not effective literacy. Further, Engels was
writing in 1843-4, and the succeeding years of slump and hardship,
that produced millions of signatures for the Chartist Petitions, must
also have raised the numbers of believers, for 'Conversion was
clearly correlated with periods of economic and social strain'.[1]
Engels also emphasises that even among the workers there were
vestiges of conventional religion-'the Irish, a few elderly people,
and the half-bourgeois, overlookers, foremen, and the like', which
links up with Hobsbawm's view that in the industrial towns the
chief Nonconformists were the tradesmen and smaller manufacturers. It is clear that the first section of society to become
thoroughly materialist or *demystified* was the city workers, and that
they did so as part of their main struggle.

The culture of the time polarises more and more between what
the working people were moved to create for themselves and what
could be wished on them by the propertied and their spokesmen.
In 1825 Place had manoeuvred dukes and businessmen into the
Institute on the ground that workmen couldn't afford out of their
own pockets the money to build anything worthwhile. Yet by 1841
the Owenite Society of Rational Religionists-the typically hybrid
name for what was in fact the spearhead of socialist propaganda
and educational work-had invested £32,000, subscribed mainly
by workmen, in Halls of Science with a capacity of 22,000 people.[2]
The Liverpool Hall had a lecture theatre, library, schoolrooms,
observatory, and kitchen. There were others in Halifax, Huddersfield, Hyde, Salford, Stalybridge, and Bristol-the list could be
continued. Trades Halls, also independent workers' centres and
used regularly for Chartist meetings as well as for progressive education, existed in Birmingham, Leeds, Oldham, Manchester, London.
Many had good supplies of books and periodicals.

The Midlands and North were to the fore, taking the cultural
lead in a way impossible in the age from the 1660s to 1800, when
London, centre of merchant capitalism, was all-powerful. London's
'industrial revolution' had happened with the sixteenth-century
boom in trade, when the important cities were in the old rich areas
of England, Norwich in East Anglia, Bristol in the south-western

[1] Eric Hobsbawm, *Primitive Rebels* (Manchester, 1959), 129.
[2] Simon, *History of Education*, 235, 238: this and the next eight paragraphs
draw especially on Simon, Kelly and Tylecote.

wool country. Mechanisation of textiles and intensive coal and iron working had shifted England's centre of gravity north. In the twenty years from 1801 the population of Lancashire grew faster than Middlesex's. By 1884 there were 458 people per square mile north of the Trent, 312 to the south. Chartism–the first movement to work out and claim the bulk of the political rights that have since been won and which we now take for granted–was strongest in the industrial north, weak in purely farming areas, though these were no less needy and *more* tyrannised over by the old ruling class. The first response to Chartism came from factory and especially cotton districts, and the woollen districts of Yorkshire followed a little more slowly–just as the Industrial Revolution itself had been tardier in woollens than in cottons.[1] Similarly, Professor Kelly's maps of the spread of the Mechanics' Institutes and kindred centres show how east Lancashire and the West Riding soon over-hauled London as the districts richest in such culture and how the north-east, especially Tyneside, had little to show until the time of the 'second' or heavy-industrial revolution around 1850. New ideas were everywhere. But they were able to grip the mass of the people and give rise to action only in the areas most affected by those changes in production that were at bottom responsible for the ideas themselves.

The independent cultural movement had come after the first large-scale moves by the middle class to supply the people with 'safe' education through the Mechanics' Institutes, just as Chartism had come after the middle-class Reform movement. In each case the movement from 'above', once a vanguard, had become a brake on the developments that had been set in motion, and was super-seded.

The new class-conscious or militant culture–which contained the embryo of socialism–started up often as a counter-attack against attempts at censorship. For example, political and theological works were at first kept out of many Institute libraries as 'dangerously controversial'. Although the parsons soon learned to collaborate in the towns, they were (according to James Hole, the enlightened Honorary Secretary of the Yorkshire Union of Mechanics' Institutes) a major obstacle to the founding of institutes in the countryside–where one can still feel this kind of feudal deterrent

[1] Asa Briggs, *Chartist Studies*, 3, 288, 317; T. S. Ashton, *The Industrial Revolution*, 75-6.

to the free growth of adult education: for example, when her lady-
ship lets it be known that she would rather 'her' workpeople did
not join a W.E.A. class.

What was taught and discussed in the two kinds of centre makes
their class basis plain. For example, economics was rare in the
Institutes as late as 1841–even though the more advanced middle-
class spokesmen were urging that politics should be brought in to
counter-balance the enthusiastic discussions of it in the Chartist and
Socialist Halls. Many promoters of the Institutes belonged to the
Central Society of Education, which said in 1837 that 'In towns
where the working population forms a dense mass–where strikes,
trades unions, and combinations have been so ruinous to the
merchant, the manufacturer, and the workman–it is of the utmost
importance that the principles which affect national wealth and
industry should be most thoroughly understood'–the context shows
that the principles taught would be chosen to exclude the tradition of thought represented by Owen, Hodgskin and William
Thompson. The Society's hint that strikes can only harm 'the
public'–a public from which the strikers are somehow left out–is of
course still dirt-common today.

The Institutes reveal by their mixed nature the struggle inside
the working-class against conformist ideas. A few openly allied
themselves with Radicalism and aimed at getting the ideas of
Cobbett, Owen, and the Utilitarians to the working people.
Occasionally they provided a platform for Radical or Chartist
speakers. In 1835 the Corn Law Rhymer, Ebenezer Elliott, was
telling the Sheffield Institute at its Annual Meeting: 'Your enemies,
the legislating or landed class . . . dared not examine the foundation'
of society, but 'that is no reason why you should not examine it'–
just as Hodgskin had taught. But the 1841 Report of the State of
Literary, Scientific, and Mechanics' Institutions had to admit that
these could not approach the devotion and energy that went into
the trade unions, friendly societies, and Chartist Clubs: 'Who, it
was asked, had seen a working man proselytising on behalf of a
mechanics' institute?' Perhaps the most revealing slant on the
alignment of this culture is the fact that during slumps, with
lowered wages and widespread unemployment, the institutes did
badly, whereas these were just the times when trade unionism,
Co-operation, and Chartism gained support. The workers knew
which institutions they most needed.

In the institutes, according to Mrs Tylecote, the working man was usually studying for the sake of his own career rather than to better his ability to lead his class. A writer in one of the cheap Chambers publications, which were generally Malthusian, and talked down to the people,[1] admitted that many of the workers thought the bosses had some secret motive in backing the institutes, especially where they were attached to a factory. Some workers, he said, attended to curry favour, others stayed away to show their independence.

It must be remembered that these centres were not a mere extra or spare-time hobby. Cultural facilities were then so meagre–owing to the failure of the new industrial society to provide for the huge growth of population–that adult education was a lifeline for people in a way that it hardly is now.[2] The numbers that attended show what a crying need was being met. In Yorkshire, in sixteen large towns with more than 10,000 people, 1 in 53 were members of institutes; in fourteen small towns between 5000 and 10,000, 1 in 37; in twenty-seven towns with less than 5000, 1 in 27; and in villages in the Ripon area, 1 in 8. The reason was, of course, the famine in education. In 1842, according to the Report of the Factory Inspectors, there was not a single public day-school for poor children in an area of 105,000 people around Oldham and Ashton-under-Lyne,[3] and when the Sheffield Institute was founded 1 in 200 could not read and 40 in 200 could not write.

Educational advance did not come only through pressure in the name of education for its own sake. The most militant workers were also the most enlightened in their ideas of cultural development. William Lovett, writer of the Charter, planned (in a book he wrote in prison) a new type of education that in detail after detail–his stress on apparatus and experiment, on visual aids of all kinds from models to relief maps, on science as a basic subject, on English composition as description of what the child knows at first hand–foreshadows the kind of teaching that has come into practice in our lifetimes. Again one is struck by the power of the intellect, un-distorted and unshackled by any need to defend a stunted *status quo*, which can so leap ahead of its own time.

[1] Craig, *Scottish Literature*, 300.

[2] Anthony Greenwood, M.P., speaking in Leeds in 1964 on the Jubilee of the Yorkshire W.E.A., recalled his father Arthur Greenwood saying that to him in Leeds in 1914 the evening classes were 'like a window through to the sky'.

[3] J. L. and B. Hammond, *The Town Labourer* (1949 ed.), I, 64.

The politicians who were manipulating for their own ends the democratic drive of the people could still speak of the workers as only a political brute-force. Cobden–the Radical Manchester businessman who regretted the spread of barracks (to put down unrest) because they sent down the value of property–regarded votes for everyone, not as a basic right, but just as 'something in our *rear* to frighten the Aristocracy'. The President of the Manchester Chamber of Commerce wanted the workers to come into the struggle to repeal the Corn Laws because 'until they do the Aristocracy will never yield–I grieve to say that the brickbat argument is the only one that our nobles heed'.[1] But already history had left these men behind. Working-class thinkers were analysing society and politics more deeply than the Establishment. The record of Chartist and kindred culture bears out the words of the Edinburgh economist and M.P. Leonard Horner, when he was looking into 'that remarkable traffic in books round Glasgow by itinerant retailers'. He considered that there was 'nothing in the interior economy of our country so important to know, as the progress of instruction among the industrious classes' (i.e. factory workers), and no better protection against 'enemies of reform' than 'the effects of knowledge readily and solidly diffused through the great body of the people'.[2]

Once again this militant culture was not confined to studies. The Mechanics' Institutes used to worry about the successful competition from 'casinos and singing saloons'–I take it these were what Disraeli describes in chapter 10 of *Sybil* (1845). He gives a rich and delightful description, worthy of Dickens, of a pub called the Cat and Fiddle with a special hall known as 'the Temple of the Muses'. Here several hundred people drink and smoke, the walls are painted with scenes from Shakespeare, Scott, and Byron, a 'lady in a fancy dress' sings 'favourite ballads' and a 'gentleman' sings comic songs. 'The most popular amusements, however, were the "Thespian recitations"; by amateurs, or novices who wished to become professional. They tried their mettle on an audience which could be critical.' The favourite songs Disraeli mentions are 'Cherry Ripe' and 'Scots Wha Hae': '"Don't you remember, Dusty, when we used to encore that German fellow in 'Scots Wha Hae'? We always had it five times. Hang me if I wasn't blind

---

[1] John Morley, *The Life of Richard Cobden* (1906 ed.), 507; *Chartist Studies*, 348.
[2] *Memoirs and Correspondence*, ed. Leonard Horner (1853), II, 304-5.

drunk at the end of it." ' It would be easy to make light of such
amusements. One young workman in the scene says, pointing to a
picture, ' "That's the Lady of the Lake. I've seen her at the Circus,
with real water".' But the merriness of the fun and the love of
eloquent poetry were neither brutal nor brainless–contrast bingo
and American comic-books. The customers at the Cat and Fiddle
also included the local militants. The chapter ends with an only
half-humorous conversation between a young group, among them
the secretary of a 'Literary and Scientific Institute' in a slum area:

> 'I think one of the greatest grievances the people have is the
> beaks serving notice on Chaffing Jack to shut up the Temple
> on Sunday nights.'
> 'It is infamous,' said Mick; 'ain't we to have no recreation?
> One might as well live in Suffolk, where the immigrants come
> from, and where they are obliged to burn ricks to pass the
> time.'
> 'As for the rights of labour,' said Harriet, 'the people goes
> for nothing with this machinery.'
> '. . . Labour may be weak, but capital is weaker,' said
> Devilsdust.

Between the effective end of Chartism in the early 1850s and the
Great Unrest that lasted from the later 1880s to 1914, cultural
opportunities expanded. Unions of skilled workers were foremost in
the campaign for 'universal, compulsory, secular education' which
won part of its aims by the Education Acts of 1870 and 1872.[1] By
the later 1880s the unskilled men and women too were waking
from their 'long winter's sleep'. First the girls who made the matches
in Bryant and May's London factory, then the casual labourers
from the Thames docks, then the South London gas workers were
organised to strike, put demands, and maintain themselves while
they were on strike.[2] These were the first efforts at resisting the
evils of the crisis caused by the hotting up of Britain's competition
with other rising powers. These years leading up to the Great War
were a time of extraordinary hardship. The first reasonably complete and scientific surveys of the people's livelihood that had ever
been made showed that in York, for example, 27·84 per cent of
people earned too little 'for the maintenance of merely physical

---

[1] Simon, *Studies in the History of Education*, 360-6.
[2] Engels in *On Britain*, 520-4 (letters of 1889-90); *Tom Mann's Memoirs* (1923),
79-91; Dona Torr, *Tom Mann and His Times*, I (1956), 280-303.

efficiency' (the London figure computed a little earlier by Charles Booth was 30·7 per cent); and applying this 'poverty line' to a large sample of country people on the eve of the War it was found that in all counties except five the average wage was below the line.[1] Slump followed slump; at a time when wages were falling, from the middle 90s till just before the War, the value of the pound dropped by one-third; there were rarely less than a million out of work; and malnutrition was rife.[2] Such hardship, combined with the already far-flung organisation of the working people, gave a massive boost to trade unionism, though the troughs themselves temporarily slackened militancy. From 1892-1910 the total of union members rose by about a million, or 66 per cent.[3] Such a figure clearly has behind it a tidal wave of militancy, and we can read time after time in the eye-witness accounts how listless workmen would be hanging around in back streets or waste ground, the labour speaker would arrive, and the men would be galvanised at the touch of the new powerful ideas–attacks on the arms race, explanations of how monopolies were growing and intensifying exploitation.[4]

What happened in an hour at a meeting was repeated in more gradual and long-lasting ways by means of a new type of workers' institution. Modern adult education comes into being in the thick of the Great Unrest. The University of Oxford's extra-mural classes were considered to have lapsed into catering mainly for middle-class students whose educational opportunities were ample anyway. So Ruskin College was founded (with funds provided in 1899 by an American). It was for working-class students and modelled itself partly on the halls that had grown up round the universities in Manchester and Liverpool to enable poor students to live cheaply by sharing household expenses and helping each other with their studies. To start with, at Ruskin, they even cooked for themselves, and they crammed a forty-eight-week term into a year. It is said that they set up a separate college because the students were

[1] B. S. Rowntree, *Poverty*, 1900 (1922 ed.), 117-8; Rowntree and M. Kendall, *How the Labourer Lives* (1913), 31-2.

[2] A. L. Morton, *A People's History of England*, 494, 509; Cole and Postgate, *The Common People*, 497-8. More relevant details are given below, in ch. 7, 144-5.

[3] S. and B. Webb, *The History of Trade Unionism*, 473.

[4] E.g. Torr, *Tom Mann and His Times*, 347; E. J. Hobsbawm (Ed.), *Labour's Turning Point* (1948), 157, 161.

'deterred by a mixture of pride and shyness' from going to the usual university and college lectures–a natural reaction to the upper-class tone of Zuleika Dobson's Oxford. And they wanted subjects, useful to their class, that were unpopular at the old-established colleges–political science, political economy, and economic history.[1] It is the theme that we have seen running through from the time of Thomas Hodgskin.

In 1903 the Workers' Educational Association was founded to do, like Ruskin, what the university extra-mural system had lapsed from; and the W.E.A., like Ruskin, had to start without any help from government. At the same time the Central Labour College (for years the left wing of the workers' education movement but now replaced by a system of regional committees controlled by the T.U.C.) was being founded with subscriptions from left-wing unions. Its initiator was the socialist principal of Ruskin, Dennis Hird, who considered that Ruskin was failing to equip students specifically for militant struggle. Here was an educational movement with its roots in the politically-conscious working people. Politicians of all parties, Anglican parsons and bishops, consented to serve as patrons of the W.E.A., as of the institutes fifty years before. But the movement itself was inseparable from labour militancy. Ruskin students were free to spend their week-ends in labour agitation in any constituency they chose. The Labour College was the propaganda centre for the Manchester Syndicalist Education League. This had been founded in 1910 by delegates representing sixteen trades councils and 60,000 workers, men convinced by the terrible poverty of these years, and by the crawling and compromising of the Lib.-Lab. members in Parliament, that politics was futile and the only hope for the working-class was the winning of state power through a series of general strikes that would force the owners of industry to throw in their hand.

Once again working men were paying for and building their own kind of centre. We read in the life of Ernest Bevin–himself a pioneer organiser of the transport workers–how in 1897 forty Baptists in Bristol broke away from their chapel and in three years had 350 in their own Sunday School. By 1911 they had built their own chapel for £3000, raised from among themselves. Here as

[1] Elie Halévy, *The Rule of Democracy (1905-1914)* (1961 ed.), 86-7; the next three paragraphs draw especially on Halévy.

elsewhere the chapel was helping to nurture labour leaders–often by repulsion rather than positively, though Primitive Methodists in particular had an outstanding record as union leaders in the countryside.[1] Bevin used to attend a Sunday afternoon discussion class led by a Glasgow artisan turned Baptist minister. A hymn was sung, followed by a discussion in which agnostics, free-thinkers, radicals, socialists all took part. He also went before breakfast on Sundays to an Adult School–part of a nationwide organisation– where 300 men met for hymns and hymn practice, followed by systematic reading and debate. The subjects show the progressive slant of the times–women in industry, Christianity and poverty (how reconcile a benevolent omnipotent God with the hardships they saw around them?).

Bevin's career shows how Nonconformist culture was being secularised and turned progressive from inside itself or, if it would not change, it was left behind. It was in Christian institutions that Bevin learned to argue a case. But he found his growing socialism frowned on in chapel circles–organised religion was content to explain away inequality as 'a part of the natural order'. The final stage in his early culture was, as with many Labour M.P.s, study in classes jointly arranged by unions and Workers' Educational Association. When he came to see that he had outgrown the chapel, he joined the town Socialist Society (which was affiliated to the Social Democratic Federation) and became unpaid secretary of the Bristol Right-to-Work Society.[2] The same mixture of forces was at work in Aneurin Bevan's development. He learned to think and debate partly from his father and partly at Baptist and Congregational Sunday schools, where his arguments about evolution angered his teachers. Presently a group broke away and with the help of socialists from Merthyr they founded the Tredegar branch of the Independent Labour Party.[3] Thus in a few months of their own lives these men enacted the fundamental development in our culture: from the religious to the secular, from the transcendent to the here and now.

As in the 1820s, or in the '30s and '40s, the same impulse was at work in both intellectual life and the industrial struggle. This militancy over the whole field is voiced in a fully conscious way

[1] See Reg Groves, *Sharpen the Sickle!*, e.g. 40-1, 110.
[2] Alan Bullock, *The Life and Times of Ernest Bevin*, I (1960), 8-16.
[3] Michael Foot, *Aneurin Bevan*, I (1966 ed.), 20.

by J. M. Mactavish, a docker member of the Shipwrights' Union, in a speech to the W.E.A. Annual Conference at Oxford in 1907:

> I have not come here as a suppliant. . . . I refuse to sit down at the rich man's door and beg for crusts. . . . I demand for my class all the advantages that Oxford has it in her power to offer, and I claim it as a right of which we have been unjustly deprived–unjustly for us and for Oxford too. . . . For, remember, democracy will be achieved with or without the assistance of Oxford; but if the University of Oxford continues to hold herself aloof from the working classes, then we shall end by thinking of her, not for what she is, but for what she has been. . . . In point of fact, workmen's sons come to Oxford to escape their class, not to relieve it. . . . We want her in future to inspire them, not with the desire of succeeding, but with that of serving society–we have need of you. But you have need of us.

This is a classic statement of the case for cultural equality: the novel of this trend is Thomas Hardy's *Jude the Obscure*, published in 1895.[1] And Mactavish came from one of the very areas (Clyde docks, Lancashire and Cheshire cotton spinners, Welsh and north of England coalfields) which three years later were to start a wave of strikes so militant that many, among both bosses and union leaders, thought it was the start of a revolution.[2]

Such phases show how changes in the foundations of society–changes in production and the social relations that depend upon it–can pass through and transform our culture. Such times are hardly exceptional or abnormal: the phases surveyed in this chapter account for a good half of the century between the Napoleonic and Great Wars. And the effects were not short-lived. Workers who had attended the Halls and Institutes helped the fight for universal education twenty years later. The railway strikes of the Great Unrest led to the penal legislation against unions which helped to arouse mass support for the Labour Representation Committee, nucleus of the Labour Party in 1906.

To this kind of process we owe all that we understand today by socialism. We can apply to it the words Lenin used to describe

---

[1] Edward Thompson amplifies this point, in the context of an important discussion of the relation between 'educated' and 'customary' experience, in his lecture 'Education and Experience' (Leeds, 1968), 18-20.

[2] See below, ch. 7, 145-6.

Marx's thinking, in a speech to the Youth Leagues in 1920: 'Everything that had been created by human thought [was] re-shaped, criticised, tested on the working-class movement'. Conclusions were drawn 'which people, restricted by bourgeois limits or bound by bourgeois prejudices, could not draw'.[1]

[1] V. I. Lenin, *On Socialist Ideology and Culture* (Moscow, n.d.), 46.

CHAPTER 5

Hard Times and the Condition
of England

DICKENS's flair for expressing matters of common concern *in their own style* shows in the very title of the novel in which, for once, he dealt with the average life of his time.[1] Most of the twenty-five possible titles for *Hard Times* and the fourteen he short-listed suggest, usually by a cliché or a pun, the theme of human life ground down by calculation and routine: for example, 'According to Cocker', 'Prove It', 'Hard Times', 'Hard Heads and Soft Hearts', 'A Mere Question of Figures'.[2] 'Hard Times' stands out in that it was the phrase which came most naturally, when weariness or hardship had to be voiced, to the people with whom the novel is concerned: the men, women and children whose lives were being transformed by the industrial revolution. It is very much a vernacular phrase, common in folk songs especially between 1820 and 1865[3] but not in pamphlets, speeches, or the papers, however popular or radical. 'Hard times' (or 'tickle times', 'weary times', 'bad times') usually meant a period, often a slump, when scanty food and low wages or unemployment bore particularly hard. Much less often it could mean the more pervasive state in which people felt that the essential and permanent conditions of their lives hemmed them in inflexibly, as in the refrain of a song from the knitting mills of South Carolina around 1890:

> Every morning just at five,
> Gotta get up, dead or alive.
> It's hard times in the mill, my love,
> Hard times in the mill.

[1] Compare the third page of the best single study of Dickens, George Orwell's essay in his *Critical Essays* (1951 ed., 3).

[2] John Forster, *The Life of Charles Dickens* ('Gadshill Edition', n.d.), II, 144-5; Phillip Collins, *Dickens and Education* (1963), 146.

[3] E.g. 'Jone o' Grinfilt's Visit to Mr. Fielden', *c.* 1835; 'Gooin' T' Schoo'' and 'Hard Times', *c.* 1864 (John Harland, *Ballads and Songs of Lancashire*, 175, 508, 512); 'The New-Fashioned Farmer', *c.* 1840 (John Ashton, *Modern Street Ballads*, 191); 'Hard Times' (Ben Brierley, *'Ab-o'th-Yate' Sketches*, Oldham, 1896, 270-2; the song is much earlier than the volume).

Every morning just at six,
Don't that old bell make you sick?
It's hard times in the mill, my love,
Hard times in the mill . . . .

Ain't it enough to break your heart?
Have to work all day and at night it's dark.
It's hard times in the mill, my love,
Hard times in the mill.[1]

The rightness of Dickens's judgement lay in his seizing on the popular phrase and using it for a novel which is not about a time of special neediness but rather about a kind of bondage to routine and calculation so integral to the culture of industrial societies that much of it is still with us.

Both theme and title, then, are typical at once of Dickens's fellow-feeling for the mass of people and of his flair for sharpening the topical to a pitch of memorable art. His novels in general, and *Hard Times* more than any other, are so saturated in the habits, social forms, and events of his own age, and enter so directly into its struggles, that we can best understand why such works appeared at just that juncture if we consider the trends in his own development and in English literature as a whole that had led up to the situation at mid-century. Dickens himself was notable for not drawing much on the art-literature that came before him. He delighted in and owed much to the hearty comedians among eighteenth-century novelists, especially Smollett, but it is at least as relevant to note that he began his career as a reporter, writing against time on breathless journeys around the country from one political meeting to another; that he was famous among the journalists in the gallery of the House of Commons, where he reported for seven years, for the extraordinary speed and fullness of his reports; that his first wish artistically was to act at Covent Garden because 'I believed I had a strong perception of character and oddity, and a natural power of reproducing in my own person what I observed in others'; and that his first novel, *Pickwick Papers*, began as the letterpress for a series of 'cockney sporting-prints' issued in monthly parts.[2] He thus differs in kind from Jane Austen, who carried on from Johnson and Sheridan, and George Eliot, who carried on from Jane Austen and Dickens. Dickens raised an estab-

---

[1] *American Industrial Ballads*, side 1, band 5.
[2] Forster, *op. cit.*, I, 60-63, 58, 67-8.

lished form, the novel, to new levels by fusing all manner of popular
elements and new cultural media, and this is typical of how an art
grows at a time of rapid, drastic social change, when artists must
take in and digest the startling new experiences, assailing them
from all sides, which the conventional art of the time finds it hard
to cope with.

Dickens also arrives after a prolonged lull or barren phase in
British writing. By 1824 Shelley, Keats, and Byron are dead, and
Wordsworth's powers have failed him; Jane Austen dies in 1817,
Maria Edgeworth publishes nothing of interest after 1812, and
Scott's best vein is quite done by 1824. The Twenties and Thirties
are thus, in literature, a flat calm, stirred only by the faint ripples
of Tennyson's first books; and when energy returns to literature it
is in the form of an urgent concern with what came to be called the
'Condition-of-England question'. From about 1838 Dickens is
brusquely modernising the novel, driven by his sense of the topical,
his consuming fascination with his own times. His modernity is
extraordinary: how many people faced with these words–'plain to
the dark eyes of her mind, as the electric wires which ruled a
colossal strip of music-paper out of the evening sky were plain to
the dark eyes of her body'–would place it in the 1850s? Yet it is
from *Hard Times*. Clearly the 'accident' of Dickens's individual
genius is crucial in modernising fiction at that juncture, just as the
'accidental' deaths of those leading Romantic poets were crucial in
causing the lull. Yet the lull also corresponds with what contemporaries called the Thirty Years' Peace (from 1815 to 1848), and
what ends the lull is the upheaval that includes the outcry against
the New Poor Law of 1834 (an ingredient in *Oliver Twist*), the
Chartist campaign from 1838 onwards (an ingredient in Disraeli's
Sybil), and the Year of Revolutions, 1848 (an ingredient in the
radicalism of Elizabeth Gaskell and George Eliot).[1] Altogether it is
as though our culture (including folk song, political parties, and
trade unions as well as the main arts) had been cudgelling its brains
for ways of dealing with the new life–life dominated by the industrial system–and had now found what was needed.

The historical image of this period–the breakneck growth of the
railways, the congested towns and great oblong mills swarming
across Lancashire–is so familiar that we can't pretend to keep it

[1] *Mary Barton*, Preface; *George Eliot's Life*, ed. J. W. Cross, 98-9, letter to
J. Sibree.

out of our minds as we read *Hard Times*. Equally, it would be
wrong—a failure to drink in what Dickens offers—if the novel were
allowed to trail after that history, used merely to attach a few
picturesque personifications and episodes to a body of material we
think we already know. But it would be another kind of missed opportunity not to use the novel as a source of insights into a specific
phase in that long train of social experience which has brought us
to where we are. Dickens himself was writing with this purpose—to
incite thought and help mould attitudes to burning problems; and
Hard Times is 'about' a specific time, the Forties, whereas others
even of his most social novels tend either to satirise types that could
have been found at many a time (e.g. the stony-hearted businessman in *Dombey and Son*) or else to draw historical elements freely
from several different times (as in *Bleak House*). In *Hard Times*
Dickens was striving to articulate the parts of a civilization, with a
minimum of flights down fanciful by-ways, and with an insistence
on the typical and even the average which suited the industrial and
mass aspects of that age. It was the age in which cities like the
original of Coketown multiplied by three within a lifetime and
Britain 'changed over from a rural to an urban civilization' inside
two generations. It happened fast enough to cause actual bewilder-
ment. We can read in the diary of a man who must have been very
much like Stephen Blackpool how when he set out on Good Friday
1860 to walk through his native parts of twenty-eight years before—
the industrial villages around the eastern side of Manchester—he
found that 'everything was changed':

> Villages have grown into large towns, and country places
> where there was nothing but fields are now covered with
> streets, and villages and large factories and workshops every-
> where. I made enquiries [at] many a place after people who
> had lived there, but they were either dead or gone to America
> or gone somewhere else. I only saw one woman whom I knew,
> but she did not know me and would not believe me when I
> told her I was very tired.

Again, from the Black Country comes a song with the refrain 'I
can't find Brummagem'. Once, this sense of being literally lost in
the new surroundings would have been confined to London with
its uniquely fast development in the eighteenth century. Now it was
widespread. According to the Census taken three years before *Hard
Times* was written, of the 3,336,000 adults living in London and

61 other English and Welsh towns, little over one-third had been born in the town where they now lived.[1]

Of course many things could be made of such material. But one broad approach that we can now see, from its frequent occurrence, to have been positively enjoined upon artists by the life of those times is a radical or humane concern with hard conditions, a vehement desire to bring home to public opinion, in terms both compassionate and warning, that it was *not tolerable* that the ordinary conditions of living for so many should be damaging to physical and psychological well-being or that rich and poor, employers and working people, should live at such different standards and be arrayed against each other in class struggle. This is the 'Condition-of-England question', so named by Carlyle in his essay 'Chartism' of 1839–Carlyle to whom *Hard Times* was dedicated and a quotation from whom was printed on the balance-sheet of the fund collected for unemployed workers during week fourteen of the Preston lock-out which Dickens went to report when gathering copy for the novel.[2]

Dickens had thus found his way to a subject from the heart of industrial civilization quite early in his artistic maturity. It is surely the novels in which social institutions are turned into rich and ramifying dramatic symbols that are in Dickens's *oeuvre* what the tragedies are in Shakespeare's, and the series of these novels starts with *Dombey and Son* in 1846-8. It is a measure of the urgency and directness of Dickens's concern in *Hard Times* that whereas in *Dombey* the business that dominates Dombey's life is scarcely typical of English commercial activity at that stage, and is vaguely specified into the bargain, for *Hard Times* Dickens was so bent on 'getting it right' that he went to Preston (in January 1854) for material. Much of what he saw there he turned straight into fiction: for example, the 'coldly and bitingly emphatic' master or owner on the train north, who extolled Political Economy and insisted on the total irrelevance of human sympathy to questions of labour or production; or the professional speaker whom Dickens heard at a Sunday meeting of locked-out cotton workers and whom in his article he

[1] Cole and Postgate, *The Common People*, 305 and table opp. p. 450; 'The Diary of John Ward of Clitheroe, Weaver, 1860-1864', in *Transactions of the Historic Society of Lancashire and Cheshire*, Vol. 115 (1964), 138; *Folksongs of the Black Country*, ed. M. and J. Raven (Wolverhampton, 1964), 20-22; Lewis Mumford, *The City in History* (1966 ed.), 532.

[2] 'On Strike': *Household Words*, No. 203 (11 February 1854), 556.

dubbed 'Gruffshaw'. ('On Strike', pp. 553-4, 557.) It must also
be said that Dickens had to go and gather copy because he had
never known the industrial heartlands at first hand (apart from an
occasional visit to relatives in Manchester). Both aspects, his real
concern and his comparative inexperience in this field, must be
kept in mind when we are pondering the truth of the novel as an
image of the life centred on the factory system.

To put it in this way is not to beg the question of whether or not
Hard Times really is an 'industrial novel'. My opening discussion of
its title should already have shown that Dickens's concern entailed
his dealing in the same breath, continually, with both the immediate
facts of mill-town life and the less direct, the all-pervading *cultural*
effects of the new intensive production. The novel is about the ways
in which iron conditions were felt to have closed round people's
lives. I say 'felt' as though the matter were not clear-cut, for it is a
fact that people were often making heavy weather of perfectly con-
venient new arrangements: for example, Dickens was fascinated by
transport, and people tended to grumble about the sheer punctuality
and orderliness of the railways compared with the old coaching.[1]
Yet many contemporaries were not being captious or just torpidly
averse to change when they expressed concern at the condition of
England and considered they were beset by unprecedented troubles.
Dickens was writing towards the climax of a phase during which, it
can now probably be said,[2] the standard of living for large sections
of the people fell, as the first manic onset of the industrial revolution
took its toll and had not yet yielded its compensating benefits. We
have also to remember that encroachments on freedom of behaviour
aroused militancy quite as readily as evils like wage-cuts or the
price of flour. The many petitions against the enclosing of common
and waste ground were only the first of many protests against the
process whereby the actual scope or room in which to live was
curtailed. Dickens's lifetime saw the beginning of the end for the
old cottage industry. The family which in the time of, say, Defoe
had carded, spun, and woven, washed and bleached as a team was
now scattered from home out into the mills, there to be knit together
again as a class no longer based on blood-ties–the Hands of
Bounderby and Gradgrind. Instead of work following the rhythms

[1] Humphrey House, *The Dickens World* (1960 edition), 140.
[2] See J. D. Chambers, *The Workshop of the World* (1961), esp. 219-20, and
E. J. Hobsbawm, *Labouring Men* (1964), esp. 87-8.

of close personal relations–work until the piece was finished, a journey to sell it, and then perhaps a long week-end until the money was finished–now the men, women, and children must submit to a rigid time-table laid down by a management avid that every minute should be worked to the full. Experience narrowed. The surroundings of the work and the work itself were the same day in day out. Where once a man might have had several jobs–for example, the German iron miners who wore their furnace-skins of white calf's hide while haymaking in their own meadows[1], now each person was likely to work at one job only and his sole means of livelihood was the sale of his power to work at that job.

The point is not that the quality of life deteriorated in some absolute way: so general a matter is impossible to decide for or against, and even if one breaks it down into seemingly verifiable parts, it turns out that, for example, the notorious horrors of the early factories were parallelled by the physically vile conditions in which many handloom weavers worked at home.[2] The point for *Hard Times* is that people had become less a law unto themselves, the stuff of their lives less variegated, and it is this sense of lives clamped under a grid that haunts Dickens throughout his work, whether he is writing about imprisonment itself or about the more impalpable sorts of bondage that are the theme of *Hard Times*. In such matters it is necessary to hear the testimony of the people who lived at the point of change: for example, the following verse from a song about the transition to powered weaving (staple industry of Coketown), written by the Gorton weaver John Grimshaw:

> So, come all you cotton-weavers, you must rise up very soon,
> For you must work in factories from morning until noon:
> You mustn't walk in your gardens for two or three hours a-day.
> For you must stand at their command, and keep your shuttles in
>   play.

Grimshaw was a notable songster, but singing was precisely what the mill-owner felt obliged to forbid in case it interfered with production. The handloom weaver had either talked or sung while he worked: 'When not talking he would be humming or singing snatches of some old ballad.' And in a weaving-shop before steam

---

[1] J. H. Clapham, *The Economic Development of France and Germany, 1815-1914* (1936 edition), 89-90.
[2] E. Royston Pike, *Human Documents of the Industrial Revolution in Britain* (1966), 332-3.

came in, 'let only break forth the healthy and vigorous chorus "A man's a man for a' that"', the fagged weaver brightens up. His very shuttle skytes boldly along, and clatters through in faithful time to the tune of his merrier shopmates!' By mid-century this was forbidden: in mill after mill placards were up with such rules as 'Any person leaving their work and found Talking with any other workpeople shall be fined 2d. for each offence', and similarly for 'Talking with any one out of their own Ally', or 6d. (the equivalent of £1 today in terms of real wages) for 'talking to another, whistling, or singing'.[1] Here is the policing and hemming-in of the human being that moved Dickens to his reiterated message, put into Sleary's mouth in *Hard Times*: '"People mutht be amuthed. They can't be alwayth a learning, nor yet they can't be alwayth a working, they an't made for it."' In *Hard Times* the rigid system that cages people in is located squarely in or rather is seen actually to consist of the mill-town itself, especially in that passage from Chapter 5 that sets the keynote or fixes the image of the dominant scene:

> It was a town of red brick, or of brick that would have been red if the smoke and ashes had allowed it. . . . It was a town of machinery and tall chimneys, out of which interminable serpents of smoke trailed themselves for ever. . . . It had a black canal in it, and a river that ran purple with ill-smelling dye. . . . It contained several large streets all very like one another, and many small streets still more like one another, inhabited by people equally like one another . . .

In face of this insistence on a specific real location, it seems wilful to rarefy the novel's theme along metaphysical lines: 'Coketown with its troubles is merely the purgatory in which individuals suffer.'[2] What Dickens is intent upon is a specific society which had become unbearable for historical (and therefore remediable) causes.

In stressing the directness of the links between the novel and mill-town life, one is not somehow missing or coarsening its thematic subtlety. Certainly Dickens did not intend an 'industrial novel' if by that one means a barely-fictive report on troubles in,

[1] Aspin, *Haslingden 1800-1900*, 33, 37-8; William Thom, *Rhymes and Recollections of a Hand-loom Weaver* (1845 edition), 14; *Stubborn Facts from the Factories by a Manchester Operative* [James Leach], in Pike, *Human Documents*, 63; John Grimshaw, 'Hand-loom v. Power-loom', in Harland, *Songs of Lancashire*, 189.

[2] John Butt and Kathleen Tillotson, *Dickens at Work* (1957) p. 212, commenting on the scene in which Blackpool is sent to Coventry.

say, Manchester or Sheffield: for example, he decided against
depicting a strike. This led to disappointment among early reviewers
who evidently assumed that he should have written a straight
industrial piece and not made this aspect 'subordinate and inci-
dental' to the educational aspect.[1] But Dickens was shirking nothing.
To be as trenchant as he was about the owners and their pet schools
was itself to take sides and declare one's commitment in the matter
of the condition of England. Dickens was writing at a time when
the periodicals could smell radicalism a mile away, and in the most
unlikely places. *Jane Eyre* had been censured for 'moral Jacobinism'
and anti-Christian 'murmuring against the comforts of the rich and
against the privations of the poor', although I would have thought
that Charlotte Brontë had leaned as far back to square with conventional taboos as a remarkable artist well could without sinking
herself entirely. Charles Kingsley's *Alton Locke, Tailor and Poet* (1850)
had just been given hostile reviews in *The Times*, *Blackwood's*, the
Edinburgh Review, and the *Quarterly* for advocating socialism cunningly disguised as Christianity. Philanthropic cotton-masters were
warning village institutes about the tendencies implicit in *Mary
Barton*.[2] Indeed the trenchancy of Dickens's social criticism now
began to jeopardize his reputation, throughout the second half of
his career, in the eyes of both the conservative and the go-ahead,
from Macaulay with his objection to the 'sullen socialism' of *Hard
Times* to an American, Whipple, who considered it childish to
oppose 'the established laws of political economy', which he considered on a par with those of the physical universe.[3] It took artistic
determination to come as near the heart of the industrial matter as
Dickens did, and equally it led to several swerves into evasion as the
good-hearted radical novelist strove to come near the truth without
committing himself too ruinously.

The stress on schooling is certainly no evasion. This linking of
classroom and mill turns out to be one of Dickens's most telling
ways of composing his sense of English civilization into a coherent,

[1] Dickens, *Letters*, ed. W. Dexter (1938), vol. II, p. 554; *The Letters of Mrs.
Gaskell*, ed. J. A. V. Chappell and Arthur Pollard (Manchester, 1966), p. 281;
Collins, *Dickens and Education*, p. 150.
[2] Kathleen Tillotson, *Novels of the Eighteen-Forties* (1961 edition), 260, n.1;
John Saville, 'The Christian Socialists of 1848', in *Democracy and the Labour Move-
ment*, 158, n. 2; Mabel Tylecote, *The Mechanics' Institutes of Lancashire and Yorkshire
Before 1851*, 271, n. 3.
[3] George H. Ford, *Dickens and his Readers* (New York, 1965), 102-3.

many-sided image. Both school and town were owned, or at least controlled, by the same men, the masters, some of whom were fanatically eager to try out on the populace the theoretical social systems which they had drawn up on strict Utilitarian principles. Some of the first efforts to redeem the hell of what Mumford calls the 'insensate industrial town' went into restoring the common land in the form of parks, beginning with Dickens's Coketown, Preston, in 1833-5. But the spirit of the movement was distinctly Gradgrind. The park at Derby, for instance, was 'tastefully laid out in grass intersected by broad gravel walks, and planted with a great variety of trees, shrubs, and flowers botanically arranged' – admission free on Sunday *except* during hours of church service, or 6d. (equivalent to £1 now) on weekdays. Here was what the Hands got in place of the two- and three-hundred acre commons on which townsfolk a generation before had run races, played at knur and spell, or courted among the bushes.[1] Again and again the trouble with the 'utilitarian economists and Commissioners of Fact' satirized by Dickens is not so much their basic aims as the detailed arrangements they thought necessary to achieve them – the fanatical tidy-mindedness which had so little sense of the freedom, the room for free movement, that we need as organic, sentient beings. Under the Poor Law of 1834, which was engineered by Edwin Chadwick (former secretary to the founder of Utilitarianism, Jeremy Bentham), a destitute man could get no poor-relief unless he entered a workhouse (and more than a quarter of a million had done so by the Forties). To discourage people of low moral fibre from succumbing to the lure of an easy life, Chadwick and company worked out 'a discipline so severe and repulsive as to make them a terror to the poor': 'minute and regular observance of routine', for example silence during meals; confiscation of all personal possessions; total separation of men and women; and separation of husbands and wives, if still fertile, partly to make easier '*the requisite classification*' (my italics).[2] And all this was grafted onto the economic system favoured by the Utilitarians – *laissez-faire*, which in its tendency to produce uncontrolled slumps might have been designed to turn able-bodied and industrious workmen into paupers. Dickens was never more surely in touch with rightful popular feeling then when,

---

[1] J. L. and Barbara Hammond, *The Bleak Age*, 79-86.
[2] *English Economic History: Select Documents*, ed. A. E. Bland, P. A. Brown, and R. H. Tawney (1914), 663; Thompson, *Making of the English Working Class*, 267-8.

in this particular novel, he made rigid systematism the centre of his target rather than the more glaring sorts of material evil.[1] In the words of a contemporary, the attempt to apply the New Poor Law 'did more to sour the hearts of the labouring population than did the privations consequent on all the actual poverty of the land'.[2]

Why did Dickens dwell so much on the educational forms taken by the new fanaticism? Partly because it was there, among the young, that one could see most strikingly how the still plastic human being was forced into an iron mould; partly because the schooling systems favoured by go-ahead cotton masters were themselves like living satires on Utilitarianism in practice, even before Dickens had recreated them in the mode of satire. The Gradgrind model school with its regimen of pure fact is in no way an allegory or symbol of what a cult of fact would run to if carried to an extreme. It has been suggested that what Dickens is really getting at is the Victorian fascination with compendiums, encyclopedias, statistical accounts, etc., and that Bitzer's 'definition of a horse' owes something to what could be found in publications like Charles Knight's *Store of Knowledge*.[3] The fact is that the first two chapters of the novel are an almost straight copy of the teaching system in schools run by the two societies for educating the poor. In the Manchester Lancasterian School a thousand children were taught in one huge room, controlled by a kind of military drill with monitors and a monitor-general, and taught by methods derived from the Catechism. Groups of facts, mechanically classified, were drummed in by methods that might have been meant to squash forever the children's urge to find out or understand anything for themselves:

> A lesson on natural history would be given thus. The boys would read: 'Ruminating Animals. Cud-chewing or ruminating animals form the *eighth* order. These, with the exception of the camel, have no cutting teeth in the upper jaw, but their place is supplied with a hard pad. In the lower jaw there are eight cutters; the tearers, in general, are absent, so that there is a vacant space between the cutters and grinders. The latter

---

[1] In his previous novel, *Bleak House*, he had dealt powerfully with material neediness and squalor, especially in the brickfield and Tom-all-Alone sequences.

[2] S. Kydd, *The History of the Factory Movement*, 1857: *cit* Asa Briggs, 'The Local Background of Chartism', in *Chartist Studies*, 11.

[3] John Holloway, 'Hard Times', in *Dickens and the Twentieth Century Reader*, ed. John Gross and Gabriel Pearson (1962), 159-62.

are very broad, and are kept rough and fit for grinding the
vegetable food on which these animals live, by the enamel
being disposed in crescent-shaped ridges . . .'

MONITOR. What have you been reading about?
BOY.   Ruminating animals.
MONITOR. Another name for ruminating?
BOY.   Cud-chewing.
MONITOR. What is the root of the word?
BOY.   'Rumen', the cud . . .
MONITOR. You read in the lesson *the enamel is disposed in crescent
              shaped ridges*. What is the enamel?
BOY.   The hard, shining part of the tooth.
MONITOR. What part of our tooth is it?
BOY.   The covering of that part that is out of the jawbone.
MONITOR. What do you mean by disposed?
BOY.   Placed.
MONITOR. The root?
BOY.   'Pono', I place . . .   (*Bleak Age*, pp. 143-7)

This of course is precisely Bitzer's '"Quadruped, Graminivorous.
Forty teeth, namely twenty-four grinders"', and so on. It only
remains to add that the inventor of this system, Joseph Lancaster
(a Quaker), claimed to have 'invented, under the blessing of
Divine Providence, a new and mechanical system of education',
and that the inventor of a similar rival system, Andrew Bell (an
Anglican), called his 'the STEAM ENGINE of the MORAL
WORLD' (*ibid.*, pp. 149-50). Given this kind of thing Dickens had
no need to invent: the satire was already there in life, and not on
some lunatic fringe but in a widespread, dominant, and much-
admired system. (On grounds of authenticity alone, apart from
deeper considerations, this aspect has not lost its relevance. I was
present, as teacher, in a class in a Scottish city school in 1959 when
one of Her Majesty's Inspectors spent twenty minutes trying to get
the boys to define a table. As he was about to leave, he turned and
asked them to repeat the hard-won definition. None of them could
remember it.)

Dickens was not seizing on a very unusually glaring or ludicrous
part of the culture and making more of it than it signified. There
were the closest links between heartless schooling and worse than
heartless factory discipline. One of the worst sides of the early
factories was the hours and conditions of work for very young
children. It turns out that some of the atrocious punishments added
to the already draconic routine were copied from Lancaster:

Lancaster worked out an elaborate code of rewards and punishments among which was 'the log', a piece of wood weighing four to six pounds, which was fixed to the neck of the child guilty of his (or her) first talking offence. On the least motion one way or another the log operated as a dead weight on the neck. Needham [owner of a cotton mill in the Peak district of Derbyshire] clearly tried to copy this progressive idea of the age. More serious offences found their appropriate punishment in the Lancasterian code; handcuffs, the 'caravan', pillory and stocks, and 'the cage'. The latter was a sack or basket in which more serious offenders were suspended from the ceiling. Needham clearly borrowed this idea, too, though his children are alleged to have been suspended by their arms over the machines.

That will not surprise anyone aware of what the factory system was like in its early days. But few, I think, have realized that schools too went in for that kind of inhuman forcing. Lancaster laid down that classroom offenders should walk backwards round the room with the yoke of wood on their necks, and a child who was kept in was tied to his desk to save the expense of keeping a teacher on to supervise him. 'What impressed the governing classes was the orderliness that prevailed.'[1]

If Dickens had been topical only, instead of topical, farsighted, and profound, he might have concentrated on specific abuses: for example, physical hardships that could quite easily be remedied. The Nottingham spinners whose bones were deformed, joints inflamed, and limbs ulcerated with long hours standing at the machine were presently given chairs to sit on, the thousand children stupefied by the Lancasterian drill were curtained off in 'classrooms' of fifty each (on the advice of a Utilitarian).[2] But hardship was not the only trouble and might not even be the case: in the Preston cotton mills themselves, according to the inspecting surgeon, health was generally better than among the other townsfolk.[3] Dickens was concerned rather to question the intrinsic nature of industrial organisation in which the worker has nothing to do but mind a machine, with no variety of work or psychological outlet in the form of some say in the running of the concern, and in

[1] Stanley D. Chapman, *The Early Factory Masters* (1967), 204; Frank Smith, *A History of English Elementary Education, 1760-1902* (1931), 74-5; Mary Sturt, *The Education of the People* (1967), 25.

[2] Engels, *The Condition of the Working-Class in England in 1844*, in Marx and Engels, *On Britain*, 188; Sturt, *op. cit.*, 89.

[3] Bland, Brown, and Tawney, *English Economic History*, 609-10.

which productivity is pursued at the expense of the human satisfaction it is supposed to serve. The industrial image that haunts *Hard Times* is of machinery that runs itself, as though without the volition of the human beings it nevertheless compels to attend it:

> Time went on in Coketown like its own machinery: so much material wrought up, so much fuel consumed, so many powers worn out, so much money made . . . the piston of the steam-engine worked monotonously up and down like the head of an elephant in a state of melancholy madness . . . all the melancholy-mad elephants, polished and oiled up for the day's monotony, were at their heavy exercise again . . . no temperature made the melancholy-mad elephants more mad or more sane. Their wearisome heads went up and down at the same rate, in hot weather and cold, wet weather and dry, fair weather and foul. The measured motion of their shadows on the walls was the substitute Coketown had to show for the shadows of rustling woods; while, for the summer hum of insects, it could offer, all the year round, from the dawn of Monday to the night of Saturday, the whirr of shafts and wheels.

The complement to the machines are the workers – whole humans reduced to Hands:

> A race who would have found more favour with some people, if Providence had seen fit to make them only hands, or, like the lower creatures of the seashore, only hands and stomachs. . . . A special contrast, as every man was in the forest of looms where Stephen worked, to the crashing, smashing, tearing piece of mechanism at which he laboured. . . . So many hundred Hands to this Mill; so many hundred horse Steam Power.

This compound insight is in the classic line of labour analysis: in literature, from Blake and Dickens through Robert Tressell to Alan Sillitoe; in discussion, from Cobbett and Hodgskin, Engels and Marx, Ruskin and Morris, through Kropotkin to the Workers' Control and Work Enlargement movements at the present time. Engels puts the thing with characteristic lucidity: factory work 'is, as the manufacturers say, very "light", and precisely by reason of its lightness, more enervating than any other. The operatives *have little to do*' (my italics). Marx rises to images of industrialism whose scalding force and richness of physical evocation draw, it seems to me, on Carlyle and Dickens as well as on his own genius. In 1829 Carlyle wrote in 'Signs of the Times': 'On every hand, the living artisan is driven from his workshop, to make room for a speedier, inanimate one. The shuttle drops from the fingers of the weaver, and falls into iron fingers that ply it faster.' (Note the impersonal passive there.) We have seen what Dickens wrote in 1854. In 1867 Marx wrote in the first volume of *Capital*:

> [Manufacture] seizes labour-power by its very roots. It converts the labourer into a crippled monstrosity, by forcing his detail dexterity at the expense of a world of productive capabilities and instincts; just as in the States of La Plata they butcher a whole beast for the sake of his hide or his tallow. Not only is the detail work distributed to the different individuals, but the individual himself is made the automatic motor of a fractional operation, and the absurd fable of Menenius Agrippa, which makes a man a mere fragment of his own body, becomes realized. . . . Here we have, in the place of the isolated machine, a mechanical monster whose body fills whole factories, and whose demon power, at first veiled under the slow and measured motion of his giant limbs, at length breaks out into the fast and furious whirl of his countless working organs.[1]

This, in its sheer openness to the newly released energies, its sense of their mingled enormity and potency, is akin to passage after passage in Dickens where he evokes the pace, the swarming detail, and the potentiality for good and ill of his age.

Given this deep and manifold rootedness of *Hard Times* in its age, it may seem less presumptuous to offer to assess the truth of its image of the life that centred on the factory system. This can be done, so long as we approach through the kind of art that is there in the novel; for presumably if there is a flaw in the *truth* of its image, this will show as failure or uncertainty in the art. I take it that something like the following would be generally acceptable as an account of how the novel works: By creating motifs and *personae* distinguished by a few bold, vivid, and repeated traits, far-flung and complex forces are organised into one homogeneous 'fable'. This simplifying mode is no doubt something that must be 'accepted', by which I really mean that we may well have to take it as a mixed blessing, something which, after all, is clearly a

---

[1] Engels, in *On Britain*, 188; Carlyle, quoted from Raymond Williams, *Culture and Society, 1780-1950* (1961 edition), 86; Marx, *Capital*, vol. I, Part IV–chapters on 'Division of Labour and Manufacture' and 'Machinery and Modern Industry': Modern Library edition, New York (n.d.), 396, 416-7.

condition of the vitality–the trenchant social attack, the whole-hearted humour, and the graphic presentation–of Dickens's kind of art. It is surely a less repressible impatience that we feel with the outstanding weakness in the novel: that is, the Stephen Blackpool part, the mixture of sentimentality and melodrama in the giving of his life and his unacceptability as representative worker (the sole representative apart from Rachael, and she is only a female replica of him). The question is whether this element–which could be written off as the usual Victorian tear-jerking, obligatory and easy to disregard–flaws the truth of the total image of life centred on the factory system.

Presumably there is no need to show in detail that Stephen and Rachael are too good to be true and that their sufferings are exploited for maudlin purposes. It is the more insidious aspects of Stephen's role that call in question Dickens's managing of the political aspect. Saddling Stephen with a monstrous drunken spouse is in keeping with that Victorian way of martyring the hero or heroine (compare Janet's husband in George Eliot's 'Janet's Repentance' or Rochester's wife in *Jane Eyre*).[1] But the special effect here is to isolate Stephen as much as possible from his work-fellows, and this is geared to the trade-union theme through a decision not to subscribe to the union regulations which is so flimsily motivated that no credible or even intelligible account of it ever comes out. Stephen's reasons are meant to be given in two speeches from Chapters 4 and 6 of Book II: ' "I ha' my reasons–mine, yo see–for being hindered; not on'y now, but awlus–awlus–life long!" ', and Louisa's statement and question to Rachael, which is never answered: ' "He fell into suspicion with his fellow-weavers, because he had made a promise not to be one of them. . . . Might I ask you why he made it?" ' This blur makes us begin to think that Dickens is not even implying an adverse judgement of trade-unionism but is sliding out of dealing with it at all. Stephen, by being singled out as a lonely martyr, has been made easy to pity; the well-to-do reader could take his part without being drawn for a moment into discomfiting thoughts of a whole martyred *class*. The figure of Slackbridge completes the unsatisfactoriness: his foaming rhetoric is done with splendid *brio*, but his extravagant denunciation of a highly personal decision is not credible, and his only other

---

[1] See above, ch. 2, 45-7.

appearance is when he is trotted on (in Book III, Chapter 4) purely to abuse Stephen again, on the occasion of Bounderby's poster offering a reward for his arrest.

This part of the novel is thus peculiarly shaky; and its upshot is to imply that working-class militancy and working-class decency are mutually exclusive. On this Leavis comments that 'when Dickens comes to the Trade Unions his understanding of the world he offers to deal with betrays a marked limitation. . . . Trade Unionism [is shown] as nothing better than the pardonable error of the misguided and oppressed, and, as such, an agent in the martyrdom of the good working man.'[1] To leave it at that, however, and to insist that 'Dickens's understanding of Victorian civilisation is adequate for his purpose; the justice and penetration of his criticism are unaffected' is to postpone the disturbing question: how could Dickens have felt free to travesty so important a movement? That it is a travesty, a mere echo of popular and stubborn misconceptions, is easily proved: House shows it in some useful pages of *The Dickens World* (pp. 205-11), and we know that much the commonest kinds of union meeting were not to hound individuals but to decide when and where to put in wage claims, to hear information and messages of support from other branches or unions, to hand out strike pay, and the like. Indeed what Dickens wrote from Preston makes it sound as though it was partly his disappointment at finding the town in so uninflamed a state that led him both to make little of the union aspect and to graft on some extraneous excitement when he did present it.[2] But the damage done to the novel is, in my view, minimised if one sees it as a failure of sociological accuracy. For one thing, does an artist have quite this obligation to known facts? True, he will fail to arouse our deepest interest if he diverges wildly from, while plainly basing himself on, a familiar state of affairs. But may he not hit off a *general* type—for example, the huffing-and-puffing sort of demagogue—while colouring in only enough topical detail to make the

---

[1] F. R. Leavis, *The Great Tradition* (1948), 245.

[2] Diary of John Ward of Clitheroe', e.g. 140, 150 (on the bringing in of blacklegs from Coventry), 156, etc.: James B. Jefferys (ed.), *Labour's Formative Years, 1849-1879* (1948), 61 (resolutions of delegates at the Preston meeting, 29 January 1854); Forster, *op. cit.*, II, 147-8: 'I am afraid I shall not be able to get much here. Except the crowds at the street-corners reading the placards pro and con; and the cold absence of smoke from the mill-chimneys; there is very little in the streets to make the town remarkable.'

persona come alive? The main problem is more subtle, and leads to deep-rooted factors in Dickens's view of social life. Let us rephrase the question already put and ask: why did Dickens pick *that* side of his theme for his exhibition of Virtue and Pathos? Or (to take the matter beyond guesswork and into the realm of verifiability): were there really no possibilities or makings, in the area from which Dickens got his material, for an image of industrial man as *fully human though sore-pressed*?

This area was Preston in the winter of 1853-4. The city was a heartland of radicalism: it so happened that all male townspeople had the vote and it therefore attracted one radical leader after another to fight the constituency. Great numbers had welcomed Cobbett when he fought an election there in 1826, and Henry Hunt, the 'matchless orator' was its M.P. (thus breaking a virtually feudal monopoly of the seat) from 1830-32.[1] The Preston employers had long been known for their opposition to unions and as late as 1860 it was said that 'increases in wages are sometimes granted elsewhere, in Preston never'. Four strikers had been shot dead by troops in 1842. 1853 was, nationally, a year of intensive labour activity which won wage rises and shortened working hours, and in June there started what became 'by far the biggest industrial struggle in the cotton trade since the general "turn out" of 1842'. The power-loom weavers asked the employers to restore a 10 per cent wage cut enforced in 1847 on the weaving of all fabrics. Most of the masters refused even to meet the workers' representatives, and many of them were fired. To support these men and further the wage claim, unions were re-formed and at some mills strikes were started. The Masters' Association of Preston locked out their workers from September, declared they would not re-employ them unless they renounced trade-union membership, and launched prosecutions against the union leaders to help break the strike (the charges were then dropped). To help the workless, funds were raised in many places (including London) by specially-formed Trades' Committees, which are presumably what Dickens is getting at under the gratuitously pompous coinage 'United Aggregate Tribunal'. As late as April, three weeks after *Hard Times* began to

---

[1] *The Autobiography of William Cobbett*, ed. William Reitzel (1967 edition), 202; Winifred Proctor, 'Orator Hunt, M.P. for Preston, 1830-32', in *Transactions of the Historic Society of Lancashire and Cheshire*, vol. 114 (Liverpool, 1963), 129-30, 141-53.

run as a serial, strikes were still breaking out all over mid-Lanca-shire, at Wigan, Burnley, Bacup, Padiham.[1]

The reader of Dickens (as of most well-known treatments of Victorian working-class life with the exception of Elizabeth Gaskell's *North and South*) would imagine that the workers who were putting up this struggle and going through this ordeal were a wretched, sullen lot, cowed by factory and city life unless they were inflamed by trouble-makers from outside. The first-hand reports of behaviour and morale show that the prevailing tone was one of resilience, self-reliance, solidarity. In a town where between twenty and thirty thousand had been workless for twenty-three weeks, the spirit of meetings was good-humoured determination. When dele-gates from the (left-wing) Labour Parliament asked to be heard, the weaver chairman would say that money or constructive comment were welcome but not ' "politics and differences among us when what we want is 'armony, brotherly love, and concord" '. When a professional speaker got up and began in exactly Slack-bridge's 'O my friends' vein to denounce plots involving a neigh-bouring town's alleged failure to contribute, 'the persuasive right hand of the chairman' fell gently on the man's shoulder and at once stopped him. Yet in his novel Dickens conveys that organised labour was so much self-deceiving agitation, which in passing squashed the rights of individuals, and that its platforms were hogged by mere politicoes. He knew that it was not so, for the above eye-witness account is his own, from his article 'On Strike'.

Notice that my point is not the question of simple truth to life but rather the question as to whether the essential springs of humanness were failing under industrial conditions. In that key Coketown passage early in the novel, Dickens writes that the 'many small streets still more like another' were 'inhabited by people equally like one another', and this, taken with his treatment of the Horse-riders, suggests that it is only among the travelling people, the rovers from outside settled and disciplined society, that the full humanness of spontaneity, togetherness, wholehearted fun, and tenderness can still thrive. It turns out (again from Dickens's own account and also from many other sources) that the Preston spinners

---

[1] 'Chartism and the Trade Unions', in *Our History* (Autumn 1963), 10; Thorold Rogers, *Six Centuries of Work and Wages* (1884), 410-11; Cole and Filson, *British Working Class Movements*, 483; Jefferys, *op cit.*, 60; *Household Words*, No. 213 (22 April 1854), 226.

and weavers had a whole culture, and a traditional and rooted culture, of fun and imagination and common effort, which they kept up in the heart of, and indeed adapted to, the industrial struggle. 'Behind the chairman,' at the Preston meeting, 'was a great crown on the top of a pole, made of parti-coloured calico, and strongly suggestive of May-day.' Comic poems were written to drum up contributions to the unemployed fund, people contributed under playful nicknames ('The chirping blacksmith, six pence'), and humour was used especially to prod laggards into paying up. On the handbills we read:

> If that fiddler at Uncle Tom's Cabin blowing room does not pay, Punch will set his legs straight.
> If that drawer at card side and those two slubbers do not pay, Punch will say something about their bustles . . .
> If squinting Jack of Goodairs does not pay up in future, Punch will stand on his corns.
> If those piecers at Dawson's new mill do not pay better, young Punch (old Punch's urchin) will come and break their ends . . .
> If that young spark, Ben D., that works at Baxter's Mill does not pay to his trade, Punch will tell about him eating that rhubarb pudding that was boiled in a dirty night cap.
> If Roger does not pay, Punch will tell about her robbing the donkey of its breakfast to stuff her bustle with.[1]

When we come upon the first bits of circus slang in Chapters 5 and 6 of *Hard Times*, we quicken at once, after the bullying formalities and dry precisian assertions of the Gradgrind set. Plainly the author himself is enjoying the quirky idiom of Sleary's troupe (and we also notice that Bounderby is affronted by its outlandishness). The perspective of the novel would have been transformed, and brought still nearer to the real currents of life under industrial conditions, if Dickens had been able to allow that there were kindred things to enjoy and an unquenched capacity for enjoyment at the heart of Coketown.[2] The more we find out what actually happened at that time, the more we realise that militancy was a lifeline—a well-spring of hope, a channel for popular energies, as well as an indispensable lever—amidst the direst conditions. Preston

---

[1] 'On Strike', 556; Jefferys, *op cit.*, 62.

[2] In quite specific ways militancy was using the same media as the traditional amusements: e.g. in Leicester a room regularly hired by horse-riders was let for Chartist meetings (*The Life of Thomas Cooper*, Written by Himself, 1877 edition, 163).

at Hunt's election in December 1830: the radicals, 'in a high state
of exaltation', paraded the streets with 'music, flambeaux, a lighted
tar-barrel and three flags, one of them tri-coloured'. Glasgow during
the Reform campaign of 1831: 'The whole people in that place
and in the adjoining towns walked in procession into the Green,
divided into their crafts, societies, villages, and parishes, with
colours and emblems . . . with about 500 flags and 200 bands of
music.' Leeds at the start of Chartism in 1838: 'At the demonstrations the Moor [Hartshead Moor, then called Peep Green] was
like a fair, with huts erected for the sale of food and drink, and
wives and families accompanying their menfolk. From Bradford,
Huddersfield, Halifax, Dewsbury, and other towns in the West
Riding the delegates marched in formation–often several thousands
strong–with banners flying and bands playing.'[1] But the Preston
high spirits in 1854 are all the more impressive for bubbling up,
after that long workless winter, on occasions that were not special
or stirring.

The relevance for *Hard Times* can be put in two ways. We may
say that Dickens excelled when satirising the employers' habit of
discrediting every rightful demand of the Hands (as in that ludicrous
recurring image of Bounderby's about 'turtle soup and venison,
with a gold spoon') but tended to waver into the sentimental or
unconvincing when obliged to focus on the Hands either as private
people or as a class liable to take social initiatives. Or we may go
further and say that it was *not possible* to write well when taking the
line that militancy was a kind of aberration. On this crucial issue he
repeatedly veils radical indecision under a kind of fair-mindedness
typical of the gentleman of his time (or the liberal today) who sees
much too clearly to deny clamant injustice but cannot commit
himself to any course of action that might end it. When Dickens
assures us that 'these men [the Coketown workers], through their
very delusions, showed great qualities' even when they 'went astray'
by combining, or that 'every man felt his only hope to be in his
allying himself to the comrades by whom he was surrounded; and
that in this belief, right or wrong (unhappily wrong then), the whole
of that crowd were gravely, deeply, faithfully in earnest', he is
speaking with a usual voice of the middle class. It is the voice of

---

[1] Proctor, 'Orator Hunt', 143; Henry Cockburn, *Journal* (1874), I, 15 (entry
for 4 May 1831); J. F. C. Harrison, 'Chartism in Leeds', in *Chartist Studies*, 77,
n. 4.

E

Elizabeth Gaskell in chapter 3 of *Mary Barton*, blaming John Barton's bitterness at the death of his starving child partly on 'those who, either in speech or in print, find it their interest to cherish such feelings in the working class', and of *The Times* leader on Peterloo which generously condoled with those massacred in spite of the folly of the 'half employed and half starved' in letting themselves get 'puffed up by prodigious notions of their strength, and inflamed by artful pictures of their grievances'. Indeed it turns out that the notion of politics as an imported disease, with its implication that, left to themselves, masters and men would live in harmony, was precisely the line of the Bounderbys—the Preston cotton masters. In their manifesto of 15 September 1853 they deplored the 'designing and irresponsible body' who were interfering 'with the relation between master and servant' and creating 'where it does not exist . . . a feeling of dissatisfaction and estrangement'.[1]

Dickens, it seems, repeatedly leans to the mass of the people, then draws back, because to commit himself would have been to wake up from the dream of harmony between classes. His criticism of a desperately harsh and unequal society is weakened to make it less uncomfortable, whether to himself or to the reader, and Stephen's latent function turns out to be to suggest that the right way to take the inevitable suffering is with dignified restraint, and alone. His dying words about the murderous condition of the mines are at once given the cast of something to be wished or prayed for rather than struggled about by his still later plea (clearly a message from the author) that '"aw th' world may on'y coom together more"'. In specific situations this could only mean that the mill workers should give up their struggle, with its hard-won momentum and solidarity, in favour of arbitration (the suggestion that ends 'On Strike'), or that they should give up politics—the 'froth' and 'unsound counsel called the People's Charter'—in favour of agitation on practical matters like clean streets and cholera epidemics, all of which would somehow give rise to good government and 'a better understanding between the two great divisions of society'.[2] Do not the first-hand records of militant activity—the songs, memoirs, and union documents—show that so much spirit, so rich

---

[1] *The Times*, 19 August 1819; Jefferys, *op. cit.*, 60.
[2] 'A Home Question': *Household Words*, No. 242 (11 November 1854), 292; 'To Working Men': *Household Words*, No. 237 (7 October 1854), 169-70.

a human nature, flowed into struggle that to pooh-pooh it or opt out of it by setting up some ideal above the battle was to risk one's art going soft and blurred? In taking for his subject the very core of industrial civilisation—its consequences for people's upbringing, feelings and relationships, and life's work—Dickens had set himself the most exacting test of ability to see truly. In the struggle to live humanly, the working people were exerting every kind of intelligence, courage, and elasticity, the masters were blocking, curbing and denying their humanness at point after point. In such a situation all are stultified, and Dickens embodies this most memorably in Louisa and her relationship—the lack of it—with her father. But more was needed, and if one tried to imagine the great industrial novel that never did get written, one might suggest that the masters cried out to be satirised, the mass of the people to be presented with clear-eyed realism. In so far as Dickens fails in the latter, his novel sags; in so far as he excels in the former, it succeeds, and thereby earns the currency which has made 'Coketown' the classic name for the early industrial city.[1]

[1] See, for example, Lewis Mumford, *The Culture of Cities* (1940 ed.), ch. 3, esp. section 11, and plate 11.

CHAPTER 6

Fiction and the
'Rising Industrial Classes'

ONE of the more massive tasks to which the nineteenth-century novelists rose with such energy and plenitude of imagination was making sense of the more far-flung and powerful social forces that reach into the lives of all of us. The contemporary changes in living were so fast, they embroiled such quantities of peoples and materials and forced elements so new and disquieting onto the attention, that the writers, for all their energy and plenitude, tended to fall back on methods suited to the much smaller units that hitherto had been their natural scene–the village, the family, the big house. The smaller the unit and the more domestic the life, the more easily it could be managed by the masterful or goodhearted individual (or undermined by a single fiend or villain). Hence the unreal manipulations so often brought in to resolve the ramifications of a novel by Scott or Dickens or Tolstoy or George Eliot. As Mitchell puts it in a passage quoted already:

> This formal plot element . . . becomes more and more dominant as the book nears its end, while the social critique, though still remaining strong, becomes more and more a by-product of the formal plot. So, artistically, the latter sections of Dickens's novels (for that matter it seems to me the last sections of the vast majority of eighteenth or nineteenth-century English novels) tend to fall considerably short of the rest of the book.[1]

If the critic fails to recognise this–both the phenomenon and its cause–he is left with no way of either defining or explaining the weaknesses that follow, in novels that have set themselves large subjects, from pivoting too wide a significance on personal relations between individuals. For example, here are the conclusions (in a run-together form) of a recent study of *Bleak House*, 'acquisitiveness', and the 'rising industrial classes':

[1] See above, ch. 3, 83.

Rosa (standing for reinvigorated tradition) is united with honourable industrialism. It is a human solution to a rivalry of powers. The sins of the 'fathers' are resolved in and through love. Dickens's emblematic marriage, although perfectly at home at the level of character, suggests a solution to the urgent problems of the time. Provided the personal relationship is right, it will spread out and cleanse society. It will oil Chancery procedure, invigorate Parliament, reform slum landlords, and make telescopic philanthropists re-align their sights. Dickens does not show us a system actually reformed, but we are meant to recognise that the varieties of System will get cured of their constrictive or self-regarding ailments as soon as a personal love directs itself outward socially. Dickens knows, on the realistic level, that in fact one tyranny is competing with another; but he has offered his social diagnosis elsewhere in *Bleak House*. The union of Rosa and Watt signifies his social prescription.[1]

This seems to waver between recognising the fallacies of over-personalising a large social situation and falling into them. Mr Blount's first use of 'resolved' is all right since it refers only to the rounding off of the work of art, but when it turns into a 'solution', and to the urgent problems of the time no less, the fallacy has come in, since this can only mean that someone (whether Dickens or Mr Blount) does believe that, somehow, more individual efforts at friendliness, between strategically right parties, could reform a heartless social order and that, if one believed so, one could work in a practical way towards that end. This is such arrant wishful thinking that it is then half withdrawn—Dickens 'does not show us a system actually reformed', he knows that 'in fact one tyranny is competing with another'. But a final effort to clinch the question of whether personal relations could possibly be managed so as to better society—or, if not, what else could—is then fudged, or shelved, by the phrase 'on the realistic level'. If Dickens did know on the realistic level that in his society one tyranny (the hereditary landlords, the Dedlocks) was competing with another (the new industrial capitalists, the Rouncewells), it was presumably on the unrealistic level that he suggested his social prescription of a spreading, cleansing personal love. In that case, what is left of his suggestion, as anything like a serious effort to understand modern

[1] Trevor Blount, 'The Ironmaster and the new Acquisitiveness: Dickens's Views on the Rising Industrial Classes as Exemplified in *Bleak House*': *Essays in Criticism*, xv, 3 (October 1965).

society, that love could melt or wish away exploitation and acquisitiveness?

Some such fallacy has so hovered round the discussion of literary and social matters alike that the question can best be taken further through a novel that leads directly from matters of literary treatment to the main history of the industrial epoch—George Eliot's *Felix Holt* (1866), subtitled 'The Radical', another important book from the decades which followed the Hungry Forties and the start of the 'second Industrial Revolution'. Chapter 30 of *Felix Holt*, like the chapter of Lawrence's *Women in Love* called 'The Industrial Magnate', opens out endless perspectives into those lines of social development that have brought us to where we are now. It presents, in the speeches of the nameless trade-unionist and of Felix at an election meeting, two kinds of radicalism: the first a rendering of what must have been said on many a platform from about 1815 onwards, and the second George Eliot's own kind of ardent humanism. The workman's speech is the most plausible and telling political utterance I know of in our literature,[1] and from the first images of the man we sense that we are getting the real thing: 'a grimy man in a flannel shirt, hatless and with turbid red hair, who was insisting on political points with much more ease than had seemed to belong to the gentlemen speakers on the hustings', his 'bare arms . . . powerfully muscular, though he had the pallid complexion of a man who lives chiefly amidst the heat of furnaces'. The man's speaking style is equally well done, over a stretch of several pages: it has the momentum, the insistences and repetitions, the immediate striking-power which are indispensable if such utterance is to carry across. This quality of writing shows George Eliot to have been quite unusually open to the viewpoint, idiom, and whole culture of the underdog and militant mass-representative. But her final sympathy is not with this man.

His speech is written to show him as a fully enlightened spokesman for his class: he doesn't care only for immediate party ends—

> 'It isn't a man's share just to mind your pin-making, or your
> glass-blowing, and higgle about your wages, and bring up
> your family to be ignorant sons of ignorant fathers, and no
> better prospect; that's a slave's share; we want a freeman's

[1] Not that the competition is strong: the only immediately comparable thing is the conversation among the miners which Disraeli dramatises convincingly in Book 3, ch. 1, of *Sybil*.

share, and that is to think and speak and act about what
concerns us all, and see whether these fine gentlemen who
undertake to govern us are doing the best they can for us.
They've got the knowledge, say they. Very well, we've got the
wants. . . .'

Just before this Felix has given a loud 'Hear, hear!' and the crowd
have looked round at him with his 'well-washed face and educated
expression'. The speaker then puts his main arguments for democratic control over the legislature–in which he echoes Gerrard
Winstanley the Digger's classic appeal for justice *in this life*–and
ends with a point that roots the speech perfectly in real politics.
He has attacked the ruling-class, but in that post-1832 pre-1867
England he must make do with a member of it as his representative: hence the business-like bluntness with which he ends up, '"And
if any of you have acquaintance among county voters, give 'em a
hint that you wish 'em to vote for Transome,"' and he steps down
from the stone and quickly walks off.

The whole thing is so right and complete that one can't think of
anything (except perhaps more responses from the crowd) that is
either necessary or plausible for the dramatic rendering of such a
piece of life from such a time. The author's clinching comment,
however, in introducing the immediately following speech, is that
Felix's expression 'was something very different from the mere
acuteness and rather hard-lipped antagonism of the trades-union
man'. These phrases are in themselves perfectly apt; what is not
acceptable is the implication that there was some finer alternative
attitude which could replace or seriously compete with that kind of
militancy. The state of social struggle at that time was such that
only antagonism, allied to acuteness, could conceivably have made
any headway in quickening people to a sense of all they lacked.
This was the age in which the miners were moulding bullets in their
cottages and the government was building barracks all over
England because it could no longer trust the soldiers not to be
subverted if they were lodged in billets.[1] It was the age in which a
wave of slump was liable to throw one-third of the workers in a
textile town into pauperdom.[2] When the people gathered to
protest against these conditions, they were attacked and sabred by

[1] Hammonds, *The Town Labourer*, I, 91-5.
[2] Arnold Toynbee, 'Are Radical Socialists?', 1882, in his *The Industrial
Revolution*, 221-2.

men of Harold Transome's class—the gentleman-volunteers at
Peterloo. When things have reached such a pass, hard-lipped antagonism is so irresistibly wished upon people of spirit that to try
and base one's ideal 'above it all' is to place veils between oneself
and reality.

Unreality is indeed what mainly tinges the image of Felix in
what follows. He wears a working man's brown velveteens but the
author is careful to make him an odd man out, 'with a dress more
careless than that of most well-to-do workmen on a holiday', and
this oddity she of course presents as a virtue. This virtue is not one
which she is able to ground in convincingly-rendered mien,
behaviour, or speech:

> Even lions and dogs know a distinction between men's glances;
> and doubtless those Duffield men, in the expectation with
> which they looked up at Felix, were unconsciously influenced
> by the grandeur of his full yet firm mouth, and the calm
> clearness of his grey eyes, which were yet somehow unlike
> what they were accustomed to see along with an old brown
> velveteen coat, and an absence of chin-propping. When he
> began to speak, the contrast of voice was still stronger than
> that of appearance. The man in the flannel shirt had not been
> heard—had probably not cared to be heard—beyond the
> immediate group of listeners. But Felix at once drew the
> attention of persons comparatively at a distance.

We are not told by what mesmerism or miracle of elocution Felix
draws people from afar. The association of 'clear' eyes with moral
loftiness is of course sentimental pot-boiler's stock-in-trade, and
that blurred 'somehow' is quite unlike George Eliot's typical good
prose. It is vague in order to be evasive, and what she is evading is
saying, with the open snobbery of an ordinary 'lady novelist', that
Felix has the supposed virtues of a 'gentleman' in spite of his 'low
origins'. The alleged 'grandeur' of his presence is not done in words
that bring to the mind's senses an image anything like solid enough
to bear the moral weight laid on it. In the speech itself, as in all
Felix's dialogue, proletarian directness is meant to be done by the
occasional homely phrase, 'he pours milk into a can without a
bottom' and the like. But the run of the speech, especially the pre-
arranged syntax and smoothly sequential linking of the sentences,
doesn't suggest any kind of utterable English, unlike the trade-
unionist's speech in which one phrase triggers off another. What
Felix comes out with is really Victorian printed homily. It might

be argued that a self-educated Victorian artisan would in fact have expressed himself rather stiffly. But this is not pointed up in any way, it is not distinctly marked off from the author's own moralising prose, and the effect in dramatic terms, especially coming after the lifelike trade-unionist, is to shrink Felix's speech to the status of a message coming at us direct from the author.

This message is that the vote (and the other democratic demands then being put by the Chartists) matters little unless 'men's passions, feelings, desires' can be refined:

> 'That's very fine,' said a man in dirty fustian, with a scornful laugh. 'But how are we to get the power without votes?'
> 'I'll tell you what's the greatest power under heaven,' said Felix, 'and that is public opinion – the ruling belief in society about what is right and what is wrong, what is honourable and what is shameful. . . . How can political freedom make us better, any more than a religion that we don't believe in, if people laugh and wink when they see men abuse and defile it? And while public opinion is what it is – while corruption is not felt to be a damning disgrace – while men are not ashamed in Parliament and out of it to make public questions which concern the welfare of millions a mere screen for their own petty private ends, – I say, no fresh scheme of voting will much help men in our condition. . . .'

and he goes off on a denunciation of 'treating' voters till they are too drunk to know what they're doing and vote for the men who bought them the beer. It is a sorry anti-climax after the building up of Felix as a saviour and sole mouthpiece of the redeeming truth. Studies of mid-nineteenth-century voting suggest that fear of eviction was often a more potent influence than the treating. But the paramount factor here, which George Eliot manages to evade, is that corruption was petty compared with the fundamental class bias in the political system. Insofar as Felix is arguing that the trade unions 'expected voting to do more' towards an equal society than it possibly could, we can agree, for the mass of people had largely helped towards a middle-class hegemony in society by allowing their own power to be channelled into the struggle to enfranchise the £10 householders. As the most penetrating contemporary journalist put it, 'They had united all *property* against all *poverty*.'[1] But Felix is shaped to embody quite a different sort of protest. He

---

[1] Bronterre O'Brien, quoted by Asa Briggs in *Chartist Studies*, 295.

stands for a moral betterment that is above mere politics, and thus
he has behind him the wishful liberalism of George Eliot's tradition.
In this respect it is only the distinction of her style that sets her
off from the claptrap typified by Charles Kingsley in *Alton Locke*
(1850), a novel expressly aimed at removing politics to the realm
of pious philanthropy:

> 'Yes,' she continued, 'Freedom, Equality, and Brotherhood
> are here. Realise them in thine own self, and so alone thou
> helpest to make them realities for all. Not from without, from
> Charters and Republics, but from within, from the Spirit
> working in each; not by wrath and haste, but by patience made
> perfect through suffering, canst thou proclaim their good news
> to the groaning masses, and deliver them, as thy Master did
> before thee, by the cross, and not the sword.[1]

The unreality of the position shows through in Felix's promise that
' "if you go the right way to work you may get power sooner without votes" '. All this could mean in practice would be something
like syndicalism, and of course George Eliot does not mean that!—
any more than Felix actually produces his 'right way' in the
course of the novel. All George Eliot can offer, through Felix,
is high-mindedness, unrooted in any particular activity or movement.[2]

This was not only preachifying in mid-air. In its place and time
it ignored the crucial truth, more and more evident as each political
phase wore on, that the struggle for the vote and other democratic
rights was itself a deep-reaching force for moral growth. This was
seen early on, by Francis Place the tailor, who knew the campaign
for the 1832 Reform from the inside. In that year he wrote that
militancy 'has impressed the morals and manners, and elevated the

---

[1] Ch. 41: 1889 ed., 304.

[2] It is significant that the ending of *Felix Holt* should have come in for exactly
the same kind of interpretation as *Bleak House*—the same overdoing of how much
one personal relationship can signify, the same reluctance to draw conclusions
from key unrealities in plot and characterisation: '[Felix's] assertive rectitude,
though quite untypical, in orientation, of any working-class Radical leader of the
period, has *a certain* positive quality. Holt voices, *however inadequately in terms of the
realities of the day*, the sense of pride in his class, and its protest against the election-
rigging and trickery of the established political parties. And *calculated though the
ending is*, there is significance in terms of social values in Esther Lyon's renunciation
of her right to Transome Court . . . and her joining with Felix in his struggle to
better the lot of his class.' (my italics: Ian Milner, '*Felix Holt, The Radical* and
Realism in George Eliot', in *Journal of Modern Philolo* , Prague, 1955, II-III,
169)

character of the working-man. . . . In every place as reform has advanced, drunkenness has retreated'.[1] Place of course did not make speeches on the moral insignificance of the franchise but worked for it with every ounce of his devotion and shrewdness. By the end of George Eliot's life (1880) or shortly after it, with the growing union organisation of the unskilled,[2] those closest to the struggle could see time and again how the militancy despised and feared as barbarous by the middle and upper classes was in fact a civilising force. Once the East End worker 'develops his own type and makes it count by means of organisation', as Engels put it in a letter of 1889, 'Scenes like those which occurred during Hyndman's procession through Pall Mall and Piccadilly will then become impossible and the rowdy who will want to provoke a riot will simply be knocked dead.' A foremost leader of labour in those years, Tom Mann of the Amalgamated Society of Engineers, saw how this was working in the north of England. In a letter of about 1888 he wrote that as Marxism spread in Lancashire and the Social Democratic Federation developed more branches, 'The Blackburn men will testify that as a result they became respected where they had formerly had to be constantly ready for fisticuff work, & Darwen developed even better.'[3] This was not at all confined to an exceptional few advanced socialists. In a passage that seems to me classic—it deserves to be known as a milestone in the growth of our civilisation—Ben Tillett, the dockers' leader, sums up the after-effects of the 1889 agreement on a higher minimum wage, a rate for overtime, regular gangs, notice or money when men were dismissed, and regular signing-on times (to stop the bestial fight for work-tickets at the docks):

> We had established a new spirit; the bully and the thief, for a time at least, were squelched; no more would the old man be driven and cursed to death by the younger man, threatened and egged on to murder by an overmastering bully. The whole tone and conduct of work, of management of the men, was altered, and for the best.
>
> The goad of the sack was not so fearful; the filthiness and foulness of language was altered for an attempt at courtesy, which, if not refined, was at least a recognition of the manhood of our brothers.

[1] Wallas, *Life of Place*, 145.
[2] See above, ch. 4, 103.
[3] *On Britain*, 521; Torr, *Tom Mann and his Times*, 255.

From a condition of the foulest blackguardism in direct-
ing the work, the men found a greater respect shown them;
they, too, grew in self-respect, and the men we saw after the
strike were comparable to the most self-respecting of the other
grades of labour.

The 'calls' worked out satisfactorily; organisation took the
place of the haphazard; the bosses who lazed and loafed on
their subordinates were perforce obliged to earn instead of
thieving their money; the work was better done; the men's
lives were more regular as their work was–the docker had,
in fact, become a man!

The man became greater in the happiness of a better supplied
larder and home; and the women folk with the children,
shared the sense of security and peace the victory at the docks
had wrought.[1]

There is how modern man has won his way forwards, developing
himself in the course of meeting those needs with which his way of
life has faced him. Yet–deflected and domineered-over, it seems,
by the old notions of salvation for the individual soul–thinking
about such matters is still weak in the sense of what we are collec-
tively. The novel, which is bound to work through the characteri-
sing of individuals–whatever may be made of this in sum–has
suffered accordingly. The first critic to realise the quality of *Felix
Holt* and, in doing so, to distinguish between the implausible Felix
and the fine Transome part was F. R. Leavis; yet in discussing *why*
it was that George Eliot couldn't help idealising Felix he can only
suggest that she was 'relying on her "moral consciousness" un-
qualified by first-hand knowledge'.[2] At least as important, I would
have thought–for she did know the country workman yet still
idealised Adam Bede–is the tendency in our culture to value the
purely moral above the merely social, to set a space between
practical and ideal activities. For this comes in again and again to
deform the presentation of society in the best of our classic novels
since the Industrial Revolution. In *Women in Love* Lawrence takes
the critique of 'hard-lipped antagonism' to an extreme and can see
nothing but smash and grab and a debased levelling-down in the
concerted struggles of the working people at the start of this century.[3] At least this is only a minor element in that novel and, as I

[1] Ben Tillett, *A Brief History of the Dockers' Union*, 1910, quoted from *Tom Mann's
Memoirs*, 89-90.
[2] *The Great Tradition*, 52.
[3] See below, ch. 7, esp. 144-6, 150-3.

argue below, one that Lawrence fails to incorporate into the valid drama of the book. In the case of *Howards End*, which is E. M. Forster's attempt at the sort of comprehensive coverage of modern civilisation that Leavis claims for *Women in Love*, the novelist tries to embody a *rapprochement* between intelligentsia and businessmen through the central relationship of the book, the Wilcox-Schlegel marriage. The tantalising thing about it is that Forster with part of himself quite realises that individual love or friendship cannot bring together a whole people deeply divided by interest, upbringing, and way of life: he emphasises, for example, the futility of Margaret and Helen's hoping to change Leonard Bast (to make him the free and developed person he craves to be) by taking him home for tea-parties with intelligent conversation. Yet by having Margaret marry Mr Wilcox, with her eyes open, and with no final loss of her loving attachment to him even in the teeth of his repeated flouting of what she holds most valuable, Forster is staging what he has already shown to be unrealistic; indeed, time after time he almost openly challenges us to demur.[1]

Forster's social radicalism has been keen but intermittent,[2] and it is significant that the experiences which, for a time, floated him off the shoals of barrenness as a writer were those he had in India, where the facts of inequality, inhumanity, and exploitation were so clamant that wishful ideals could hardly have survived. In *A Passage to India*, which has recently been praised by a distinguished psychologist for showing how colonialism vitiates relations between people,[3] the only vestige of the over-personalising fallacy is the occasional aphorism – 'One touch of regret . . . would have made . . . the British Empire a different institution', 'Indians know whether they are liked or not . . . and that is why the British Empire rests on sand', and so on.[4] But nothing in the body of the drama supports this kind of view of the empire: the frictions between races – which in many ways have replaced those between classes, with the evolution of capitalism into imperialism – are followed out

[1] Esp. the end of ch. 22 when Margaret is looking into Wilcox's eyes: 'What was behind their competent stare? She knew, but was not disquieted.'

[2] The only place where he aligns himself with the have-not's, as distinct from ironically exposing the failings of his own class, appears to be the essay 'Me, Them and You' in *Abinger Harvest*.

[3] G. M. Carstairs, Foreword to *A Dying Colonialism* by Frantz Fanon (1970 ed.), 8.

[4] Chs. 5, 29 (Penguin ed., 50, 253).

unflinchingly, from the touches of unease that mar Fielding's friendship with Aziz, down to the last, perfectly-imagined moment of acknowledged conflict between Indian and Englishman as they ride along the rocky trail.

It is easier to face matters squarely when they are sited abroad, and this must be one of the reasons why during the past sixty years more good novels by English writers have been set abroad than in their own country.[1] When the situation is close to us, we are prone to retreat into ideals rather than face the lifetime of wearing practical effort that a genuinely social solution necessarily demands: for example, we pretend to ourselves that far-flung communal matters could be solved by a 'change of heart' or by pursuing some 'higher purpose' or abstract end not grounded in the situation in which we find ourselves. In a world moulded by industrial revolutions it would be more sensible to realise that man makes himself by meeting specific needs, most often of a social-practical kind, in the course of which his human nature is changed and new ideas arise. This is not to subordinate feelings and relationships to some brute process but rather to see more exactly why the course of our lives—including feelings, relationships, and thoughts—is as it is.

[1] E.g. by Conrad, Forster, Lawrence, L. H. Myers, Joyce Cary, Graham Greene.

CHAPTER 7

Lawrence and Democracy

'Trade, the invidious enemy; Trade, which thrust out
its hand and shut the factory doors, and pulled the
stockingers off their seats, and left the web half-finished
on the frame; Trade, which mysteriously choked up
the sources of the rivulets of wealth, and blacker and
more secret than a pestilence, starved the town.'

LAWRENCE, 'Goose Fair'

THE chapter of *Women in Love* called 'The Industrial Magnate' is
crucial for anyone concerned to assess the changes in civilisation
brought about by the modern developments in industry and the
large-scale organisation of society that flows from it. Lawrence's
special convictions, and prejudices, are as strikingly figured here as
anywhere. The sequence is one of the most telling tests of whether
Lawrence achieves what Leavis claims for the novel, that it is a
'presentation of twentieth-century England – of modern civilisation
– so first-hand and searching in its comprehensiveness as to be
beyond the powers of any other novelist he knows of.'[1] Presumably
such comprehensiveness can't be verified solely by intuition.
Doesn't such a claim entail that the work be largely true to what is
known to have been the case in the relevant particular situations?
I suggest that the reader's experience, as he reads his way through
the very fully embodied epitome of Gerald's immediate family past
and on into the more historical sequence that opens 'There was a
crisis when Gerald was a boy, when the Masters' Federation closed
down the mines because the men would not accept a reduction',
must be to notice that the prose mode has changed – it has moved
back from individuals evoked in their relationships, to look out over
a large tract of country peopled by a class. It is no less powered by
a confidence of insight than before, yet it offers far fewer of those
particulars than can act as touchstones for a writer's large view.
At the same time it offers an opinion of how things were going for
the industrial workers – the majority of English people – which on

[1] F. R. Leavis, *D. H. Lawrence: Novelist* (1955), 149.

143

the face of it is not to me convincing. The historical mode of the passage lays it open to verification against what is known to have been the case, and since the relevant particular situation is the militant movement among working people on the eve of the Great War, it is the facts of this that we need if our sneaking sense that Lawrence has here given in to prejudice is to be confirmed or not.

The nub of Lawrence's diagnosis–it may be called the essence of his response to socialism, or democracy–lies in two clusters of sentences from the sequence, the first on militancy and the second on equality (the two are barely separable):

> Seething mobs of men marched about, their faces lighted up as for holy war, with a smoke of cupidity. How disentangle the passion for equality from the passion of cupidity, when begins the fight for equality of possessions? . . .
>
> And then it came to an end, and the men went back to work. But it was never the same as before. There was a new situation created, a new idea reigned. Even in the machine, there should be equality. No part should be subordinate to any other part: all should be equal. The instinct for chaos had entered.

'Holy war' cuts two ways: it suggests the men were in earnest, it also suggests that they were clothing a base motive in high-minded trappings. What was the actual state of affairs? The novel is set during what historians call the Great Unrest, which began a year or two after Lawrence's birth with the riding and clubbing down of a massive demonstration of the unemployed in the autumn of 1887 ('For more than a fortnight, Trafalgar Square was in a state of siege') and the first big efforts at militant organisation by semi-skilled and unskilled workers a year or two later.[1] During the generation that followed, when Lawrence was getting his first conscious impressions of life, there were rarely less than one million men out of work. Sharp economic crises set in in 1902-4, 1908-9, and 1914, the last ended only by the boom resulting from the war. Prices rose steeply. £1 at the 1895 rate could buy only 14/7 worth of goods by 1914. Between 1906 and 1909, just before Lawrence began to write, the cost of living rose by 6 per cent while wages fell by 2 per cent. Between 1893 and 1908, in effect the years leading up to the events in 'The Industrial Magnate', profits went up by 29·5 per cent and wages (not real but nominal) by 12 per cent.

[1] Torr, *Tom Mann and His Times*, 262 and ch. 17.

The workers' 'simple view was that, as the power to produce wealth grew greater, the standard of living ought to rise with it'.[1]

Those are not 'mere statistics'. Economic setbacks meant not only frugal living but lethal hardship. One of the first detailed surveys of how most people were living found that 'The life of a labourer is marked by five alternating periods of want and comparative plenty'. Or to take the body of people *Women in Love* makes typical of the workers, 'the miners lived by turns in comfort and destitution'.[2] This hard, insecure life engendered a will to organise against exploitation and loss of livelihood. From 1892 to 1910 the total of trade-union members rose by about a million, or 66 per cent. In the years including the crisis described by Lawrence, another million joined, which was an increase of 10 per cent a year. 'No less significant is the fact that the increase has not been confined to particular industries, particular localities, or to a particular sex, but has taken place, more or less, over the whole field.' Trade unionism came to maturity as the recognised representative of the working people with the series of industrial Acts of 1906-13 which at last gave the beginnings of a comprehensive machinery for securing a minimum wage and a form of semi-disinterested arbitration on wages, hours, and conditions. It was the beginning of the end for the virtually blackmailing system of 'agreements' which had held down earnings since the early days of workmen's 'combinations'.[3]

Perhaps as important as a sign of the state of mind of working people under capitalism just before the War is the fact that it was a heyday of Direct Action—strikes aimed at forcing the hand of the government on issues not directly connected with betterment of material wellbeing. During 1913-14 there was a spasm of industrial 'insurrectionism' (stopped only by the War)—an 'outburst of exasperated strikes' that sprung demand after demand on the employers. The aim was to draw every worker into a union and with this strength to thrust Parliament aside and drive the unions to the forefront as the sole effectively democratic organ that represented the whole people in their struggle to organise life justly. This

[1] Morton, *People's History of England*, 494, 509-10; Cole and Postgate, *The Common People*, 476, 497-8.
[2] B. Seebohm Rowntree, *Poverty*, 169-70; Elie Halévy, *Imperialism and the Rise of Labour* (1951 ed.), 253.
[3] Sidney and Beatrice Webb, *The History of Trade Unionism*, 473-5.

wave of syndicalism was behind the 1910 strikes in the north of England and Welsh coalfields, the Clyde dockyards, and the cotton mills of Lancashire and Cheshire. As an employer remarked to a high official at the Board of Trade during the international strike of seamen: 'It is a revolution.'[1]

Those basic facts about life in England at that time seem to me to amount to a claim on the novelist that he shall not ignore the social needs and social values that are implied by them. Lawrence characterises the struggle for the means of life as a war shot through with greed for possessions. Of course 'cupidity' will have entered in. But should it be *interpreted* with a stress on the degeneracy of the human nature involved? The famous Welsh syndicalist manifesto of 1913, *The Miner's Next Step*, had as its thirteenth point: 'That a continual agitation be carried on in favour of increasing the minimum wage and shortening the hours of work until we have extracted the whole of the employers' profits.'[2] Was this the 'passion for equality' or the 'passion of cupidity'? It is hard to be sure of the state of mind of a million people from three generations back. But there is circumstantial evidence. In the first place, someone trying to save his family from a perpetual switch between 'comfort and destitution' seems more likely to be thinking of survival than of 'the plush furniture, and pianofortes' which Birkin-Lawrence treats as the goal of work in the pits.[3] Secondly, the miners in many parts of Britain couldn't but look on the mines and the mining country as their own:

> The miners, who often owned their cottages, who had contributed to the cost of building those little chapels, Methodist, Baptist, or Congregationalist, dotted about all over the countryside, and among whom mining was an hereditary profession, had come to regard themselves as joint-owners of the soil and the coal measures beneath it.[4]

Thirdly, there was a growing feeling, spreading out from the more hellish places in the industrial system, that the mass of the people were owed a decent life and must now rise and take it. The worst hardships had become notorious. Rowntree found in 1899, taking York (correctly) as an average smaller city, that for 30 per cent

---

[1] Webbs, *History*, 665-7; Halévy, *The Rule of Democracy, 1905-1914*, 453, 456.
[2] A. L. Morton and George Tate, *The British Labour Movement, 1770-1920* (1956), 239.
[3] Ch. 5.
[4] Halévy, *Rise of Labour*, 253-4.

of families their incomes were too small to maintain 'merely physical efficiency', the main causes being low wages and large families. The periods of worst poverty and the sapping of bodies and spirits that resulted occurred 'In childhood—when his constitution is being built up', 'In early middle life—when he should be in his prime', and 'In old age'.[1] People so maltreated were being undermined in every way. In a street in east London, most of the two hundred families lived in a single room.

> Not a room would be free from vermin, and in many life at night was unbearable. Several occupants have said that in hot weather they don't go to bed, but sit in their clothes in the least infested part of the room. What good is it, they said, to go to bed when you can't get a wink of sleep for bugs and fleas?

Beatrice Webb summed up what she had seen as a seamstress in the attic workshops of cheap-clothing makers and as a gatherer of information for Booth's survey:

> It is not so much the actual vice, it is the low level of monotonous and yet excited life; the regular recurrence to street sensations, quarrels and fights; the greedy street-bargaining, and the petty theft and gambling. The better natures keep apart from their degraded fellow-citizens and fellow-workers, live lonely and perforce selfish lives, not desiring to lead their more ignorant and un-self-controlled neighbours. . . .
> The fact that some of my workmates—young girls, who were in no way mentally defective, who were, on the contrary, just as keen-witted and generous-hearted as my own circle of friends—could chaff each other about having babies by their fathers and brothers, was a gruesome example of the effect of debased social environment on personal character and family life. . . .
> The violation of little children was another not infrequent result. To put it bluntly, sexual promiscuity, and even sexual perversion, are almost unavoidable among men and women of average character and intelligence crowded into the one-room tenement of slum areas, and it is the realisation of the moral deterioration involved more than any physical discomfort, that lends the note of exasperated bitterness characteristic of the working-class representatives of these chronically destitute urban areas.[2]

Such was the motivation of the 'holy war'. Such was the life which for a century had been warping the bones, rotting the lungs,

---

[1] Rowntree, *Poverty*, 171.

[2] Beatrice Webb, *My Apprenticeship* (1938 ed.), 285-6 (quoting from *Life and Labour of the People in London*, ed. Charles Booth), 325, 368 n. 1.

crushing the spirits of working people by the million. The pent-up
rage at it issued in that tide of militancy which came seething
through the muddy channels of society and rose to a crest of outright revolution in Russia, Germany, Hungary. Not to understand
this—wilfully to curtail your perspective so that its source is not
considered but only one or two of the more ignoble results—is the
surest way to distort your view of industrial civilisation.

It might be objected that the Nottinghamshire miners Lawrence
knew and sprang from lived very differently from the unskilled
workers of east London. But people were not insulated against the
troubles of their worst-off fellows. For one thing, many bad conditions were widespread. In York the housing even of people 'in
receipt of moderate but regular wages' (62 per cent of families)
was so jerry-built that it would 'soon tend to degenerate into
slums'. A year or two before Lawrence's novel was finally published,
after the War, the Sankey Commission found that in many mining
areas housing was 'scandalously bad'.[1] It was not luxuries that
people craved but the elementary means of a happy family life.
Secondly, the docks where many east Londoners found their work
were often the well-spring of a militancy that spread through the
country, from distribution back into production. Engels in the
1880s saw the awakening of east London from its 'passive poverty,
broken by starvation', its 'vegetative' lack of political awareness
and organisation, as the start of a great class stirring which would
be 'an example for the provinces'. This was the trend throughout
the next thirty years. The dock strike in 1889 was followed by a
national mining strike in 1893. The syndicalist strikes of 1910
embroiled both docks and coalfields. Then 'suddenly, in August
1911, the pot boiled over. There was a spirit of revolt in the Labour
world.' In June and July the dockers struck, and stopped the port
of London. Unauthorised railway strikes broke out in the provinces
and a national strike followed which threatened to bring industry
to a standstill. Large numbers of troops were sent out through the
country, ready to fire on the workers if they became angry at
unsuccessful negotiations.[2] We can see that the workers' interests

[1] Rowntree, *Poverty*, 185, 187; Webbs, *Trade Unionism*, 519.
[2] Engels, letter to Bernstein of 22.8.89: Marx and Engels, *On Britain*, 520-1;
Halévy, *Rule of Democracy*, 453-4; Webbs, *Trade Unionism*, 529-9: this last may
be the original of the strike-breaking described by Lawrence—the colliery train
full of redcoats, the firing on the 'mob' with one man killed.

were common ones, and if the lives of great numbers of them were (in Engels's phrase) 'utterly unbearable', the awareness of this was liable to spread like a stinging\ acid throughout their class.

Militant egalitarianism—socialism—was therefore inevitable. Lawrence with his characteristic concentration on the moral essence of any matter might concede the inevitability but still assert that it was pernicious, a dragging down of the human. Only a rabid partisan would deny that the vapours given off by the class struggle are unsavoury on all sides. A nagging concentration on material betterment—urgent for working folk if they were to save themselves from malnutrition, a destroying poverty and debt, and the workhouse—is liable to wear people down until they can think of little but 'things'. While the Coal Commission was sitting in 1919, Sidney Webb could say dispiritedly to his wife that 'the miners' representatives would be badly beaten if they held out for nationalisation, the bulk of the miners caring for nothing but hours and earnings.'[1] Yet this is not the whole truth—it may even be only the cynicism of an outsider misled by the prejudice of his class. Labour history is rich in instances where working people have put politically far-sighted ends before money-gain or 'cupidity'. English economists in the 1840s had been 'amazed to see the workers sacrifice a good part of their wages in favour of associations, which, in the eyes of these economists, are established solely in favour of wages'.[2] This continued to be the case. In the 1870s the Scottish engineers were offered a rise by their employers if they would drop their demand for a reduction in the 54-hour week. They refused the money, kept solidarity with the Nine Hours Movement, and won their demands.[3] To come near to Lawrence's example, in 1894 the Scottish miners were faced with wage cuts of one-quarter— consider the difference this would make to a family living perpetually on the edge of physical and domestic ruin. The slogan of the Miners' Federation of Great Britain, which organised the fight against cuts, was 'An injury to one is an injury to all'. A strike was mounted and lasted for four months while the men subsisted on strike pay, which was in many districts shared out among all those on strike although union members were outnumbered by

---

[1] Beatrice Webb, *Diaries 1912-1924*, ed. Margaret I. Cole (1952), 150.
[2] Karl Marx, *The Poverty of Philosophy* (Moscow, n.d.), 172-3.
[3] Cole and Filson, *British Working Class Movements*, 597-9.

non-members in a proportion of 2 to 1.[1] I cannot see that this kind of selfless stand against being robbed of the means of life is fairly called 'cupidity'. It looks more like the evolving of a new fellow-feeling, a new humaneness, in response to the nineteenth-century owners' use of the person as a mere wealth-getter, a Hand.

It seems from contemporary observations that the deeper trend in the workers' militancy was reaching out to ends they did not yet wholly realise themselves. In 1889 Engels was noting that 'the people themselves regard their immediate demands'—what Lawrence calls 'arrangements'—'as only provisional, although they do not know as yet what final aim they are working for. But this dim idea is strongly enough rooted to make them choose *only* avowed Socialists as their leaders.'[2] People were not striking or carrying on the 'holy war' for a few shillingsworth of consumer goods. They were ranged, the poor majority against the rich few, in a struggle against the system which did so range them in antagonistic classes. They were 'losing their agelong faith in the permanence of the system which oppressed them'.[3] This was not visionary in some weak sense, and it was not the short-lived dream of a culture which went in for utopias. If Keir Hardie and Tom Mann and Engels and the other militant minds of the nineteenth century were right, then their view of industrial struggle should have gone on being confirmed beyond their day. Here is the view of a recent expert:

> In the twenty years of high employment from 1940 the proportion of strikes about 'wage questions other than demands for increases', and (particularly) about 'working arrangements, rules and discipline' rose remarkably: from one-third of all stoppages to three-quarters. . . . One could say that these disputes all involve attempts to submit managerial discretion and authority to agreed—or failing that, customary—rules: alternatively that they reflect an implicit pressure for more democracy and individual rights in industry.[4]

Lawrence's failing was to mistake a particular malign side-effect of the struggle for the means of life for a deep-seated lapse in human nature itself. With this stress on 'cupidity' and the 'fight

[1] R. Page Arnot, *A History of the Scottish Miners* (1955), 74-9.
[2] Letter to Sorge, 7.12.1889: *On Britain*, 522.
[3] V. I. Lenin, *What Is To Be Done?* (Moscow, 1952 ed.), 51.
[4] H. A. Turner, *The Trend of Strikes* (Leeds, 1963), 18.

for possessions' compare the Webbs' account of how the class struggle can debase:

> . . . the capitalist, ever thinking of the rate of profit instead of social service, is reflected in the workman thinking only of wages and hours; selling himself to the highest bidder; and, on business principles, assuming that he should give as little as possible, for as short a time as possible, in return for as much as possible. This sort of sale is in its essence prostitution; and it cannot be imposed on generation after generation of workers without finally disabling them from regarding their emancipation in any other light than that of a fight for mastery of the sources of production in which they must win by 'downing' their present masters. . . .[1]

What makes the difference between Lawrence and the Webbs is that they feel positively for one side in the struggle and not for an ideal human nature in some way outside it. Being thus grounded in practice, they can see a way forward. They realise that a major debasing factor, the appropriation of the world's resources for gain and not for the common good, is alterable and not permanent. Because they see the System clearly—that is, socio-historically, they do not come down in mere ill-will or impatience on any one class suffering under it. When Lawrence passes judgement on the System—what he calls 'mechanism' or 'machinery', he does so in the spirit of 'A plague on both (or all) your houses'. This spirit is foreign to the greatest fiction, to *War and Peace* and *Middlemarch*, and equally to *The Rainbow*, which seems to me the finest novel in English. But it stops short of the Great Unrest, and glimpses industrial life, the source of socialism, only from a distance.

The other root matter in the political life of the country, along with the 'fight for equality of possessions', was organisation. Lawrence characterised the mass view of this as an 'instinct for chaos', the smash which went along with the grab of the fight for possessions.

> No part should be subordinate to any other part: all should be equal. The instinct for chaos had entered. . . . In function and process, one man, one part, must of necessity be subordinate to another. It is a condition of being. But the desire for chaos had risen. . . .

[1] S. and B. Webb, *The Decay of Capitalist Civilisation* (1923 ed.), 162.

The quick, easy transition from 'equal' to 'chaos' and the summary diagnosis, 'The instinct for chaos had entered', suggest how confident Lawrence is that his intuitions are right. They clash, however, with the intuitions, or insights, of the many writers who have thought that evolving socialism has tended towards a new kind of order. If it were to be suggested that Lawrence is uncovering, like a psychiatrist, a deeper, less straightforward, even perverse motive, analogous to a death-wish, it must be answered that it is not easy to find any facts at all to support this. Those who looked deeply into the way of life engendered by the factory system had been suggesting for many years that the new discipline forced onto people by industrial work and their crowding together into factories and cities had laid the basis for new organisations developed by the people themselves.[1] As we follow the history of European labour, we see the 'outbursts of desperation' that Lenin had studied in Russia steadily being replaced by a will to build a new kind of order once the rule of the private owner had been ended. This will, expressed in the long series of Acts to control the ownership of industry, ways of reaching wage agreements, standards of purity in products and safety in work, is too well known to require detailing. Most to the point here is that the working people's own organisations took part in the drive to make industry serve and not despoil life. For example, the English Women's Protective and Provident League, subsequently the Women's Trade Union League, organised women workers outside the cotton and woollen industries. Among its activities were the 'interchange of useful trade information', the registration of vacancies so that women need not trudge round looking for jobs, and 'facilities for ascertaining the opinions of women concerned in the operation of the Factory and Workshops' Act, as to whether the extension of such legislation is desirable. This is a question of great importance to the women, but they have seldom been consulted about it.'[2] More of what Lawrence disparages as 'arrangements'. To me it is evidence of that marvellous staunchness in trying to bring under control the colossal dust-heap of Victorian industry, in the teeth of an intimidation and wear-and-tear which today we could not endure.

---

[1] Marx and Engels, *Manifesto of the Communist Party* (Moscow, 1957 ed.), 62-4; Marx, *Poverty of Philosophy*, 172; *Capital*, 257-8, 552, 836-7; N. K. Krupskaya, *Lenin* (Moscow, 1959 ed.), 462.
[2] Cole and Filson, *British Working Class Movements*, 610-611.

The workers were developing an organisation more effective socially than the owners'. As Beatrice Webb wrote,

> It was, in fact, exactly this collective regulation of the conditions of employment, whether by legislative enactment or by collective bargaining, that had raised the cotton operatives, the coal miners and the workers of the iron trades into an effective democracy; or, at least into one which, in comparison with the entirely unorganised workers of East London, was eager for political enfranchisement and education; and which, as the chapels, the co-operative societies and the Trade Unions had demonstrated, was capable of self-government.[1]

The drive to a better livelihood ('cupidity') was inseparable from the working towards a new kind of order ('will for chaos'):

> They [the workers] were waging war upon the miseries of life: on poverty, exploitation, speed-up, overtime, arrogant employers, bad housing, the despair of a world in which a man was 'too old at forty'. . . . The workers were feeling the strength which came from the growing unity and maturity of their class, and their eyes were turning beyond the immediate questions of wages and hours to the greater question of their part in the control of industry itself.[2]

The trend is epitomised in the sittings of the 1919 Coal Commission, which developed from a tribunal on miners' wage claims into an arraignment by their representatives of capitalist mine-ownership and a demand, endorsed by the judge-chairman and carried out some twenty-five years later, for their nationalisation.[3]

Lawrence's view of the miners' movement turns out to be little different from the smear that socialism is no more than unbridled licence, every man for himself and the devil take the hindmost. This is classically answered in *The Decay of Capitalist Civilisation*:

> Now let no-one imagine that these lower classes, or the socialists who champion them, or indeed any persons with common sense, object to one man exercising authority over another. What is resented in the capitalist organisation of industry is both the number and the kind of orders given by the rich to the poor, by the owners of land and capital to the persons who gain their livelihood by using these as instruments of production. The authority of the capitalist and the landlord has invidious characteristics. It is continuous over the lives of the individuals who are ordered; it is irresponsible and cannot be

---

[1] *My Apprenticeship*, 395.
[2] Morton and Tate, *British Labour Movement*, 234.
[3] Webb, *Diaries 1912-1924*, 152-4, 155-6.

called to account; it is not in any way reciprocal; it does not involve the selection of the person in command for his capacity to exercise authority either wisely or in the public interest: above all, it is designed to promote, not the good of the whole community, but the personal pleasure or private gain of the person who gives the order. . . .

. . . the practical subjection of the mass of the people . . . disguises itself as subordination; but in genuine social ordination the director is no more free to give orders as he pleases than his subordinates are to work as they please.[1]

The critic commending Lawrence might still say that what he was capturing was the *spirit* of the workers' movement–'Really all they wanted was loot and long holidays, free beer and no bosses on their backs.' If this were so, it would surely be odd that in the years since, the nearer we have moved to socialism and the more the working people have called the tune, the more coherent and planful has been the type of society we have sought to bring about.

The term 'equality' and Lawrence's way with it is as important as 'cupidity' and 'chaos', livelihood and order. *Egalité*, that major slogan of European man, has epitomised for generations a vital aspiration. Before 'The Industrial Magnate' is reached, our minds have already been set working on 'equality' by the argument between Mr Colliery-Manager Crich, Miss Art-Teacher Brangwen, Ursula and Birkin, Hermione Roddice the aristocratic hostess, and the socialist knight Sir Joshua (Bertrand Russell). It is key in the novel, and Leavis takes it up triumphantly as though it established a great, nearly self-evident 'truth' (his own word) cardinal to his own and Lawrence's position. 'The great social idea,' Sir Joshua has said, is the 'social equality of man.' Hermione rephrases this in her emotionally attitudinising way: ' "If, " said Hermione at last, "we could only realise, that in the *spirit* we are all one, all equal in the spirit, all brothers there–the rest wouldn't matter. . . ." ' This might have seemed just gush–the gracious lady playing at being the liberal. But Birkin, treating her as a typical spokesman for the brotherhood of man, makes a reply which evidently carries Lawrence's main thought on democracy, considered as the moving principle in the civilisation of this century. Here is Birkin's *credo* (and Lawrence's[2]):

---

[1] *Decay of Capitalist Civilisation*, 49-50, 139.
[2] E.g. letter to Lady Ottoline Morrell, the original of Hermione, on 3.1.1915: *Letters*, ed. Aldous Huxley, 213.

'We are all different and unequal in spirit—it is only the social differences that are based on accidental material conditions. We are all abstractly or mathematically equal if you like. Every man has hunger and thirst, two eyes, one nose and two legs. We're all the same in point of number. But spiritually, there is pure difference and neither equality nor inequality counts. It is upon these two bits of knowledge that you must found a state. Your democracy is an absolute lie—your brotherhood of man is a pure falsity, if you apply it further than the mathematical abstraction. . . .

'. . . In the spirit, I am as separate as one star is from another, as different in quality and quantity. Establish a state on *that*. One man isn't any better than another, not because they are equal, but because they are intrinsically *other*, that there is no term of comparison.'[1]

This, in its context in the novel, which (as we have seen already) is charged with a decided view of modern society, is so likely to strike the conservative-minded as the final and devastating *exposé* of 'levelling-down' socialism that the actual currency of 'equality' must be reviewed if the claim that *Women in Love* is a true image of our civilisation is to stand.

It is true that over the centuries 'levelling' has often been laughably impracticable, innocently greedly, and otherwise absurd in its remoteness from social fact. This is the egalitarianism burlesqued by Shakespeare in Jack Cade's speech in *Henry VI*:

> There shall be in England, seven halfpenny loaves sold for a penny: the three-hooped pot shall have ten hoops, and I will make it felony to drink small beer. All the realm shall be in common, and in Cheapside shall my palfrey go to grass. . . . There shall be no money, all shall eat and drink on my score, and I will apparel them all in one livery, that they may agree like brothers, and worship me their Lord.[2]

But this is only a cheerfully uncaring version of the deadly-serious protest against racking inequality which was uttered by John Ball during one of those 'outbursts of desperation' by the people at large:

> Good people, things will never go well in England so long as goods be not in common, and so long as there be villeins and gentlemen. By what right are they whom we call Lords greater folk than we? On what grounds have they deserved it? Why do they hold us in serfage? If we all come of the same father

---

[1] Ch. 8, 'Breadalby'.
[2] Part II: Act IV, scene ii.

and mother, Adam and Eve, how can they say or prove that they are better than we, if it be not that they make us gain for them by our toil what they spend in their pride? They are clothed in velvet and warm in their furs and their ermines; while we are covered with rags. They have wine and spices and fair bread; and we oatcakes and straw and water to drink. They have leisure and fine houses; we have pain and labour, the rain and the wind and the fields. And yet it is of us and our toil that these men hold their state.[1]

This was the main social idea that was taken up by generation after generation of the people in this country as they strove for a livelihood.[2] Literal levelling was attempted again by that puny, courageous sect, the Diggers, at the close of the Civil War, and it is significant that in Cromwell's Council of War in 1647, when parliamentary representation was being discussed, the squires Cromwell and Ireton had to defend private property and its moral equivalent, inequality, against the arguments of the Leveller Colonel Rainborough. If one man, they said,

> hath an equall right with another to the chusing of him that shall governe him–by the same right of nature, hee hath an equal right in any goods hee sees: meate, drink, cloathes to take and use them for his sustenance. . . . Itt may happen, that the majority may, by law, nott in a confusion, destroy propertie; there may bee a law enacted, that there shall bee an equality of goods and estate.[3]

In the age following the Civil War and the turning-point of 1688, merchant and landed capitalism flourished. But towards the end of the eighteenth century private property and inequality were again challenged, under the inspiration of the French Revolution. 'Equality', of natural rights and of parliamentary representation, was the essence of Tom Paine's teaching, which was far and away the most popular democratic doctrine current in Britain. One manifesto of the radical Corresponding Societies, for example, began by declaring that 'all men are by nature free and equal and independent of each other'.[4] As the industrial revolution went on,

---

[1] Version from J. R. Green, *A History of the English People* (1881), I, 440.

[2] It occurs in the poetry Shelley wrote at that peak of revolutionary activity, 1819, esp. 'Song to the Men of England', and in speeches and pamphlets of militant farm workers at the end of that century: see Hobsbawm, *Primitive Rebels*, 190.

[3] *The Clarke Papers*, ed. C. H. Firth, quoted in *Decay of Capitalist Civilisation*, 137.

[4] Leslie Stephen, *The English Utilitarians* (1900), I, 128.

the gross contrast between the lavish living of the wealthy and the destitution of the town poor again threw up the issue of equality. Social, and socialist, theory at last found a massive basis in contemporary social fact and 'equality' became more than a rallying cry. Mill wrote in 1873, when defining his own socialism, that he looked forward to the time when

> it will no longer either be, or be thought to be, impossible for human beings to exert themselves strenuously in procuring benefits which are not to be exclusively their own, but to be shared with the society they belong to. The social problem of the future we consider to be, how to unite the greatest individual liberty of action, with a common ownership in the raw material of the globe, and an equal participation of all in the benefits of combined labour.[1]

That definition grounds 'equality' in the practical arrangements of society, and it is the spirit of influential discussion of the matter ever since. Matthew Arnold could be virtually fascist in his views on how to discipline the militant masses. Yet he could write, in his essay on 'Equality', that 'inequality materialises our upper class, vulgarises our middle class, brutalises our lower.'[2] More purposeful discussion of equality was carried on, from their reforming or gradualist viewpoint, by the Fabians, exponents of what has been called 'the new Benthamism',[3] and it is here that we see how widely Lawrence in his devastatingness misses the mark. Equality is the pivotal idea in *The Decay of Capitalist Civilisation*, in the programme the Webbs drew up for the Labour Party in 1918, and in the thinking that runs through Beatrice's diaries. A sentence from Sidney's Fabian Lecture of 1894, 'Socialism: True and False', makes unambiguously clear what they meant by it:

> Bentham himself, the great father of political radicalism, urged that taxation need not be limited to the supply of funds for the bare administrative expenses of the state, but that, wisely handled, it also supplied a means of gradually securing the great end of equality of opportunity to every citizen.[4]

---

[1] *Autobiography*, 196.

[2] In the Conclusion to *Culture and Anarchy* he recommends the Tarpeian Rock treatment for working-class agitators. One blinks, sickened, and half-hopes that the passage is ironic. For 'Equality', see *Mixed Essays* (1879), 92.

[3] Cole and Postgate, *The Common People*, 423.

[4] Quoted from Beatrice Webb, *Our Partnership*, ed. Barbara Drake and Margaret I. Cole (1948), 106.

Equality of opportunity has been ever since the great cry, whether from communists, reforming socialists, or conservatives in the liberal guise that has become obligatory. 'Equality of opportunity', as used in the General Election of 1945, were the first words that made me realise that there was a practical ideal to live for. If each person does not enjoy the full scope available in his society to develop whatever he has in him, then his society is failing in its main purpose: that is what 'equality' means in our time.

Lawrence's destructive method is to take the term literally. He says, in effect: 'The democrat proclaims that we are all equal. Not a bit of it. We are all different, and some are superior to others. I am no-one's brother. Let him live as he likes so long as he keeps his distance.' What single element in the actual currency of 'equality' does this seriously answer? In what sense has either exact equality or the assumption that all people are intrinsically the same ever entered into the ideology of equality? Of course there have been cranky blunders. Marx had to warn the members of the First International against the utopian shibboleth of equal wages:

> . . . as the costs of producing labouring powers of different quality differ, so must differ the values of the labouring powers employed in different trades. The cry for an *equality of wages* rests, therefore, upon a mistake, is an *insane* wish never to be fulfilled. It is an offspring of that false and superficial radicalism that accepts premises and tries to evade conclusions.[1]

A little later Beatrice Webb was repudiating Bernard Shaw's fancy theory of 'absolute equality of income':

> He might have made more of the necessary connection between mechanical equality and despotism; because no democracy would tolerate it and the compulsory work that this type of equality involved.[2]

But the self-parodying excesses and flourishes of an ideology are not its root or main stem. The absolute equality, the stereotyping of people, which Lawrence sets up as his target is an Aunt Sally.

It is natural that this confusion should have arisen and that 'equality' should have been open to wild counter-attacks. Leslie

[1] Lecture now known as *Wages, Price and Profit*: Marx and Engels, *Selected Works* (Moscow, 1958), I, 426.
[2] *Diaries, 1924-1932*, ed. Margaret I. Cole (1956), 159.

Stephen in his volume on Bentham analyses shrewdly the confusion which is, strictly speaking, implicit in the term:

> The general doctrine of the 'Rights of Man'—that all men are
> by nature free and equal—covered at least the doctrine that
> the inequality and despotism of the existing order was hateful,
> and people with a taste for abstract principles accepted this
> short cut to political wisdom. The 'minor' premise being
> obviously true, they took the major for granted.[1]

In other words, considering the racking injustices of the given
unequal society, nothing *less* than equality could be laid claim to
by the radical if he was to make headway against the massed power
of vested interests. The other good reason for the rise of the term
'equality' is that it is the indispensable fulcrum of any socialist
ideology. Here appears the relevance of 'Benthamism', which
Leavis has recently given a still more malign twist in his term
'technologico-Benthamite'.[2] Taking up Lawrence's coinage 'disquality', he remarks:

> No great novelist can be a Benthamite; for him the fact that
> we can be said to be all 'abstractly and mathematically equal'
> has little to do with his interest in mankind. It is a fact that
> Lawrence is concerned with by way of protest and warning. . . .
> The truth that 'disquality' insists on has, he knows, to be
> insisted on in the modern world—and he was writing *Women
> in Love* thirty years ago, when Lenin's revolution was contemporary news. . . .[3]

The great novelist may not be interested in the social urgings behind
'equality' and the planning that it entails, but that doesn't free him
from the duty to present fairly—which in terms of his particular art
means a *fully dramatic* treatment—the sorts of situation in which
the ideas he is canvassing ('cupidity', 'chaos', 'disquality') actually
arose. It is true that the early Benthamites were inhumanly calculating: the practical outcome of the 1834 Poor Law is a poor
advertisement for their sense of what people need.[4] But the idea of
equality which underlay their absurdly utopian-bureaucratic blueprints of a new social organisation is precisely missed by Lawrence's
affirming of the spiritual separateness of each person, for the reason

---

[1] *English Utilitarians*, I, 122.
[2] See esp. *Nor Shall My Sword* (1972), 127, 151, etc.
[3] *D. H. Lawrence: Novelist*, 162-3.
[4] See above, ch. 5, 118-9.

that the Benthamites, as they groped towards a model of a planned
society, were concerned, not with each person's natural and valid
sense of uniqueness, but with the social conditions in which a
unique being might (or might not) fulfil himself. They were concerned with methods and principles of administration and distribution, the planning and spending of state finances on the welfare
of the whole and of each citizen. Whether or not a great novelist
could find such matters interesting is an open question, but Lawrence does raise them: he does make his spokesman-character say,
'"We all drank milk first, we all eat bread and meat, we all want
to ride in motor-cars"', as though this states a mere minimum of
human likeness which matters little beside the deep, the spiritual
question. The fact is that someone's spirit cannot thrive if his bones
are being spoiled for want of the free milk in his growing years
which should be a minimal right. 'The greatest happiness of the
greatest number' was of the essence for Benthamites and 'equality
of opportunity' for socialists because unless that right was claimed,
then resources, livelihood, and the right to work would fall into
the hands of a minority. What surely must interest the great
novelist is that in Victorian times 'gentlefolk' lived twice as long as
labourers in the cities and half again as long in country districts.
In York in 1898 the poorest had twice as high a death-rate as even
the best-paid workers. If you lived in Southwark, your expectation
of life was fourteen years shorter than if you lived in Hampstead,
or ten years calculated at the age of five–what an important
economist contemporary with Lawrence called 'a want not only of
the means of life but of life itself'.[1] *There* is inequality of opportunity
–of the opportunity sheerly to live! The statistics ensure that one is
keeping in touch with the living of the whole people. What they
cannot bring out is the personal toll taken by a lack of what
Lawrence calls, dismissingly, a 'fair share of the world's gear'.[2]

Of course egalitarianism has its vices, for example the philistinism
masquerading as democracy which is envious of real distinctions
and impatient of exacting standards. I said before that a 'taint of
cupidity' and a 'will for chaos', where these exist, have been among

[1] G. M. Young, *Portrait of an Age: Victorian England* (1953 ed.), 24, n. 1;
Rowntree, *Poverty*, 243: Rowntree remarks that 'it must be remembered that a
high death-rate implies a low standard of general health, and much sickness and
suffering which is not registered'; Chiozza Money, *Riches and Poverty* (1905), 195.
[2] From ch. 8, 'Breadalby'.

the unsavoury vapours arising from the class struggle. But do they define the worst distortions of mankind in conditions of inequality? In *The Decay of Capitalist Civilisation* the Webbs mention often the 'demoralising servility' bred of wealth and poverty:

> This life of unconscious theft, of which the idle members of the propertied class have an uneasy suspicion, together with the callousness and insolence that it breeds, as regards the sufferings of any but those who belong to their own class– subtly degrading as it is to the rich, has its obverse in its effect on the minds and characters of those who have not been able, in the same way, to place themselves above the world's law. The resulting servility, on the one hand, and on the other, the envy, or even the simple-minded admiration of a life which is essentially contrary to all principles of morality, is as demorali- sing to the poor as it is to the rich. . . .
> . . . although the rise and growth of a new wealthy class may not, in itself, have increased either the insecurity and penury of the mass of the people, or widened the surrounding destitution, the contrast adds a further grievance, whilst the encouragement of parasitic idleness, the sterilisation of intellect and the decay of manners among the newly enriched, are social evils parallelled only by the servility, the envy, and the cor- ruption of ideals manifest in the slum population.[1]

In their 1918 Labour Party programme they speak of 'The individualist system of capitalist production . . . with the monstrous inequality of circumstances which it produces and the degradation and brutalisation, both moral and spiritual, resulting therefrom'; and in their book on the Soviet Union they make a distinction between kinds of equality which clinches my argument:

> So long as a vocation for every man is insisted on by public opinion, and so long as all children and even all backward races enjoy genuine equality of opportunity, there is (where no class of functionless rich exists) little social harm in transient inequalities of personal earnings or possessions which involve no differences of education or manners, and therefore create no distinctions of social class.[2]

The servility criticised by the Webbs strikes me as a distortion of essential human character, of self-respect, individuality, and direct

---

[1] *Decay of Capitalist Civilisation*, 30-1, 138.
[2] Quoted from Morton and Tate, *British Labour Movement*, 291; *Soviet Communism, A New Civilisation* (1944 ed.), 969. Note that I am citing this passage purely for its idea and not to imply that such a thing was actually achieved in the U.S.S.R.

F

and honest meeting between person and person, whereas the concern with possessions Lawrence seizes on is rather a necessary and
positive drive (a wish for the means of life) gone too far.

Lawrence's seriously mistaken and unjust reaction to the movement for democracy goes with a bitter turning against almost
everything in ordinary life—this feeling pervades the novel.[1]
Birkin's most extreme remarks—'"Let mankind pass away—time it
did. . . . Humanity is a dead letter"', or '"I abhor humanity, I
wish it was swept away. . . . You yourself, don't you find it a beautiful clean thought, a world empty of people, just uninterrupted grass,
and a hare sitting up"'[2]—are more or less justified dramatically by
their contexts: Birkin is ill, at a low ebb in his life, he emerges from
this through achieving a relationship with Ursula. Yet both the
drift and the many explicit discussions amount to a suggestion that
a fulfilling life can be reached only by cutting away from everything habitual in social living. Very few of the characters work in a
way that matters or is effectively present in the novel. Birkin's
visit to Ursula's classroom is memorable, but his school-inspecting
is oddly intermittent: he is in effect a man of private means rather
than someone who earns his living. The run of workers by hand or
brain appear only as a kind of moving back-cloth or crowd of
extras against which the middle and upper-class *dramatis personae*
perform. The mass of the people are seen twice, once as 'natives'—
'Women, their arms folded over their coarse aprons, standing
gossiping at the end of their block, stared after the Brangwen sisters
with that long, unwearying stare of aborigines'—and once as a
presence in Gudrun's sexual fantasying—'In their voices she could
hear the voluptuous resonance of darkness, the strong, dangerous
underworld, mindless, inhuman. They sounded also like strange
machines, heavy, oiled.'[3] If Lawrence meant to give the whole
English social organism, if he even meant to give with adequate
fullness the people on whom he pronounces summarily in 'The
Industrial Magnate', then it is indeed odd that we no more than
glimpse the class who are three-quarters of the population. 'Comprehensiveness' is, here, out of the question.

An essential of the life conveyed by the novel is the home, and

---

[1] He himself called it 'terrible and horrible': 'The book frightens me: it is so
end-of-the-world', and Frieda wanted to call it *Dies Irae* (*Letters*, 372, 376).
[2] Chs. 5, 11.
[3] Chs. 1, 9.

here the severance from most human life is complete. Late on, when Birkin and Ursula have become something like integrated together, Birkin can still say to Gerald during the argument in the chapter 'Marriage or Not':

> '. . . marriage in the old sense seems to me repulsive . . . the world all in couples, each couple in its own little home, watching its own little interests, and stewing in its own little privacy—it's the most repulsive thing on earth. . . .
> 'One should avoid this *home* instinct. It's not an instinct, it's a habit of cowardliness. One should never have a *home*.'

This is not ungrounded in the whole novel. Lawrence shows with novelistic fullness one kind of average home in its comfortless unloveliness and genteel lifelessness—the terrace type of house from which the Brangwen parents flit in chapter 27:

> The sense of walls, dry, thin, flimsy-seeming walls, and a flimsy flooring, pale with its artificial black edges, was neutralising to the mind. Everything was null to the senses, there was enclosure without substance, for the walls were dry and paper. Where were they standing, on earth, or suspended in some cardboard box?
> . . . Ursula recognised half-burnt covers of *Vogue*—half-burnt representations of women in gowns—lying under the grate. . . . The kitchen did look more substantial, because of the red-tiled floor and the stove, but it was cold and horrid.

But when it comes to discussion of home-making as a foundation of living, in the talk between Birkin and Ursula in the key chapter 'A Chair', the drift shows Lawrence to be bitterly repelled by life now to the point of ignoring the ordinary behaviour which alone could have given 'comprehensiveness'. Rejecting the 'horrible tyranny of the fixed milieu', Birkin says about houses:

> 'Houses and furniture and clothes, they are all terms of an old base world, a detestable society of man. And if you have a Tudor house and old, beautiful furniture, it is only the past perpetuated on top of you, horrible. And if you have a perfect modern house done for you by Poiret, it is something else perpetuated on top of you. It is all horrible. It is all possessions, possessions, bullying you and turning you into a generalisation.'

By now the novel has written off all homes—the skimpy standard house as well as the old country houses and expensive commissioned articles of the very wealthy. Yet in doing so he has disabled himself as a witness to modern experience by sliding out of touch with the daily comings and goings of the people occupying those buildings, which he never again dramatises. 'Homes' are more than 'couples'. Most couples, since they have families, are in a position to know that their home is not necessarily or only a unit of jealous privacy, it is also a base of life, a place where every kind of work, energy, skill, and emotion is enhanced by its being active in the growth of human beings from the seed to the mature person.

This lack in Lawrence belongs with that childlessness, and that social functionlessness of Frieda, whose spoiling effect on his art Leavis defines with firm delicacy at one point but tends to forget in his particular critiques.[1] Ursula and Gudrun agree in explicitly dissociating themselves from all usual habits:

> 'As a matter of fact, one cannot contemplate the ordinary life—one cannot contemplate it,' replied Gudrun . . . 'with the ordinary man, who has his life fixed in one place, marriage is just impossible. There may be, and there *are*, thousands of women who want it, and could conceive of nothing else. But the very thought of it sends me *mad*. One must be free, above all, one must be free. One may forfeit everything else, but one must be free—one must not become 7, Pinchbeck Street—or Somerset Drive—or Shortlands. . . . A man with a position in the social world—well, it is just impossible, impossible!'[2]

It seems to me that for Lawrence to locate the viewpoint of his novel in characters so estranged from any community puts in the way of 'comprehensiveness' obstacles which Leavis has not considered seriously, presumably because *Women in Love* answers so well to his own nearly despairing view of the modern 'plight' or 'sickness'.

It should now go without saying, though for years it did not, that in many aspects *Women in Love* is extraordinarily fine: in particular it works for page after page at a depth in human experience which few other artists have even attempted. My experience of the book in discussion is that it gives off meaning more or less inexhaustibly, in a way that only two or three other books approach. It is all the more significant—significant of the difficulty of maintaining morale and coherence in forming one's social views—that so wise and deep an analyst of human nature should have been so prone to wildness, even silliness when he tried to pronounce on likelihoods, problems,

---

[1] *D. H. Lawrence: Novelist*, 47-52.
[2] Ch. 27.

and solutions of a social kind. His substantial prose work on such matters is the essay 'Democracy', first printed in *Phoenix*. It begins sanely, with an appeal that we should 'strip off at once all the ideal drapery' from the machinery of state and regard state organisations as conveniences. The Benthamite position is lucidly acknowledged: 'Society . . . exists . . . to establish the Average, in order to make living together possible: that is, to make proper facilities for every man's clothing, feeding, housing himself', and so on. Yet he can end:

> When men become their own decent selves again, then we can so easily arrange the material world. The arrangement will come, as it must come, spontaneously, not by previous ordering. Until such time, what is the good of talking about it?[1]

To my mind the historical record enforces the axiom that it is precisely in the course of 'arranging the material world' that people become their decent selves. There *is* no inward-turned, psycho-moral process whereby selves can be regenerated and *then* go on to reorganise social life. The fallacy implicit in Lawrence's argument here is yet another variant on the wishful idealism that we have already found in George Eliot's *Felix Holt*.[2]

More characteristic of his approach to the issue of democracy is the kind of open and vehement outburst that flares out in his letters time after time. At the time of *Women in Love* he wrote to Ottoline Morrell:

> I am not a democrat, save in politics! I think the state is a vulgar institution. But life itself is an affair of aristocrats. In my soul, I'd be as proud as hell. In so far as I am one of many, *Liberté, Egalité*– I won't have *Fraternité*. . . . In so far as I am myself, *Fierté, Inégalité, Hostilité*.[3]

We should feel, I believe, sorry for the man who is so driven to repudiate human togetherness. Not realising his own disability, he allows it to carry him on into a rage of unseeing rejection:

> What does Russell really want? He wants to keep his own established ego, his finite and ready-defined self intact, free from contact and connection. He wants to be ultimately a free agent. That is what they all want, ultimately–that is what is at the back of all international peace-for-ever and democratic

---

[1] *Phoenix*, 701, 718.
[2] See above, ch. 6, 138.
[3] Letter of 3.1.1915: *Letters*, 213.

control talks, they want an outward system of nullity, which
they call peace and goodwill, so that in their own souls they
can be independent little gods, referred nowhere and to
nothing, little mortal Absolutes, secure from question. That is
at the back of all Liberalism, Fabianism and democracy. It
stinks. It is the will of the louse.[1]

Lawrence had the advantage of having met Russell. Yet this
passage seems not only unfair but irrelevant to the political career
of a man who time and again risked his freedom, livelihood, and
reputation for beliefs such as pacifism, libertarian education, and
(at the very end of his life) humane resistance to imperialist atrocity. 'Russell' and 'democracy' seem to be acting as mere scape-
goats for Lawrence's agony at his inability, coupled with his
periodic urgent desire, to make common cause, or simply live
together, with others. It meant that the amazingly deep reach of his
insight was repeatedly nullified by an impatience with the facts of
what lay beyond his personal grasp. A crowning instance comes in
the history book which he published in the name of 'Lawrence H.
Davison':

> But Germany and Russia step from one extreme to the other,
> from absolute monarchy such as Britain never knew, straight
> to the other extreme of government, government by the masses
> of the proletariat, strange, and as it seems, without true
> purpose: the masses of the working people governing themselves
> they know not why, except that they wish to destroy all
> authority, and to enjoy all an equal prosperity.[2]

'Chaos' and 'cupidity' reappear, and are used in the teeth of the
facts to discredit a movement which, so far from 'knowing not why'
it was moving, had given out the clearest of slogans, 'Peace and
Bread'. The 'true purpose' of the Russian people was to be assured
freedom from mass slaughter, freedom from destitution, and freedom from an exploiting class—sadly though they failed to achieve
some of these. Lawrence is, again, disparaging about or else sheerly
fails to realise what is uppermost in the minds of people as they
strive together to change an unbearable way of life.

It seems that once community as Lawrence had known it in the
part farming, part mining country of the Midlands was being
encroached upon and dispersed, he could not conceive of there

---

[1] Letter to Cynthia Asquith of 16.8.1915: *Letters*, 247.
[2] *Movements in European History*, 1922 (1931 ed.), 343-4.

being anything else properly called 'community' to take its place. It is indeed the most difficult thing in the world – to keep abreast of life as it changes, to realise that mankind tends to take on only those problems that we can solve, and not to turn away in petulance or a deeper revulsion from forms of social behaviour different from the ones in which we invested our emotions when we were young. And if one is, like many writers, an unusual and highly introverted person, it is also difficult to face up to mass movements, to ally one's precious distinctiveness with anything collective. Unless the writer can do so, in the age of what has been called mass civilisation, his solidarity with his species will be impaired or broken, and his art will suffer.

Section Three

POETRY AND MODERN LIFE

CHAPTER 8

Loneliness and Anarchy:
Aspects of Modernism

FOR twenty-five years or so it has been common for reviewers or self-appointed coroners holding a *post mortem* on The Novel to regret that literary modes have relapsed into the ordinary and 'naturalistic', that the flair for radical innovation has been lost. These critics were in the first place (though they now have quite young imitators) men whose tastes had formed in the epoch of Cubism and serial music, *vers libre*, the 'stream of consciousness', Futurism and surrealism. They had come to assume that the *avant garde* of the Modernist heyday, from about 1905 to 1925, had set *the* standard for artists in modern times–that the sign of serious and original intentions in the arts was to take non-realistic or non-figurative (in the painter's sense) styles to their extremes. Viewing the matter as part of the culture, we can see that a main effect of Modernism was to set a gulf between the 'quality' and the popular. The very phrase 'modern art' as commonly used suggests that something has come over the arts which wasn't there before, something which most people–and I mean most people–dislike. A decade ago the new element was still taken to be 'obscurity' or 'distortion'. Just now it is more often some such idea as 'Life is meaningless' or 'We can't communicate'. In front of an abstract painting most people say, 'But what's it meant to be?' After a television play they object that 'it had no proper ending'.

As early as 1916 Lawrence had made the hero of *Women in Love* say: '"We are all different and unequal in spirit . . . spiritually, there is pure difference. . . . In the spirit, I am as separate as one star is from another."'[1] The tone of that is affirmative, almost proud. But this view of man as estranged or cut off from his fellows has more often been held pessimistically. It occurs across the literary spectrum, from the most stylised work to the most lifelike.

[1] See above, ch. 7, 155.

The main sufferer in Kafka's symbolic novels gets no support or kinship from his surroundings, through which he moves as though in a nightmare, acutely aware yet helpless. Dos Passos begins and ends his panoramic trilogy of the United States with a man on his own, hitch-hiking along the highways in a fruitless search for a job and a resting place. More recently the highest esteem has gone to playwrights such as Pinter, the responses of whose characters precisely fail to follow from or match their objective situations, and Beckett, whose characters only just emerge from the sandhills and dustbins in which they exist to communicate with each other and the audience.

Thus the complaint of the Fifties critics had no sooner been made than it was answered, for Pinter and Beckett are the direct offspring of the modernists. Pinter follows Kafka in presenting individuals demented or harried by routines that stop just far enough short of nightmare to remind us unpleasantly of our actual society and its entanglements. Beckett's waste-land sense of life is close to Eliot even in its verbal detail: typical dialogue from *Waiting for Godot* needs only to be rearranged a little—

> In the meantime let's try and converse calmly,
> Since we're incapable of keeping silent.
> You're right, we're inexhaustible.
> It's so we won't think. We have that excuse.
> It's so we won't hear. We have our reasons.
> All the dead voices. They make a noise like wings.
> Like leaves. Like sand. Like leaves.
> They all speak together. Each one to itself.
> Rather they whisper. They rustle.
> They murmur. They rustle.
> What do they say? They talk about their lives.
> To have lived is not enough for them.
> They have to talk about it.
> To be dead is not enough for them.
> It is not sufficient—

for it to resemble closely, in rhythms as well as in imagery and subject-matter, 'The Hollow Men'—

> Our dried voices, when
> We whisper together
> Are quiet and meaningless
> As wind in dry grass
> Or rats' feet over broken glass
> In our dry cellar

> Shape without form, shade without colour,
> Paralysed force, gesture without motion –

or 'Burnt Norton' –

> Only a flicker
> Over the strained time-ridden faces
> Distracted from distraction by distraction
> Filled with fancies and empty of meaning
> Tumid apathy with no concentration
> Men and bits of paper, whirled by the cold wind
> That blows before and after time,
> Wind in and out of unwholesome lungs
> Time before and time after.[1]

Again, when Tennessee Williams, the current playwright whose work has reached the widest audience, writes in his preface to *Cat on a Hot Tin Roof* (1955), ' "We're all of us sentenced to solitary confinement inside our own skins." Personal lyricism is the outcry of prisoner to prisoner from the cell in solitary where each is confined for the duration of his life', we recognise the ideology of *The Waste Land*: for example, those lines near the end with its imagery of psychosis and anarchy, 'We think of the key, each in his prison/Thinking of the key, each confirms a prison', which Eliot glosses from F. H. Bradley's *Appearance and Reality*: 'my experience falls within my own circle, a circle closed on the outside.'[2]

The unrivalled repute of these writers has lent so much prestige to the view of life as irretrievably isolated that it has become for a time the scarcely resistible ideology of the literary intelligentsia. To speak up for the reality of human communication, of the feelings and experiences we all share and can rely on having in common as kindred creatures, has been to draw the charge of being superficial and complacent, a 'consenting liberal'[3] heedlessly at his ease in a world that more thoughtful souls reject. Commenting on Pinter's *Dumb Waiter* a critic writes: 'As within ourselves, on the one hand open abysses of bottomless inanity, on the other loom the fearful crags of an irrational, implacable cruelty.'[4] To this it is

---

[1] *Waiting for Godot* (1959 ed.), 62-3; Eliot, *Collected Poems, 1909-1935* (1936), 87, 188.

[2] Further discussed below: chap. 9, 208.

[3] Frederick Grubb's name for me in a passage where he challenges my view of *The Waste Land* as defeatist: *A Vision of Reality* (1965), 57.

[4] J. W. Lambert in *New English Dramatists*, 3 (Penguin, 1961), 9.

surely not self-deceiving to rejoin that I, and you the reader, probably do not feel inane at bottom, and that cruelty in our century (as in any other) is far from irrational or inexplicable. But this rejoinder, though correct, would not explain why so many people in our time, especially artists, have come to think that irremediable isolation is the essence of human life.

A recent almost self-parodying case of isolation literature suggests a clue: the play *No Quarter* by Barry Bermange. It was written for the stage yet it takes place in total darkness in a huge hotel with blown fuses—hence its suitability for broadcasting (in the Third Programme, November 1962). The *Radio Times* willingly interpreted: 'If indeed "some are born to endless night", their darkness may be social, political, religious.' Here the depressed morale of the playwright is abetted by the publicist with his lax assumption that a whole many-sided way of life can be hit off by a single symbol. Paul Ferris commented in the *Observer* (November 18 1962):

> Radio reflects intellectual pessimism more thoroughly than any other large-scale medium, probably because the core of intellectuals at Broadcasting House are left alone, without the pressures of success and daily public interest. Things are always blowing up or falling down in Third Programme plays.

This hints with shrewd wit at one fundamental cause for the loneliness and anarchy at the heart of so many recent novels, plays, and poems. The author who produces his work as a commodity never quite meets his public. In this sense he is objectively isolated. And he has been able to become all the more convinced that those who attend to him are few and remote from him because he is bound to compete with newspapermen, pop-singers, advertisers who sell to millions. Thus the writer who is not trying for a smash hit—whose work is meant to reach gradually into our minds and imaginations—may well despair before he has won a hearing, or despise it when he gets it. The original writers who have won a hearing in recent times have often dealt with sex, which must further discourage a genuine talent who is concerned with other matters. Overawed by his beleaguered position, the writer retreats into himself, and comes to assume that his loneliness is *humanly typical*.

By itself this process—clearly inherent in the art of a machine age where production and marketing are run on capitalist lines—might not have been enough so to establish loneliness and anarchy as the dominating cult. But it seems to have been inherent, too, in the division of society into classes. A. L. Morton, a critic who trained as a historian, has written of the 'middle classes to whom even the idea of voluntary association is alien',[1] and this is fundamental. The middle-class person, to confirm his position in the world, his success, his self-respect, wants above all to stand single. His house is at least *semi*-detached and he will not have waited for it on a Council list. He will aspire to transporting himself singly to his place of work in his own car. He will think of sending his children to schools where they can get an education different from the average. In his very feelings he tries for separateness: togetherness would feel too ordinary, mediocre, unsuccessful, 'common' in both senses. To succeed is to differentiate yourself from the ruck by putting your own interests first. Most people nowadays are in fact workers, in that they have nothing to live on but the sale of their labour-power, whether paid for in salary or in wage–by the week or by the month. Yet it is notoriously difficult, and has only in the past few years become possible on a worthwhile scale, to organise trade-union activity among the sections of people who *feel* themselves to be 'middle-class', in particular white-collar workers such as teachers, bank clerks, and doctors, for they are inhibited from acknowledging that their situation is shared with millions–with the overwhelming majority. Thus middle-class life actually is poor in types and images of the social, the shared.

All this does not mean that the average businessman, white-collar worker, or bungalow-dweller will readily recognise his own image in a novel by Kafka or a play by Beckett or Tennessee Williams, or that such social material will appear explicitly in the literature itself (although in notable cases it has, for example Arthur Miller's *Death of a Salesman*). It is rather that a position shared by many and, in a competitive commercialised society, aspired to by many more contributes to the social emotions that colour our lives and thus–sometimes deviously, sometimes with documentary directness–moulds the image of life created by the arts.

If this explanation of the cult of loneliness is right, it should hold good also for that other aspect of modernism, 'distortion' or 'obscurity'. It was this that struck people first. For most readers the

[1] 'The Arts and the People': *The Challenge of Marxism*, ed. Brian Simon (1963), 139.

idea that 'modern poetry' is obscure and unpleasant and generally 'unpoetic' probably originates from passages like the opening of Eliot's 'Prufrock':

> Let us go then, you and I,
> When the evening is spread out against the sky
> Like a patient etherised upon a table . . .

Why (the common reaction runs) has the poet chosen that morbid, clinical image for a lovely thing like a sunset? Why, at the start of *The Waste Land*, does he call April 'the cruellest month' when everyone (including the poets of old, such as Chaucer) knows that spring is a delightful time of renewed freshness? Why does Brecht (in a poem from *Hauspostille*, 1927) write like this about trees and birds, country things, as lovely as sunsets:

> Towards morning in the early grey the fir trees piss
> And their vermin, the birds, begin to cry.
> About this time in the city I empty my glass,
> Fling away my butt, and sleep restlessly.[1]

Why, at about the same time, was Stravinsky using discords as freely as harmonies in his music for the ballet *The Rite of Spring*, and why was Picasso sticking ugly, inartistic things like nails, brown paper, and newspaper clippings onto his paintings?

This cluster of items is so evidently a family and so central to the best art of the time that it cries out for explanation—unless we are content to treat the arts as apparitions that materialise out of unfathomable darkness and pass away like dreams. Certainly, those family likenesses inside modernism have often been noted and historical links have been groped for. Thus a leading historian of the period, Alan Bullock, draws together the main innovations at the turn of the century, in social history, the sciences, and the arts, and tries to formulate them as a qualitative leap in the growth of civilisation. His generalising on the strictly historical side is firm and concretely based: 'In the years 1870-1913 the international economy, measured by increase in industrial output per head, expanded more rapidly than ever before or since. . . . Industrialisation had been accompanied by a great increase in urban popula-

---

[1] The poem is 'Concerning Poor B.B.' It is translated by H. R. Hays in *Selected Poems* of Brecht (1959), 14-17, but I have changed this version considerably since it is not accurate.

tions,' and so on. But the conclusion that he plainly feels his data call for is, when it comes, a wistful anti-climax: 'surely, the break-up of the old patterns in so many different spheres at roughly the same point of time cannot have been accidental'. But no explanation follows.[1] It might be thought that the biographer of Hitler and Ernest Bevin was simply out of his depth in the history of art and ideas. But what help could he have got from his literary colleagues? In one current essay Graham Hough caustically repudiates the notion that 'revolutions' in the arts can be correlated at all consistently with simultaneous upheavals in the main life of the time.[2] In another, Walter Allen offers the same cluster of innovations as does Bullock, briefly raises the question whether they belonged to the ferment of the Great War, concludes from the dates that they can't have (Freud, Chekhov, Picasso, Stravinsky, Joyce had all set out on their new paths before 1914), and seems to think that the possibility of explaining modernism historically has thereby been invalidated. All he can fall back on is Virginia Woolf's epigram, 'On or about December 1910 human nature changed.'[3] The theoretical mistake here is basic. The critic has looked for his connections inside too narrow a time-span and failed to see that an evident kinship between historical and artistic events is more likely than not to be in the form of *cognate* descent from a common root.[4] To theorise cogently on these matters it is as necessary to be critically precise about the art itself as to be well up in the historical facts. It is therefore best at this point to look afresh at the novel qualities which come into literature at that epoch.

Modernism strikes one as a deliberate disruption of the beautiful. Actually the dreariness of many a daybreak is caught in Brecht's lines with the utmost accuracy, as is the terror of barbaric ritual in Stravinsky's music or the flattening out and immobilising of stratus clouds at sunset in the image from 'Prufrock'. But in the past artists had usually tried to create images that were not only true to their subjects but also pleasing in themselves. It is true that some previous poetic 'revolutions' had made an impact rather like Eliot's, for example Wordsworth's short-lived attempt, just after the French

---

[1] 'The Double Image': *The Listener*, March 19 1970, 369, 373.
[2] Cited and discussed in my 'Towards Laws of Literary Development': *Mosaic*, V, 2 (Winnipeg, 1972), 13-15.
[3] *Tradition and Dream* (1964), 1-3.
[4] This idea is worked out fully in my chapter in G. H. R. Parkinson (Ed.), *Georg Lukács* (1970), 204-7.

Revolution, to write poetry in 'the language of conversation in the middle and lower classes of society' –

> And he is lean and he is sick,
> His little body's half awry
> His ancles they are swoln and thick
> His legs are thin and dry.
> When he was young he little knew
> Of husbandry or tillage;
> And now he's forced to work, though weak,
> —The weakest in the village.
>
> ('Simon Lee' from *Lyrical Ballads*, 1798)

We know how uncouth this seemed to a public accustomed to the literature, from Dryden to Dr Johnson and Jane Austen, meant exclusively for the well-to-do and 'refined'. Earlier, Donne had had to break the graceful flow of the Elizabethan songsters in order to make love poetry as deep and surprising as passion itself: for example, the first lines of the first poem in his *Songs and Sonets* overturn Beauty even more rudely that Eliot's 'etherised patient' –

> Busie old foole, unruly Sunne,
> Why dost thou thus,
> Through windowes, and through curtaines call on us?

Neither in the seventeenth century nor in the nineteenth, however, did the break with Beauty last as long or disrupt as much as it has in our time. The Simon Lee material, for example, was soon relegated to the novels of a Scott or an Elizabeth Gaskell, and the 'social novel' was still considered a lowly form, hardly Literature at all. A shake-up as prolonged as the modernist revolt against conventional models of Beauty, order, and coherence suggests, as a matter of common sense, some quake in the order or morale of society.

Modernism did indeed appear towards the climax of the Great Unrest in Britain when, as we saw in the previous two chapters, men and women were streaming into the unions and other forms of militant activity as never before. But such a raw parallel between literature and history explains little by itself. Writers and other artists cannot necessarily seize on change as it occurs and all at once find the means of transforming their art to bring it abreast of changing life. The thing prepares itself more gradually.

In Britain poetry the tap-root of modernism was the work of

Hopkins, who as early as the 1870s is melting down and re-creating diction and poetic form to make them responsive to the very point at which conflicting impulses flow and recoil:

> Not, I'll not, carrion comfort, Despair, not feast on thee;
> Not untwist—slack they may be—these last strands of man
> In me or, most weary, cry *I can no more*. I can;
> Can something, hope, wish day come, not choose not to be . . .
> ('Carrion Comfort', 1885)

This is nominally a sonnet but the intensity of the feeling has strained metre and rhyme-scheme to bursting-point. Without the least touch of wilfulness or obscurity, and with the utmost linguistic resource (indicatives used like imperatives, all unnecessary connectives stripped away), the poet has rendered his whole feelings as they come, rather than a congealed or stylised type of them at some removes from the psychological event. This style of Hopkins has been called (by F. R. Leavis, in conversation) 'the revolt of the English language against Tennyson'; and Tennyson was then the lyric voice of the Establishment, Queen Victoria's favourite, writing poetry that dignified the feudal, ancient, and ceremonious. Not that it was the politically conformist side of Tennyson that stirred Hopkins to revolt, although in the year of the Paris Commune he did write a remarkable letter in which he looked forward, half in alarm and half in hope, to 'the Communist future'.[1] What mainly stirred Hopkins seems to have been the struggle of his own feelings (as a priest sworn to chastity and worried that even his poem-making was a self-indulgence) to find expression at a time when poetry was supposed to keep a beautifully unruffled surface.

This does not, however, exclude the foundations of life at that time from a decisive role at the basis of the literary tradition. For why was Victorian poetry lofty, unruffled, Tennysonian? I suggest that it was because it had to maintain the equanimity of middle-class culture in face of the Bleak Age—the swarming slums, the ruining of rural Britain, armed struggle between the workers and the owners. Even the first generation of Romantic poets had hankered to escape, to the countryside, the vanishing England of the yeomen farmers, the Mediterranean past. But that impulse was

---

[1] To Robert Bridges on August 2 1871: 'Horrible to say, in a manner I am a Communist . . . it is a dreadful thing for the greatest and most necessary part of a very rich nation to live a hard life without dignity, knowledge, comforts, delights, or hopes in the midst of plenty—which plenty they make.' (*A Hopkins Reader*, ed. John Pick, 1953, 225-6).

at least still fresh, and it was also the cry of the people at large, for example the dispossessed villagers who were petitioning Parliament against enclosures of common land and the drift of young folk to the towns. Whereas Shelley could reach his peak—could for the first time concentrate and intensify his style—in response to the reign of terror that culminated in Peterloo in 1819, the second generation of Romantics never wrote a notable poem that was also socially radical. Poetry could find no way of associating itself with the forward impulses of life at large. Matthew Arnold must be counted, by virtue of 'Dover Beach' and the most trenchant passages from his polemic essays, as a man whose sensibility was in touch with the front line or growing-points of his time; yet his poetry as a whole fails to penetrate beyond that kind of second-hand high style that Hopkins saw to be typical also of Tennyson and called 'Parnassian'.[1] The poet is no longer at home in the world, he has no appetite for the typical experiences of his time and so for his style must fall back on ever fainter echoes of earlier work. Thus Arnold's other key poem, 'The Scholar Gypsy', is largely Keats's 'Autumn' ode watered down, and where it does sharpen to distinctive phrasing it is only to resign from the position of concerned witness which I take to be the irreducible vantage-point for an artist of any stature. In 1804 Blake could write—

> I will not cease from Mental Fight,
> Nor shall my Sword sleep in my hand
> Till we have built Jerusalem—

whereas by 1853 'mental strife' is to Arnold an 'infection' and 'modern life' a 'strange disease' from which the sensitive soul is urged to flee.

Even if Hopkins's poems had been published before 1918, it seems unlikely that they could have much dislodged the sensibility of the Victorians, for the tendency of his concerns was little different from Tennyson's or Arnold's: for all the energy of his response to life, in his heart of hearts he wishes to escape from the blight and spoliation which he sees as typical of modern man's activity, he yearns to curl up inside some ideal refuge.[2] Nevertheless, the degree

---

[1] Letter to Alexander Baillie, September 10 1864: *Hopkins Reader*, 74-6.

[2] See especially 'The Sea and the Skylark' and 'God's Grandeur' of 1877, the sonnet on the unemployed, 'Tom's Garland', and the letter that goes with it, which attacks 'Socialists and other pests of society': to Robert Bridges, February 10 1888 (*Hopkins Reader*, 165).

of disturbance which he allows into his versification is an early sign that people would not be content indefinitely with the assumption to which the Victorians subscribed at least in their perorations (e.g. the close of *In Memoriam*): namely, that the cosmos steered by its automatic pilot was in good hands and headed towards an assured goal. For generations poetry had either thrown a lustre over the old-established institutions, the monarchy and aristocracy, learning, the Church, or if it was radical-minded and therefore dissatisfied with the actual order of things, it had set its heart on ideal forms, the True, the Beautiful, and the Good. Many churches and crowns were shaken or went smash in the Great War and the revolutions that followed it. The appalling experiences in the trenches, the bestial squalor and slaughter, the idiocy of the leadership, made it impossible ever again to refer with the same assurance to the dignity of man, etc. In the best documentary of that turning-point, Robert Graves's *Goodbye to All That*, the poet writes (reviewing the values of the men at war): 'Patriotism. There was no patriotism in the trenches . . . Religion . . . not one soldier in a hundred was inspired by religious feeling of even the crudest kind.' The smallest touches bring out how mass suffering had so steeped people in the atrocity of what men could do to each other that the least effort to rise 'above it all' was suspect. On one occasion near Loos, the men 'were singing songs to the accompaniment of an accordion and a penny whistle. Only at one time, when a "mad-minute" of artillery noise was reached, they stopped and looked at each other, and Sergeant Townsend said sententiously: "That's the charge. Many good fellows going west at this moment; maybe chums of ours."'[1] Graves's recoil from the least attempt to hallow or moralise the atrocity is closely akin to Sassoon's angry *exposé* of the old ruling-class which he identifies, accurately, with the Higher Command and the staff officers. In *Counter-Attack* contemporary subject-matter bursts back into poetry but the versification, the metre and the rhyming, is quite undisrupted by the violence of the content. The two best poets of the time, Rosenberg and Owen, both broke with Beauty and took to abrupt irregular rhythms and imperfect rhymes in the poems they wrote amongst the mud and gunfire at the Front. Brecht, who also saw service in the War and wrote one of its classic poems (the 'Legend of the Dead Soldier'), was fully conscious of the modern need for irregularity.

[1] (1929), 240-1, 217.

In his essay 'On Rhymeless Verse with Irregular Rhythms' he says about the problem of adapting the old heroic metre of Marlowe: 'I needed elevated language, but was brought up against the oily smoothness of the usual five-foot iambic metre. I needed rhythm, but not the usual jingle.' The argument that he then develops reaches the very centre of the subject and it is, as it must be, at once aesthetic and sociological:

> My political knowledge in those days [*c.* 1923] was disgracefully slight, and I didn't think it my task formally to iron out all the discordances and interferences of which I was strongly conscious. I caught them up in the incidents of my plays and in the verses of my poems; and did so long before I had recognised their real character and causes. As can be seen from the texts it was not a matter just of a formal 'kicking against the pricks'–of a protest against the smoothness and harmony of conventional poetry–but already of an attempt to show human dealings as contradictory, fiercely fought over, full of violence.[1]

Although it has been necessary to stress the ways in which the Great War disrupted Beauty, again we have to notice that the root of this process lies further back and is equally common among artists who never saw combat. In their letters from 1914 onwards Pound and Lawrence come out against all kinds of laxity in poetry and in favour of work that impinges sheerly by accurate presentment of particulars and a speaking directness. In March 1913 Pound wrote:

> Don't use such an expression as 'dim lands *of peace*'. It dulls the image. It mixes an abstraction with the concrete. It comes from the writer's not realising that the natural object is always the *adequate* symbol. . . .
> Don't allow 'influence' to mean merely that you mop up the particular decorative vocabulary of some one or two poets whom you happen to admire. A Turkish war correspondent was recently caught red-handed babbling in his despatches of 'dove-grey hills, or else it was 'pearl-pale' . . .
> Don't be 'viewy'–leave that to the writers of pretty little philosophic essays.

And in January 1915 he wrote to Harriet Monroe:

> Poetry must be *as well written as prose*. . . . Objectivity and again objectivity, and expression: no hindside-beforeness, no

---

[1] *Brecht on Theatre*, ed. John Willett (1964), 116. The poem referred to began as a song from his war play, *Drums in the Night*, which he wrote about 1920, two years before his Marlowe adaptation.

straddled adjectives (as 'addled mosses dank'), no Tenny-
sonianness of speech; nothing—nothing that you couldn't, in
some circumstance, in the stress of some emotion, actually
say. . . . Language is made out of concrete things. General
expressions in non-concrete terms are a laziness; they are talk,
not art, not creation.[1]

This, in its closeness to Hopkins on the 'Parnassian' (which Pound
could not have read), confirms that here we have a line of development intrinsic to the art itself: the medium under its own momentum, so to speak, is moved to purge itself of the fatty layers that
have come to blur its features.

The other major reason for the recreation of literature at that
time is extrinsic: it has to do with the function or role of the medium
in the culture as a whole. We have seen how Graves mistrusted
sententiousness—the least larding on of a moral. The heyday of
sententiousness is described by Lewis Mumford in a pregnant
passage from *The Culture of Cities*:

> . . . in the bleak industrial towns *national* politics became drama,
> battle, sport: its orators were the chief actors, its protagonists
> were the greatest prize-fighters, its parliamentary leaders were
> the leading generals, and its election bouts, with their speeches
> and their torchlight parades and their hysterical mass enthusi-
> asms, were the principal occasions for emotional release: more
> universal even than the revival meeting. . . . Sonorous oratory
> served the double function of stimulant and anaesthetic:
> exciting the populace and making it oblivious to its actual
> environment. In the ranks of the Trade Union movement itself
> mere political windbags rose to leadership: men who com-
> manded crowds in order to sate their narcissism: copious in
> emotion, diffident, fumbling in action.[2]

The original minds of the time sharpened their irony on that
rhetoric: Marx and Arnold are at one in their way of bringing the
facts of poverty and debasement hard up against the slogans of a
Roebuck, rhapsodising over the 'unrivalled happiness' of the
'Anglo-Saxon race, the best breed in the whole world!', or a

---

[1] 'A Few Don't's': see *Literary Essays of Ezra Pound*, ed. T. S. Eliot (1960), 5-6;
The Letters of Ezra Pound, 1907-1941, ed. D. D. Paige (1951), 91; compare Lawrence
to Catherine Carswell, January 11 1916: 'break the rhyme rather than the stony
directness of speech. The essence of poetry with us in this age of stark and un-
lovely actualities is a stark directness.' (*Letters*, 307-8.)
[2] *Culture of Cities*, 182.

Gladstone, boasting in his Budget speeches of 'this intoxicating augmentation of wealth and power'.[1] But the afflatus generated by the Workshop of the World was then still in the ascendant; the official poet was still in effect obliged to see in life itself a corresponding trend towards one far-off divine event. Such rhetoric inevitably lost its credibility and was seen to be gross when the social system failed to master the mass evils—poverty, demoralisation, the drift towards war. Artistic effort became polarised between the perfectionism of the aesthete, who rejected practical action in the social world as a utilitarian or 'materialist' vulgarity, and the socially-minded writer (a Wells or a Gorky) whose anger at man's inhumanity to man left him no patience, and often no time, to work scrupulously enough at his art.

In the work of the leading modernists, of Pound, Eliot, and Joyce, two elements from the *fin de siècle* show as inseparable: a sense that affirmations of social purpose are inevitably fatuous and an aesthete's concern with refining the medium. But they are of the twentieth century, not the Nineties, in their bitter concern with the 'botched civilisation', the long heritage of 'poverty and inaction'.[2] The joint outcome of this socio-literary process was that when the War (and the Irish rebellion and the Russian Revolution) sank into people's minds and disgusted them finally with the old uplift, they found a suitably purged and disenchanted poetry ready to hand: this is typified by E. M. Forster's relief, on reading *Prufrock* in Egypt at the end of the War, that here was a work which totally eschewed the large and declaratory.[3] A less fruitful result was that English poetry, in becoming skilled at refraining and eliminating and eschewing, had made itself the fitting medium for those who were negative in face of modern life—who could not see their way to identifying themselves with the more potent and ongoing impulses in either society or human nature. No-one caught the shabbiness of the industrial city in images more vivid and typical than Eliot's—

> Wipe your hand across your mouth, and laugh;
> The worlds revolve like ancient women
> Gathering fuel in vacant lots.

[1] *Capital*, I, ch. 25, section 5, 715; *Essays in Criticism*, First Series (1865), 'The Function of Criticism at the Present Time'.

[2] *Hugh Selwyn Mauberley*, V; *Dubliners*, 'After the Race'.

[3] *Abinger Harvest* (1940 ed.), 87-8.

A broken spring in a factory yard,
Rust that clings to the form that the strength has left
Hard and curled and ready to snap.

The rhythms here are dead and stopped. The poet is evoking the modern scene only to write it off. Already these poems (from before 1917) foreshadow *The Waste Land*, in which every ounce of the poet's skill in evocation, mimicry, and contrast is used to pass off as objectively typical of modern life his own particular hopelessness.[1] This is the poetry of the first slump in post-War morale, the epoch of the first hunger marches, Mussolini's taking power in Italy, and Hitler's potent appeal to the unemployed ex-Servicemen. Yet it was possible for a poet less inward-turned than the Modernists to register disenchantment and shabbiness to the full without dismissing the whole human effort as beyond redemption. Brecht's 'Concerning Poor B.B.' is in its seemingly casual way as quintessential a poem of the epoch as Eliot's, and its human range is greater. Brecht is self-critical, not superior, he can do justice to modern technical mastery, and in face of all discouragements he can suggest the irrepressible resilience of human nature:

I make friends with people. And I wear
A hard hat on my head as others do.
I say: these animals have a funny smell
And I say: no matter, I do too. . . .

Towards evening I gather some fellows around me,
We address each other as 'Gentlemen'.
They put their feet up on my tables
And say: things will get better for us. And I don't ask when. . . .

A lightweight generation, we have settled in houses
Which are indestructible, it is supposed
(As we put up the tall buildings on Manhattan Island
And the thin antennae which keep the Atlantic amused).

There shall remain of these cities only the wind that blew
    through them!
The house maketh the feaster merry: he empties it.
We know that we are makeshift
And after us will come—nothing to say about it.

In the earthquakes that are coming I am hopeful
That I shan't allow bitterness to put out my cigar's glow,
I, Bertolt Brecht, consigned to the asphalt cities
By my mother from the forest long ago.

[1] Full grounds for this judgement are given in the following chapter

The qualities of this poem anticipate Brecht's later masterpieces of humane realism—*Mother Courage*, *The Life of Galileo*, *The Caucasian Chalk Circle*. Eliot's sense of modern life as a dead end anticipates his painfully strained attempts, in the poetry and plays from 1930 onwards, to transcend this life.

This double face of modernism—both hating modern life and trying to create comprehensive images of it in all its mixture of advance, backwardness, and giddy change—is discussed by Stephen Spender, himself a second-generation modernist, in *The Struggle of the Modern* (1963). The most important point that he raises—unfortunately he assumes instead of working out the solution—is whether or not the dislocated style of modernism (the lack of normal prose logic in *Finnegans Wake*, or of consecutive argument in Pound's *Cantos*, or of a subject in abstract art of various kinds) has been *necessary* to reflect the dislocations in society: wars, revolutions, unprecedented social mobility, cultural minglings, fast technical change. This trend is one that literary intellectuals, from Ruskin to Eliot and Leavis, have usually viewed pessimistically, and Spender refers constantly to the 'confusion of values' in our time, sometimes as though it were a neutral fact, sometimes as though the defeated view of it were unquestionably true. A little thought should show that enhanced or diminished fulfilment on the part of whole societies is an extraordinarily difficult thing to establish and would need a great deal of subtly interpreted evidence. Yet even the standard historians fall easily in with the defeatist view. For example, Charles Loch Mowat in his chapter on 'Stability and Change: The Condition of Britain in the Twenties' quotes the exact figures for divorce between 1910 and 1932 but when it comes to interpreting them he is the reverse of exact: 'People were continuously "popping" in and out of bed with new bed-fellows, though not, apparently, getting much pleasure out of it.' His evidence? Two lines from *The Waste Land*:

> Bestows one final patronising kiss,
> And gropes his way, finding the stairs unlit. . . .[1]

I should have thought that the common sense of such a matter would be that if the besetting trouble in a mobile society is insecurity, the counterpart in a slow-changing one was liable to be stultification in various forms. But there is little room for such a view in the cult

---

[1] *Britain Between the Wars, 1918–1940* (1956 ed.), 218.

of loneliness and anarchy. When Eliot reviewed *Ulysses* in *The Dial* he interpreted its repeated shifts of style and mingling of ancient myth and modern life as 'perhaps the only feasible method' of giving shape to 'the immense panorama of futility and anarchy which is contemporary history'.[1] This view has been found so persuasive that most people (in my experience) don't stop to ask in which age history was, as it were, under control. Consider the following comment on *Ulysses*:

> The whole picture of Dublin which Joyce presents is of a society in hopeless disintegration extended between two masters – Catholic Church and British Empire – which exploit and ruin it. The family unit is as far decomposed as any other . . .

Usually a critic who had written that would then pass over into taking this particular vision of life, in this one book, as an evidently valid view of our whole society, regardless of whether or not there were special pressures on that writer (his health, his parental environment, his struggle to free himself from a formidable religion) which might have thrown his focus out of true. In fact that comment comes from Arnold Kettle's book on the modern novel and he is almost alone in refusing to fall for the cult of 'futility and anarchy'. A little later he writes that 'there is more of the essential feeling of the relationship of man to man and man to society in a great urban centre in the public-house ballad "I belong to Glasgow" than there is in *Ulysses*.'[2] This shows up the fallacy of arguing from an art of anxiety and dissonance to society as a whole. If, for example, the family unit in Dublin had decomposed by the 1920s, how would we account for the vividly circumstantial account of a staunch, lively working-class family that Dominic Behan gives in his memoirs of Dublin in the Thirties (*Teems of Times and Happy Returns*)? The truth appears to be that if your art is all discord and dead-end or your criticism reads this straight back into life, you are either unaware of or deliberately opposed to the humane tendencies that continue to operate even in the midst of what seems like anarchy to a conservative. Spender seems to take it as proven that modern life is uniquely unfavourable to art and to the sensitive soul generally: for example, he takes up Arnold's idea that the Romantics did not 'know enough' in the way of current thought

---

[1] *The Struggle of the Modern*, 208.
[2] *An Introduction to the English Novel*, 2 (1953), 148-9.

and suggests that somehow modern ideas have been peculiarly indigestible for the artist.[1] Yet consider how Hardy absorbed Darwin on evolution, how Lawrence absorbed Freud on sex and the unconscious, how Brecht absorbed Marx on dialectics, the class struggle, and capitalism.

Part of Spender's purpose is to explain why the second-generation modernists, the writers from 1930 onwards, failed to create work of the stature of *Ulysses* and *The Waste Land*. But he never seriously considers whether the extreme innovations of the modernists were adequate to present real anarchy once it had materialised on the doorstep and faced people with life-or-death choices and emergencies. It seems to me now that modernism has done best as a loosener-up of forms that had ossified and that its own chief works are remarkable freaks rather than masterpieces. For example, the invoking of time past through the classical allusions in *Ulysses* is a 'frame of reference' arbitrarily imposed rather than an active ingredient in the book; whereas Sartre in *The Reprieve*, deriving his fluid shifts of time and place from *Ulysses* through Dos Passos' *U.S.A.*, is able to make them work, and avoid undue obscurity, as the natural way of catching the simultaneous experience of a whole continent (Europe threatened over the radio by Hitler). Again, Brecht remains to the very end a modernist in his disruption of the picture-frame stage, for example by the use of documentary stills, the laying bare of the mechanics of production, and so on. But in his plays, after the savoured decadence of *Baal* (1918) and the satirised decadence of *The Threepenny Opera* (1928), he turned to depicting with transparent realism experiences from the mainstream of life. The second-generation modernists in England did attempt a Brechtian drama that sought to stem as directly from social struggle as a slogan or a newspaper. But the Auden-Isherwood efforts at agitprop drama were never serious enough –

> One, two, three, four
> The last war was a bosses' war
> Five, six, seven, eight
> Rise and make a workers' state . . .[2]

Brecht's stage songs are simple all right but they never jingle by glibly like political nursery-rhymes for precocious kiddies. Brecht was in earnest, forced by the direst of struggles (the fight against

---

[1] *The Struggle of the Modern*, 250-2.
[2] Auden, *The Dance of Death* (1933), 16.

Hitler) to concentrate his vision into the most unmistakable and common idioms, for example 'In Praise of Learning' (from *Mother*, 1932) with its refrain *'Du musst die Führung ubernehmen'* – 'You must take over the leadership':

> Learn, man in the asylum!
> Learn, man in prison!
> Learn, wife in the kitchen!
> Learn, man of sixty!
> Seek out the school, you who are homeless!
> Sharpen your wits, you who shiver!
> Hungry man, reach for the book: it is a weapon.
> You must take over the leadership.[1]

In all Brecht's poetry, for the stage or not, we feel a bedrock of common speech–the veritable voice of his unshakable fellow-feeling with ordinary people at work, in danger, keeping alive.

This point in the argument is another of those cruxes where we can lay bare the sources, watersheds, and confluences of literary development. The account of Brecht's coming onto a drastically purged style would be incomplete if one failed to mention his intrinsic need, as a scrupulous originating artist, to rid his medium– his media, for he was working simultaneously in poetry, song, opera, and theatre–of all those overblown effects for which the Germanic style, the style of Wagner and Strauss, had become notorious.[2] The mistake commonly made by historians of literature is to think that such a development, by being placed in the context of an art with its own tendency and momentum, is thereby removed from the realm of the historical. Thus a recent writer sums up the common view of Bartók:

> . . . at one time the harsh, percussive side of Bartók was regarded as a musical representation of the grimness of a Europe advancing into totalitarianism. In fact it was a musical revolt against the over-luscious romanticism of the post-Wagnerians and a return, in twentieth-century terms, to a more classical style.[3]

This opposes the political and the musical to each other as though they were mutually exclusive categories. The truth of the matter is

---

[1] *Selected Poems*, 93.

[2] For its manic excesses in the Twenties, see Ronald Gray, *The German Tradition in Literature 1871-1945* (Cambridge, 1965), 48-53; John Willett, *Expressionism* (1970), 113-5, 122-3.

[3] Michael Kennedy in *Radio Times*, May 1 1969, 45.

surely rather as follows: Over-luscious romanticism had been able to grow up and flourish for reasons inseparable from that very advance into totalitarianism. Germany, recently come to nation-hood, behind in the imperial race, bursting with a desire to equip herself with a fullblown tradition, aggrandised the styles and motifs already there in her Nordic and Prussian heritages. This gave a potent charge to the tendency, common to all Romantic movements in recently industrialised countries, to soar off on an orbit of escape from the shameful and rankling shabbinesses of life in the raw cities. All this was redoubled by the humiliations of military defeat and the penalties of the Versailles treaty. Any dictator will cloak himself in a high-and-mighty style—Mussolini in that of Imperial Rome, Stalin in that of Peter the Great. But observers—travellers, newspapermen, writers—are agreed that Germans bet-ween the wars used to vaunt even their oddities as though they were rare national virtues; an inflamed style had seized the whole culture. Isherwood describes a Berlin youth club in 1933:

> They showed me dozens of photographs of boys, all taken with the camera tilted upwards, from beneath, so that they look like epic giants, in profile against enormous clouds. The magazine itself has articles on hunting, tracking, and preparing food—all written in super-enthusiastic style, with a curious underlying note of hysteria, as though the actions described were part of a religious or erotic ritual.[1]

Brecht was thus reacting against a swollen falsity, now naive and now propagandist, which had arisen out of that very process (the passing over of capitalist affluence into a manic totalitarianism) which shortly forced him to flee for his life.

Such a writer (and the same is true of all the fine talents who have become Displaced Persons since the time of Marx, Engels, and Herzen) certainly experiences disorder as part of his own life. But the committed writer will still feel that he is in touch with—even that he is grappling with—the forces of disruption, whereas the modernist is more likely to conceive disorder as the absurdly random, cruelly inexplicable condition of an existence that has him trapped. To put this descriptive formulation as a judgement, it seems to me, on the basis of those comparisons between the poetry of Brecht and Eliot, the drama of Brecht and Auden-Isherwood, and the fiction of Sartre and Joyce, that without a fairly drastic

---

[1] *Goodbye to Berlin,* 1939 (1952 ed.), 304.

exposure to experience a writer could not have enough material
with which to match the extraordinary technical complications of
the modernist modes. The work was all too liable to turn into a
kind of glorified cryptogram or fade into abstraction.[1] The best of
the English poets who followed Eliot in the Thirties, W. H. Auden,
is fatally inclined to intellectual doodling, and it is significant that in
his prime his best work should so often have got its material from
the heartlands of the struggle on the Continent (I am thinking of
'A Bride in the 30s', 'A Summer Night 1933', the first part of the
poem for Yeats, and 'Spain'). That literary generation, which
came between the two main waves of modernism, appears now to
have been striving to break out of solipsism and loneliness *via* the
work and comradeship of the Left. Unfortunately our labour
movement was then deeply confused and compromised. In Germany
a long history of Marxist initiatives, the terrible post-War slump
and inflation, and the struggle with the Fascist gangs had kept the
Left strong: in the Reichstag the year before Hitler took power,
there were 100 Communist members and 121 Social-Democrats
out of 570. In a situation of war, hunger, economic collapse, and
terrorism, the lines on which a humane artist must work could
hardly be clearer. From this springs the extraordinary richness and
the progressive commitment of German art before and even during
the Nazi regime: the plays and poems of Brecht, the satire of Karl
Kraus, the drawing of Grosz and Kathe Kollwitz, the paintings of
Otto Dix and Hans and Lea Grundig, the music of Hanns Eisler
and Kurt Weill, the fiction of Anna Seghers.

My effort here is not to establish any foolproof law to the effect
that it takes a strong fighting socialist movement to underpin an
important modern literature; what is at issue is the causes of the
relative strengths and weaknesses of Western literature at this
stage. In America, labour could not shake the government any
more than it could in Britain. Yet the Twenties and Thirties

---

[1] It will be obvious that so large a matter is wide open for discussion and
cannot be made good here. But I am not alone in this way of thinking: compare
John Willet in the chapter of his *Theatre of Bertolt Brecht* called 'The English
Aspect': 'our most gifted writers become autobiographical and soft-centred;
they concentrate on style (or technique) to the point of affectation; they often go
against the grain of our language by wrapping up their meaning or trying to pass
off triviality as deep thought. There is a lack of toughness in their work, in many
cases a lack of humour, too, and the spark that comes from contact with a wide
public is lacking.' (1960 ed., 220.)

produced an outstanding school of novelists, Hemingway, Scott Fitzgerald, Dos Passos, Farrell, Nathanael West, John Steinbeck. And the period had seen a struggle to establish the rights of working-people like what had happened more than a generation before in Britain: reigns of terror against the unions, near-civil war in some areas, *causes célèbres* which swung liberal opinion leftwards. From this struggle sprang new forms: the protest songs of the singing union-organisers, the Living Newspaper theatre, the part-documentary novel which borrowed methods from the sociologists. The writers, unlike their British counterparts, could find effective forms for their humane commitment–the campaign against the frame-up of Sacco and Vanzetti, the enquiry into the terrorising of the Kentucky miners,[1] the tribunal which cleared Trotsky of Stalin's charges–and it was in the same spirit that they developed an art whose very methods were moulded by a passionate responsibility for the daily life of their country. Dos Passos in his prime combined this with a cosmopolitan knowledge of what the *avant garde* were doing and as a result he could attempt, in *U.S.A.*, something beyond any British writer: the fusing of popular techniques (song, newspaper, political speech) with the modernist innovations to create a work that was complex and yet as accessible as the nine-teenth-century realists. In practice he did sacrifice breadth to depth: too many of his characters are interchangeable ciphers. But he did manage in an unprecedented way to present in a single work a whole society in flux, presented with a socialist understanding of the forces conflicting in it, and it could not have been done without modernist methods: free ranging in time outside the confines of a linear plot; transcript and parody of language from many sources, including the non-artistic; the handing over of the writer's personal style to a kind of composite medium (in painterly terms, a collage) which aims, not at Beauty or the harmonising of all elements into a seamless unity, but at the imaging of experience on many levels, inside many identities, at once.

Modernism has thus helped to fertilise even those writers whose interests are too wide to be contained in the more specialised experimental modes. I cannot but think that there is something self-defeating in that the *oeuvre* of each is too much a one-track thing that varies little from work to work despite nominal differ-

---

[1] See, for example, *Harlan Miners Speak* (1932): the editor-writers include Dos Passos, Theodore Dreiser, and Sherwood Anderson.

ences of character, theme, and situation. Kafka could not finish his novels, and wanted them destroyed; Joyce's crowning work, *Finnegans Wake*, will never be read by more than a small number of specialists; Beckett's latest theatre piece, *Breath* (1970), is so short and non-articulate that it must represent a contempt for any kind of communication at all. Can one be happy about a tradition in which the finest talents spend themselves in such ways? Nevertheless, work which has held large and thoughtful audiences (in theatres, in prisons, and on TV) in as strong a spell as *Waiting for Godot* and *The Caretaker* have done could not be failing to strike chords in present-day living. It is said that shortly before he died Brecht was thinking of rehearsing *Godot* with the Berliner Ensemble; and Arnold Wesker is on record that *Godot* was one of the things that stimulated his trilogy: 'Beckett seemed to be saying in an odd sort of way the kind of thing I try to stress in *Roots* about the terrible lack of communication that reduces us to the rumblings of Lucky, the man in chains.'[1] This is indeed a lesson in the unpredictable lines along which the arts can develop and as such should check any philistine impatience people may have with the seemingly farfetched. My own taste is for the artists of humane commitment, and one of these, the Soviet sculptor Neizvestny, has both interested himself in modernism and gone to the limits of the lifelike in his superb war pieces: for example, the memorial to death-camp inmates which shows a head squeezed between two slabs with one eyelid *dented* like metal; or the 'All Clear' of 1957, again a head, with one hand pulling off a gas-mask as though it were the man's own skin and flesh.[2] Neizvestny has written in *Iskusstvo*, the journal of the Soviet Union of Painters: 'The contemporary artist is a man whose view of the world is equal in its complexity to the contemporary conceptions of the structure of the universe.' He has also been reported to have doubts, regarding John Berger's work, whether 'the move from Freudianism to sociology is a good thing in English art criticism.'[3] Thus not only Western artists but also an artist who has been moved—in many ways forced—by his society to concentrate on public subjects, subjects given by history, wishes

---

[1] Laurence Kitchin, *Mid-century Drama* (1962 ed.), 195.
[2] The first piece is remembered from a newspaper photo seen about ten years ago; the second is in John Berger's *Art and Revolution* (1969), 100.
[3] 'Wanted—An Art of Ideas': *Observer*, 16.2.63; Stanley Mitchell, 'Impressions of Russia': *New Left Review*, 18 (January/February 1963), 53.

to affirm the importance of those depths which have been opened to us by the psycho-analysts, the stream-of-consciousness novelists, the nuclear physicists, and the molecular biologists.

It looks as though in the foreseeable future our literature will develop by interactions between three lines of work. There is the second wave of modernism, which I have represented by Beckett and Pinter. There is the renewal of realism and naturalism[1] in the new-wave plays and films, the radio ballad, the folk-song revival, and the vernacular novel:[2] this rich movement was not foreseen by those who ten or fifteen years ago still thought that imaginative prose had reached its limit in Joyce, that verse in drama had found its last resting-place in Eliot's plays, and the modernists' vision of life as lonely and chaotic was the only one that could be taken seriously in our time. There are also the working-class writers such as David Storey and David Mercer who started by creating life-like images of their home communities and have since expanded their work by absorbing the philosophical and psychological ideas of Sartre and Laing without losing their concern for people in ordinary situations.

[1] I have in mind the definitions of these terms worked out by Michael Egan. He sees realism as the mode which takes seriously the life of the contemporary ruling class, e.g. in the nineteenth-century novel the middle class, and naturalism as the specific form of realism which around 1900 brought to bear a similar seriousness on the life of working men and women and the poor in general.

[2] See below, chs. 12-14.

CHAPTER 9

The Defeatism of *The Waste Land*

> 'Is the time we live in prosaic?' 'That depends: it must
> certainly be prosaic to one whose mind takes a prosaic
> stand in contemplating it.' 'But it is precisely the most
> poetic minds that most groan over the vulgarity of the
> present, its degenerate sensibility to beauty, eagerness
> for materialistic explanation, noisy triviality.' 'Perhaps
> they would have had the same complaint to make
> about the age of Elizabeth, if, living then, they had
> fixed their attention on its more sordid elements, or
> had been subject to the grating influence of its every-
> day meannesses, and had sought refuge from them in
> the contemplation of whatever suited their taste in a
> former age.'
>
> GEORGE ELIOT, 'Leaves from a Note-Book'

T. S. ELIOT'S *The Waste Land* is the outstanding case in modern
English literature of a work that projects an almost despairing
personal depression in the guise of an impersonal picture of society.
Women in Love is a much more substantial case of the same thing,
but the response it demands, the mixture of elements it involves, is
far less simple. In my experience, however, both encourage in
readers, and especially in inexperienced ones, a sort of superior
cynicism: the 'educated man'[1] is flattered by the feeling that he is
the sole bearer of that fine culture which the new mass-barbarians
have spurned or spoiled. Eliot has characteristically slid out of
responsibility in the matter by means of his remark that *The Waste
Land* pleased people because of 'their own illusion of being dis-
illusioned'.[2] It seems to me that the essential, and very original,
method of his poem, and the peculiar sense of life that it mediates,
are such that they invite that very response, and get it from the
most considerable critics as well as from young cynics.

---

[1] This phrase is put in inverted commas to draw attention to the fact that it is
now invariably used to mean 'someone who has stayed at school till 18 and gone
on to higher education'; this implies that all the rest, with their *ten years* of schooling, are uneducated.

[2] 'Thoughts after Lambeth', in *Selected Essays* (1951 ed.), 368.

195

Before considering the poem itself it will be as well to quote a case of that view of the modern 'plight' which the poem has licensed or seemed sufficient grounds for. Summing up the social state of affairs which he sees as the basis for the poem's 'rich disorganisation', F. R. Leavis writes:

> The traditions and cultures have mingled, and the historical imagination makes the past contemporary; no one tradition can digest so great a variety of materials, and the result is a break-down of forms and the irrevocable loss of that sense of absoluteness which seems necessary to a robust culture.[1]

This is challenging in that it implies a more precisely-focused view of what modern rapid change has done to us than is usual in admirers of 'the organic community'. But consider what it leads on to:

> In the modern Waste Land
> > April is the cruellest month, breeding
> > Lilacs out of the dead land,
> but bringing no quickening to the human spirit. Sex here is sterile, breeding not life and fulfilment but disgust, accidia, and unanswerable questions. It is not easy to-day to accept the perpetuation and multiplication of life as ultimate ends.

(New Bearings, 93)

The logic of this is by no means consecutive; the critic is moving, with shifts that seem unconscious, between life and the poem treated as a true report on life. When he says that 'sex here is sterile', although the immediate reference of 'here' seems to be the 'world' of the poem, the quick shift to 'to-day', which must refer directly to actual life here and now, suggests that Leavis considers the experience in the poem a self-evident, perfectly acceptable version of the world we and the poet live in. But it is far from self-evident: consider the extraordinary body of evidence needed before one could begin to consider whether sex here and now is sterile. . . . Yet it is typical of those who have taken *The Waste Land* as a true image of our civilisation that they seem not even conscious of the difficulties of seeing whole cultures clearly. Is this enormous inadvertence their own? or can it be laid also at the door of the poem itself?

The artistic range of the poem is extraordinary and it does impress us as embodying–compared, say, with Pound's *Cantos*–

[1] *New Bearings in English Poetry* (1950 ed.), 90-1.

rich and intensely-felt resources both of experience and of other
literature. From the variety of methods one stands out: that way
of running on, with no marked break and therefore with a dead-
pan ironical effect, from one area of experience, one place or time
or speech or style or social class to another. The changing view and
valuation of the woman protagonist in section II, 'A Game of
Chess', is created by the modulations of the style, which are at first
slight and dependent on our literary knowledge. The woman is
imaged as Cleopatra but a Cleopatra who lives indoors, immured
in expensive furnishings:

> The Chair she sat in, like a burnished throne,
> Glowed on the marble, where the glass
> Held up by standards wrought with fruited vines
> From which a golden Cupidon peeped out
> (Another hid his eyes behind his wing)
> Doubled the flame of sevenbranched candelabra
> Reflecting light upon the table as
> The glitter of her jewels rose to meet it. . . .

By this point she has become Belinda from *The Rape of the Lock*,
living in a world of 'things', make-up, clothes, décor of all kinds:
the objects of conspicuous consumption. But the modern poet does
not have a mocking relish for the woman, as did Pope:

> This casket India's glowing gems unlocks,
> And all Arabia breathes from yonder box.
> The tortoise here and elephant unite,
> Transform'd to combs, the speckled and the white.
> Here files of pins extend their shining rows,
> Puffs, powders, patches, Bibles, billet-doux.

There is no equivalent for the *billet-doux* in Eliot; the woman herself
does not appear until 35 lines have passed. She is obliterated by
her surroundings. By the end of the passage she is not even Belinda,
moving with assurance in her idle and luxurious *milieu*. She is
neurotic and cannot stand being alone with her own thoughts, yet
they are all she has, for the man whom we must suppose to be
standing there while she talks ('"My nerves are bad tonight. Yes,
bad"') never actually replies. The shift into overt breakdown is
given in the modulation from a quite richly literary diction –

> Under the firelight, under the brush, her hair
> Spread out in fiery points
> Glowed into words, then would be savagely still –

to a comparatively unprocessed modern spoken English (though the colloquial phrases are cunningly fitted into a staccato quatrain):

> 'My nerves are bad to-night. Yes, bad. Stay with me.
> 'Speak to me. Why do you never speak. Speak.
>   'What are you thinking of? What thinking? What?
> 'I never know what you are thinking. Think.'

The effect is of landing up with final disenchantment amidst the stalemate of personal experience as it is right now.

There is then a change of social class; the fact that this section of the poem spans the gamut from wealth to poverty implies that the poet is *covering* society. Expensive living ('The hot water at ten./ And if it rains, a closed car at four') gives way to ordinary ('When Lil's husband got demobbed, I said . . .'). Life is fruitless here too, and once again the poet conveys his sense that this life is emptied of spirit and value by modulations from unprocessed speech to 'art-speech'. The working-class women in the pub talk about false teeth, abortions, sexual rivalry between the wives of Great War soldiers in a colloquial English that sprawls over and breaks down such formal pattern as there is. The poet does not intrude until the closing line:

> Goonight Bill. Goonight Lou. Goonight May. Goonight.
> Ta ta. Goonight. Goonight.
> Good night, ladies, good night, sweet ladies, good night,
>   good night.

'Sweet ladies'–the irony is, to say the least, obvious. As well as the effect of 'sweet' itself there is the echo of the innocently hearty student song (which seems more relevant than Ophelia's mad snatch in *Hamlet*). The effect is identical with the use made of Goldsmith's ditty from *The Vicar of Wakefield* at the end of the dreary seduction in section III:

> 'Well now that's done: and I'm glad it's over.'
> When lovely woman stoops to folly and
> Paces about her room again, alone,
> She smoothes her hair with automatic hand,
> And puts a record on the gramophone.

This technique is typical of the transitions of register and tone and of the collocation of material from different cultures which are the method of *The Waste Land*. They seem to me to be unsatisfactory in two ways. The irony is just ordinary sarcasm, the simple juxtaposing of messy actuality and flattering description, as in a common phrase like 'You're a pretty sight'. The pub women and the typist are made so utterly sour and *un*lovely that the poet's innuendoes, his insistence on what has already become obvious by concrete means, has no other function than to imply his own superiority, especially his skill at extracting aesthetic subtleties from such gross materials. Secondly, using earlier literatures to embody the better way of life which is the poet's ideal depends on a view of the past which is not made good in the poem (not that it could be) and which the reader may very well not share—unless he is himself already convinced that civilisation is degenerate. Consider some further instances. The Thames as it is now is evoked at the start of section III:

> Sweet Thames, run softly till I end my song.
> The river bears no empty bottles, sandwich papers,
> Silk handkerchiefs, cardboard boxes, cigarette ends
> Or other testimony of summer nights. . . .

(Note the pointed but prudishly, or suggestively, tacit hint at contraceptives.) For us to respond as the poet means, we have to take it, on the basis of a single line from Spenser, that Elizabethan England was all pure rivers and courtly ceremony. The same sense arises from the lyrical passage which is meant to parallel the Rhinemaidens' song from *Götterdämerung*. Modern:

> The river sweats
> Oil and tar
> The barges drift
> With the turning tide
> Red sails
> Wide
> To leeward, swing on the heavy spar.
> The barges wash
> Drifting logs
> Down Greenwich reach
> Past the Isle of Dogs.

Renaissance:

> Elizabeth and Leicester
> Beating oars
> The stern was formed
> A gilded shell
> Red and gold
> The brisk swell
> Rippled both shores

Southwest wind
Carried down stream
The peal of bells
White towers.

The poet's intention is clear: modern life does nothing but sully what was once gracious, lovely, blithe, ceremonious, natural.

It is true that the poet's comparative view of old and modern culture is not quite one-sided. As Hugh Kenner has suggested, it may not be implied that Spenser's nymph-world 'ever existed except as an ideal fancy' of the Elizabethan poet's;[1] and as Cleanth Brooks has suggested, the Elizabeth passage is meant to have 'a sort of double function': historically, Elizabeth on her barge flirted so wantonly with Leicester, in the presence of the Spanish bishop De Quadra, that Cecil at last suggested that as there was a bishop on the spot they might as well be married there and then (Froude's *Elizabeth*, quoted in Eliot's note to line 279). In Brooks's view, the passage 'reinforces the general contrast between Elizabethan magnificence and modern sordidness: in the Elizabethan age love for love's sake has some meaning and therefore some magnificence. But the passage gives something of an opposed effect too: the same sterile love, emptiness of love, obtained in this period too: Elizabeth and the typist are alike as well as different.'[2] But *in the poetry* there is not a single touch that attributes sterility to the Elizabethans. Their life is perfectly handsome, imbued with vitality, unspoiled. Brooks's 'opposed effect' exists only in that note; and in so far as the note has any status in the work of art it can only be to make us suspect that Eliot, noticing the blatancy of his own *parti pris*, has tried to bring some objectivity in by the back door. Viewing the poem as a whole, can it be questioned that it is bygone magnificence that is given the advantage? and is this not an absurdly partial view of our culture—groundlessly idealising about the old, warped by revulsion from the modern? If we desire magnificence (and admiration for it seems to die hard), modern life can readily supply it: consider how eloquent a lyric could be written to honour the olympian offices and factories of General Motors at Detroit. Conversely, if one thinks of the filth, brutality, and superstition that were common in town and village four centuries ago,

---

[1] *The Invisible Poet: T. S. Eliot* (New York, 1959), 165.
[2] '*The Waste Land*: An Analysis' in *Southern Review* (Louisiana State University, 1937), III, 1, 123.

one realises how fatuous it is to make flat contrasts between then and now. History, reality, are being manipulated to fit an over-weening but unadmitted personal bias, for all the show of impersonal and carefully specific social coverage.

This cultural warp has its counterpart in the poet's way of presenting private life, for example the intercourse between the typist and her man friend. In this most cunningly-managed episode one is induced to feel, by means of the fastidiously detached diction and movement, that a scene part commonplace part debased is totally nasty. It is a much more intimate meeting between people than Eliot presents anywhere else in his work, and here is the style he finds for it:

> He, the young man carbuncular, arrives,
> A small house agent's clerk, with one bold stare,
> One of the low on whom assurance sits
> As a silk hat on a Bradford millionaire.
> The time is now propitious, as he guesses,
> The meal is ended, she is bored and tired,
> Endeavours to engage her in caresses
> Which still are unreproved, if undesired.
> Flushed and decided, he assaults at once;
> Exploring hands encounter no defence;
> His vanity requires no response,
> And makes a welcome of indifference.

The unfeeling grossness of the experience is held off at the finger-tips by the analytic, unphysical diction, for example the business-letter English of 'Endeavours to engage her in caresses', and by the movement, whose even run is not interrupted by the violence of what is 'going on'. The neat assimilation of such life to a formal verse paragraph recalls Augustan modes. But if one thinks of the sexual passages in Dryden or Pope—the passage about the 'Imperial Whore' in Dryden's version of Juvenal's sixth satire, or even the one about the unfeeling Chloe in Pope's 'Of the Characters of Women'—one realises that the Augustans did not stand off from the physical with anything like Eliot's distaste. His style is carefully impersonal, it enumerates with fastidious care the sordid details:

> On the divan are piled (at night her bed)
> Stockings, slippers, camisoles, and stays.

But here one has doubts. This is being given as a typically comfort-less modern apartment, the scene of a life that lacks the right pace, the right sociableness, the right instinctive decency for it to merit the name of civilisation. But the touch in the second line feels not quite certain: is the heavily careful technique with which the line is built up not too contrived for the very ordinary, the actually quite neutral, habit that it is satirising? When we come to 'carbuncular'—an adjective which, placed after its noun and resounding in its slow movement and almost ornamental air, is deliberately out of key with the commonplace life it refers to—we begin to feel that Eliot's conscious literariness is being used, wittingly or not, more to hold at arm's length something which he personally shudders at than to convey a poised criticism of behaviour.[1] There is a spasm of revulsion in 'carbuncular'. It is disdainful, and the dislike is disproportionately strong for its object. Queasy emotions of the writer's seem to be at work, ones that come out also in that virulent line from 'Mr Eliot's Sunday Morning Service'—

> The young are red and pustular.

Of a piece with this is the arrant snobbery of the passage—so arrant that it seems never to have been noticed.

> A small house agent's clerk, with one bold stare,
> One of the low on whom assurance sits
> As a silk hat on a Bradford millionaire.

'He is a nobody—a mere clerk—a clerk to a *small* house agent. Who is he to look assured?' If we were to tackle this passage on its own terms, which are the terms of naked class prejudice, we might well ask what warrants Eliot in implicitly uniting himself with some class 'above' the provincial bourgeoisie: could it be the fact that he himself was then working in a bank—a *merchant* bank—a *London* merchant bank? But this is merely invidious. What is most important is that a poet of Eliot's fineness should have been able to allow himself a phrase so gross, so unthinking and indiscriminate, as 'One of the low'. It is a class of idiom that belongs, and should have been left, to the Lord Chesterfields or the members of the Athenaeum in its 'great' days.

---

[1] Compare Lawrence's classic analysis of Mann and Flaubert: 'Thomas Mann, like Flaubert, feels vaguely that he has in him something finer than ever physical life revealed. Physical life is a disordered corruption against which he can fight with only one weapon, his fine aesthetic sense, his feeling for beauty, for perfection, for a certain fitness which soothes him, and gives him an inner pleasure, however corrupt the stuff of life may be. . . . And so, with real suicidal intention, like Flaubert's, he sits, a last too-sick disciple, reducing himself grain by grain to the statement of his own disgust, patiently, self-destructively, so that his statement at least may be perfect in a world of corruption.' (*Phoenix*, 312.)

As we have seen, the passage ends,

> When lovely woman stoops to folly and
> Paces about her room again, alone,
> She smoothes her hair with automatic hand,
> And puts a record on the gramophone.

The nerveless movement, the ordinariness of the detail are finely managed. And the human poverty of the scene has never been in doubt. It is the writer's means of conveying his valuation of it that is objectionable. One may or may not agree that modern civilisation has its own kinds of health. But one must surely take exception to a method which seeks its effects through an irony which is no more than pat sarcasm. It is amazing that Leavis should speak of 'delicate collocations'[1] when the contrasts are regularly so facile in their selection of old grandeur and modern squalor, so palpably loaded by a desire to find nothing worthy in the present way of life. To put the matter in terms referring directly to life: if, as Brooks says, 'the same sterile love, emptiness of love, obtained in this period [the Elizabethan] too', then why does the critique work consistently against the modern? When Leavis says that 'Sex here is sterile', does he really mean that love between men and women has deteriorated as a whole? and if so, how does he know? (One remembers similar extraordinary suggestions about orgasm then and now in *Lady Chatterley's Lover*.) The historian tells us that in Tudor England,

> Wife-beating was a recognised right of man, and was practised without shame by high as well as low. Similarly, the daughter who refused to marry the gentleman of her parents' choice was liable to be locked up, beaten, and flung about the room, without any shock being inflicted on public opinion. Marriage was not an affair of personal affection but of family avarice, particularly in the 'chivalrous' upper classes.[2]

But can we draw from this item conclusions about the comparative quality of life then and now? We surely can not, for the fundamental reason that societies with many millions of people represent a mass of experience far too great to be dealt with by summary or partial judgements. Comparison of cultures is either impossible – a self-defeating exercise – or else possible only by specific fields. The question remains why critics and other readers have surrendered so gratefully to an almost morbidly despairing view of our civilisation,

---

[1] *New Bearings in English Poetry*, 112.
[2] G. M. Trevelyan, *A Shortened History of England* (1959 ed.), 196.

why (in Edmund Wilson's words) *The Waste Land* 'enchanted and devastated a whole generation'.[1]

The critical response is seen at its most wanton in Hugh Kenner's reading of the pub scene:

> If we move from the queens to the pawns, we find low life no more free or natural, equally obsessed with the denial of nature, artificial teeth, chemically procured abortions, the speaker and her interlocutor battening fascinated at second-hand on the life of Lil and her Albert, Lil and Albert interested only in spurious ideal images of one another.[2]

'Battening fascinated at second-hand', etc., means no more than 'listening with interest to the story of someone else's experiences'. Kenner's heavy scorn comes from the general atmosphere of moral depression generated by the poem rather than from anything concretely established in the dramatic speech of that scene—here the critic's sourness outdoes the poet's. The reference to false teeth, lumped with an injurious type of abortion, as though false teeth were not simply an admirable achievement of medical science in giving comfort where nature has broken down, is a glaring case of that blind dislike of science which has become the occupational disease of the literary intellectual. It is primitivist; and it thoughtlessly ignores the experience involved.

Faced with this kind of argument that challenges the poet by relating him to the life he is imaging, the critics now riposte subtly that it is naive to 'check' art against life. A recent writer quotes Kenner's extraordinary suggestion that the small house-agent's clerk would probably have been honoured to find himself so magnificently stylised by that word 'carbuncular' and goes on to argue that this is the way art works: what matters is not the life we are being made to see anew but the artefact that results, which is sufficient unto itself and no longer relates significantly to what it was 'of' or 'about' in the first place.[3] The one virtue of this view is that it warns us against referring back to life too quickly, before we have allowed the art to affect us fully in its own special way. But to speak as though the referring back should never happen at all is wilfully to curtail our experience of art by denying its manifest

---

[1] *Axel's Castle*, 1931 (1961 ed.), 96.

[2] *The Invisible Poet*, 156.

[3] W. H. Pritchard, 'Reading *The Waste Land* Today': *Essays In Criticism*, XIX, 2 (1969), 185-6.

rich relevance to our actual living. We have heard Pritchard's argument before—in the mouth of Loerke, the sculptor in *Women in Love*, with his brutal and overbearing will. Since Pritchard calls me a 'post-Lawrentian' (which he does not mean as a compliment), I will quote a bit of the classic debate from the 'Continental' chapter of Lawrence's novel:

> 'Why,' said Ursula, 'did you make the horse so stiff? It is as stiff as a block.'
>
> . . . '*Wissen Sie*,' he said, with an insulting patience and condescension in his voice, 'that horse is a certain *form*, part of a whole form. It is part of a work of art, a piece of form.'
>
> . . . 'But why does he have this idea of a horse?' she said. 'I know it is his idea. I know it is a picture of himself, really—'
>
> Loerke snorted with rage.
>
> 'A picture of myself!' he repeated, in derision. '*Wissen Sie, gnädige Frau*, that is a *Kunstwerk*, a work of art. It is a work of art, it is a picture of nothing, of absolutely nothing. It has nothing to do with anything but itself, it has no relation with the everyday world of this and other, there is no connection between them, absolutely none, they are two different and distinct planes of existence. . . . Do you see, you *must not* confuse the relative work of action, with the absolute world of art.'
>
> . . . 'As for your world of art and your world of reality,' she replied, 'you have to separate the two, because you can't bear to know what you are. You can't bear to realise what a stock, stiff, hide-bound brutality you *are* really, so you say "it's the world of art". The world of art is only the truth about the real world, that's all—but you are too far gone to see it.'

Leavis's view of *The Waste Land* is almost the opposite of Kenner and Pritchard's sophisticated perversities. He knows very well that what Eliot is offering is a view of the real world[1]; it is one that he

---

[1] We have to note that Leavis's view of *The Waste Land* is no longer fully represented by *New Bearings*. By 1966 he had decided that it had been going too far to believe 'that the poem *was* what it offered itself as being: an achieved and representatively significant work—significance here being something to be discussed in terms of the bankruptcy of civilisation, the "modern consciousness", the "modern sense of the human situation", *la condition humaine*, and so on . . . the treatment of the theme of the dried-up springs and the failure of life hasn't the breadth of significance claimed and asserted by the title and the apparatus of notes. The distinctive attitude towards, the feeling about, the relations between men and women that predominates in the poem is the highly personal one we know so well from the earlier poems; the symbolic Waste Land makes itself felt too much as Thomas Stearns Eliot's.' (F. R. Leavis and Q. D. Leavis, *Lectures in America*, 1969, 40-1)

Since this is *incompatible* with much in *New Bearings*, it is to be hoped that it will be at least as widely read.

shares. A key term in that part of *New Bearings in English Poetry* (as in his early editorials in *Scrutiny*) is 'continuity':

> In considering our present plight we have also to take account of the incessant rapid change that characterises the Machine Age. The result is a breach of continuity and the uprooting of life. This last metaphor has a peculiar aptness, for what we are witnessing today is the final uprooting of the immemorial ways of life, of life rooted in the soil. . . . There are ways in which it is possible to be too conscious; and to be so is, as a result of the break-up of forms and the loss of axioms noted above, one of the troubles of the present age. . . .
>
> *(New Bearings,* 91, 93-4)

It would be foolish indeed not to recognise that the upheavals started by the Industrial Revolution undermined, and were liable to demoralise, masses of those people who were forced out of the countryside and drifted into the towns. But there are ways and ways of viewing this change–defeatist ways and constructive ways. The description of the old village culture that opens Engels's *Condition of the Working Class in England in 1844*[1] is closely akin to the main line of *Scrutiny* on social matters. Both belong to the central tradition of humane protest at the harrow of industrialism. But realisation of such suffering and social deterioration may lead on to a practical will to reconstruct, using the new social means, or it may lead to a really helpless fixation on the past in recoil from the raw difficulties and uncomelinesses of the life around us. To assume on little or loaded evidence that the older culture is the finer is to head in a defeatist direction. Of course a critic cannot give full grounds for his larger historical assumptions in a book about modern poetry. But if we are to keep our thought grounded, we must admit that the converse could be reasonably stated to every advantage that Leavis sees in the 'organic' culture. Those who refer warmly to 'immemorial' ways of life should realise how cramped a range of vocations they offered. To be sure there was variety in work,[2] but the village life also ground down people cruelly by the narrowness of its outlets: both Burns and Gorky rankled despairingly at its monotony.[3] When axioms are mentioned it should be remembered that they expressed fixed habits which held human possibilities within unaltering bounds. I said before that it is futile to attempt

[1] Marx and Engels, *On Britain*, 35-8.
[2] See above, ch. 5, 114-5.
[3] This is documented in my *Scottish Literature and the Scottish People*, 82-95.

overall comparisons between older and contemporary cultures. This is partly because we are now where we are; we have the means we now have; it is these alone that we can use. Therefore the only course that is of any use is to co-operate with the helpful present trends. No one saw more deeply into the anti-human effects of industrial labour than Marx; equally he knew that this was the very means, the only means, by which we might win through to the *new* good life. This balance of possibilities is repeatedly expressed in *Capital*:

> Modern Industry, indeed, compels society, under penalty of death, to replace the detail-worker of today, crippled by life-long repetition of one and the same trivial operation, and thus reduced to the mere fragment of a man, by the fully developed individual, fit for a variety of labours, ready to face any change of production, and to whom the different social functions he performs, are but so many modes of giving free scope to his own natural and acquired powers.

As a step towards this he then mentions technical and agricultural schools; to these we can now add comprehensive education and the Workers' Control and work enlargement movements.[1] And again:

> However terrible and disgusting the dissolution, under the capitalist system, of the old family ties may appear, nevertheless, modern industry, by assigning as it does an important part in the process of production, outside the domestic sphere, to women, to young persons, and to children of both sexes, creates a new economical foundation for a higher form of the family and of the relations between the sexes . . . the fact of the collective working group being composed of individuals of both sexes and all ages, must necessarily, under suitable conditions, become a source of human development. . . .[2]

This has behind it a knowledge of the modern forms of life that could hardly have been more abundant or exact, quite different from Eliot's aesthetic revulsion at canals and gasworks.

The Waste Land, then, seems to me to work essentially against life–literally to make it harder for us to live. The range of opinions it mobilises, that come welling up in response to it, are all negative. This is as true of the thought behind it as of its social reference. In

---

[1] See also below, ch. 13, 284-5.
[2] Vol. I, Part IV, ch. 15, section 9, 534, 536.

the final section Eliot uses the philosophy of F. H. Bradley. The
lines

> I have heard the key
> Turn in the door once and turn once only
> We think of the key, each in his prison
> Thinking of the key, each confirms a prison

are glossed by Eliot from Bradley's *Appearance and Reality*:

> My external sensations are no less private to myself than are
> my thoughts or my feelings. In either case my experience falls
> within my own circle, a circle closed on the outside; and, with
> all its elements alike, every sphere is opaque to the others
> which surrounds it. . . . In brief, regarded as an existence
> which appears in a soul, the whole world for each is peculiar
> and private to that soul.
>
> (Note to line 411)

One recognises here that barren extreme of positivism that denies
we can have knowledge of anything other than our own sense-data.
To say what must suffice here: if our sensations, thoughts, and
feelings were perfectly private and the sphere of each person's life
sealed off, how could it be that speech and literature themselves are
intelligible? and intelligible so fully and intimately that to reach
understanding with a person, to catch the spark or glow in the
other's eye that signals shared experience, or to 'get' a piece of
writing, can seem to take us inside another existence? That the
question of whether one mind can get through to another should
even have arisen seems a perversion of thought, and one that must
have a cause: perhaps the anxiety of the intellectual to stake out a
position for himself in which he will be inviolable by that world
whose social growth more and more threatens his position as one of
a small minority with 'finer feelings' and a monopoly of the arts.[1]

The obscurity of *The Waste Land* is itself significant. This is not
at all to condone the philistinism of those who have regarded it as
wilfully obscure. The point is that it can never become popular
reading as other, mostly earlier important work has done, for
example Burns, Byron, Dickens, and Lawrence. On the issue of
'minority culture' which this raises Leavis writes: 'that the public
for it is limited is one of the symptoms of the state of culture which
produced the poem. Works expressing the finest consciousness of the
age in which the word "highbrow" has become current are almost

---

[1] See also above, ch. 8, 175.

inevitably such as to appeal only to a tiny minority' (*New Bearings*, 104). The argument that follows is dubious at many points. In the first place, Lawrence expressed many sides of the 'finest consciousness of the age' and he has been read in cheap editions by the million (as have Gorky and Sholokhov in the U.S.S.R. and James T. Farrell in the United States).[1] The usual obstinately pessimistic reply is that 'They only read Lawrence for the sex, or the love story'. But this is only reaching for another stick to beat the times, for is it not good that a major writer should have devoted himself to the universal subjects of love and sex? Leavis goes on to say that the idea that the poem's obscurity is symptomatic of our cultural condition 'amounts to an admission that there must be something limited about the kind of artistic achievement possible in our time'. But if this were so, how account for the work of Lawrence, or of Brecht in Germany? Leavis's question 'how large in any age has the minority been that has really comprehended the masterpieces?' contains an equivocation–'really'. Of course if one sets the highest standard, 'real' (that is, full) comprehension will be attained by few; but if the numbers of even the total public reached are small, as has happened with Eliot's work, then there is indeed a significant difference between its meaningfulness and appeal for readers and that which the main novelists (from Tolstoy and Hardy to Farrell and Sholokhov) have regularly won for themselves. *The Waste Land*, in short, cannot accurately be called the representative work of the present age. To make it so implies a defeated view of our condition and indeed of the foreseeable possibilities for mankind.

What has been made of the poem illustrates two other important issues. The critics have had to meet the charge that it is a dead end, literarily and morally. 'The poet of *The Waste Land*,' Edmund Wilson writes, 'was too serious to continue with the same complacence as some of his contemporaries inhabiting that godforsaken desert. It was certain he would not stick at that point, and one watched him to see what he would do.'[2] This implies a proper distinction between Eliot's quality of art and that of Pound's *Cantos*,

[1] For documentation on the huge popular public for the best literature in a socialist society, see the following chapter, 223-4.

[2] *Axel's Castle*, 105. Compare Leavis: 'So complete and vigorous a statement of the Waste Land could hardly ... forecast an exhausted and hopeless sojourn there' (*New Bearings*, 113-4).

Joyce's *Finnegans Wake*, or MacDiarmid's later long poems, which all come recognisably from that same line of art distorted by the break-up of cultural forms. *The Waste Land* does not cut life into bits and juggle them into patterns for the sake of the intricacy or to create a significance known only to the manipulator. At the same time there turns out to be little that Wilson and Leavis can plead convincingly when they have so say what way beyond the Waste Land Eliot did find. Leavis quotes some bracing sermons from the *Criterion* where Eliot invokes 'a tendency–discernible even in art–toward a higher and clearer conception of Reason, and a more severe and serene control of the emotions by Reason' and 'the generation which is beginning to turn its attention to an athleticism, a *training*, of the soul as severe and ascetic as the training of the body of a runner' (*New Bearings*, 114). The vague 'dedication' of this is either a throwback to the more serious of the *fin de siècle* writers, notably Yeats, in their Hellenic or religiose vein or else it is a dilute version of that cult of the ascetic and strenuous favoured by the philosophers who were then beginning to provide a kind of high-minded gloss for fascism. The abstractness, the lack of any specific social reference, typifies Eliot's inveterate drift away from anything actually present in society from whch one might conceivably move forwards in a helpful way.[1]

The wider affiliations of the defeatism come out in the agreement Eliot and Leavis reach on 'eastern Europe'. The note introducing the final section of the poem says: 'In the first part of Part V three themes are employed: the journey to Emmaus, the approach to the Chapel Perilous (see Miss Weston's book) and the present decay of eastern Europe.' This is very bland. The final phrase has that characteristic air of stating the unanswerable–he could explain further if he wished but he does not condescend to. But will it bear examination? Whether or not one approved of Bela Kun's Communist government in Hungary or Lenin's in the Soviet Union,

---

[1] What Eliot moved forward to was Anglo-Catholicism in religion and 'royalism' in politics. His slogans to this effect are too notorious to need detailing here; what has not yet been worked out is the related change in his poetry. I cannot but agree with George Orwell in finding the work from *Ash Wednesday* to the *Quartets* painfully thin, dry, and brainspun in many places and in seeing this as due to their being based on untenable beliefs (see Orwell's review of the first three *Quartets*, reprinted in *The Collected Essays, Journalism and Letters of George Orwell*, 2, *My Country Right or Left*, ed. Sonia Orwell and Ian Angus, 1970 ed., 272-5, 277-9). But those poems are much too remarkable and complex to be dealt with here.

could they be said with any exactitude to represent decay? would not the most adverse account have to allow that they stood for the brutal upsurge of new ways of life? Of course Eliot may well be pitying the plumage; he had found it natural to open his poem with the experiences in exile of some aristocratic *émigrés*:

> Bin gar keine Russin, stamm' aus Litauen, echt deutsch.
> And when we were children, staying at the arch-duke's,
> My cousin's. . . .

But if decay was rife anywhere it was in the West–in Germany ravaged by the *Freikorps* and the murder gangs (connived at by the police), or in Italy which in the year of *The Waste Land* came under the rule of the man who styled himself *un apostolo di violenza* and dismissed liberty as a 'more or less putrid goddess'.[1] Drafting his poem in Margate and Lausanne during the autumn of 1921,[2] Eliot might well have been bewildered by the conflicting news from 'eastern Europe'. Ten years later the historical record had become clear enough, yet Leavis could still argue, commenting on the lines from Part V–

> Who are those hooded hordes swarming
> Over endless plains, stumbling in cracked earth
> Ringed by the flat horizon only–

that the hordes 'are not merely Russians, suggestively related to the barbarian invaders of civilisation; they are also humanity' (*New Bearings*, 104). 'Suggestively' covers a wilful indifference to the facts. *The Waste Land* was conceived during the final year of that war of intervention during which the civilised armies of Britain, America, France, and Japan had invaded Russia and caused slaughter and famine by waging war on twenty-three fronts. If there were barbarous incursions from the East anywhere in those years, it was on the part of the Japanese, who had invaded the young republic 'amid scenes of wanton violence and destruction', or the Rumanian armies whom the Allies had encouraged to 'pillage and destroy' in revolutionary Hungary.[3]

It seems that there is no end to the backward-looking views for

---

[1] Alan Bullock, *Hitler: A Study in Tyranny* (1962 ed.), 63; William L. Shirer, *The Rise and Fall of the Third Reich* (1964 ed.), 51-2; Christopher Hibbert, *Mussolini* (1965 ed.), 23, 62.

[2] Kenner, *The Invisible Poet*, 145.

[3] E. H. Carr, *The Bolshevik Revolution, 1917-1923*, I (1966 ed.), 361; R. Palme Dutt, *World Politics, 1918-1936* (1936), 45-6.

which the poem supplies confirmation. Surely it is time that it was seen for what it is—not as a centrally wise diagnosis of 'mass civilisation' and its ills but as the acme of conservatism made into art. It should be placed along with Dryden's *Absalom and Achitophel* as one of the very few remarkable works of literary art in our language to have been conceived, framed, and pointed expressly to convey a politically reactionary view of life.

CHAPTER 10

The New Poetry of Socialism

OPINION in this country is so accustomed to treating politics as the affair of the smart operators, mad Continentals, and perhaps understandably rebellious peoples in the 'underdeveloped countries' that it isn't surprising to find writers who with one hand profess a commitment to socialism while with the other, in a spirit of ostentatious honesty, they write articles that play down the inspiration which socialism can be shown to have been to artists for the past century. Politics as a force bearing on literature is commonly imaged as a whale that swallows writers whole. Left-Socialists should be able to think more clearly than that. Yet one of the few sustained pieces in recent years that discusses literature under the aspect of political history, Gabriel Pearson's 'Romanticism and Contemporary Poetry',[1] seems to fall over backwards to avoid allowing collective values any integral part in literary sensibility.

He starts from a point of literary history, which I accept, that romanticism developed out of the disruption of the older cultures in Western Europe that had felt themselves to be 'sustained either by unified social or by religious sanctions'. This thesis is familiar from such classics as the essays in which Arnold discusses the Romantic's want of knowledge and ideas or Eliot's essays that touch on the 'dissociation of sensibility'.[2] Pearson, however, goes much further than earlier writers. He argues that the dissociation of sensibility, with its effect of laying acute stress on the more private emotions, is *still the major factor* in making our poetry what it is. And he will not have it that *any other valid basis for poetry has yet emerged.* If it were true that socialism, Marxism, communism had not yet brought into being any distinctive forms or styles, in the

---

[1] *New Left Review*, 16 (July/August 1962).
[2] See especially the essay on Blake: 'one remarks about the Puritan mythology its thinness . . . about Blake's supernatural territories, as about the supposed ideas that dwell there, we cannot help commenting on a certain meanness of culture.' (*Selected Essays*, 321)

several generations that have passed since the First International or the October Revolution, then indeed we would have to search the heart of our ideology and see whether there is something fundamentally anti-human in our beliefs and our practice.

The justification for my assuming that romanticism may fairly be set over against the collective values of socialism lies in Pearson's view of romanticism as self-regarding:

> [The romantic poem] does not consist in a series of observations about the world. Instead, the poet tries to watch himself observing the world, tries to catch himself in the act of experiencing. This is why so much romantic poetry appears not only entirely egocentric, but also reflexive, as though the poems always wanted to be experiences of experiences, or poems about poems.

He also asserts that 'all worthwhile modern poetry is romantic'. This is a statement which I would hope no reader of poetry, whether socialist or not, would allow to pass without testing it against the work of Bertolt Brecht and of Hugh MacDiarmid. Brecht is known for his 'alienation-effect', his effort to make an art which did not invite the identification of the reader or viewer, did not tempt him with any emotional luxury, but tried rather to *show*— to present life as it is in a way that deliberately provoked him into reaching an opinion of the 'case' before him. He wanted the theatre audience to say, not 'Yes, I have felt like that too—Just like me—It's only natural—It'll never change—The sufferings of this man appal me, because they are inescapable—That's great art; it all seems the most obvious thing in the world—I weep when they weep, I laugh when they laugh', but rather 'I'd never have thought it—That's not the way—That's extraordinary, hardly believable—It's got to stop—The sufferings of this man appal me, because they are unnecessary—That's great art; nothing obvious in it—I laugh when they weep, I weep when they laugh.'[1] MacDiarmid's corresponding stress on the objective consisted, in the first part of his career, of his synthesising a new poetic language that owed nothing to the nineteenth-century sentimental style and, in the second part of his career, his attempt to stretch poetry (as Pound had done in the *Cantos*) so that it could take in a great range of modern knowledge.

---

[1] 'Theatre for Pleasure or Theatre for Instruction', *c.* 1935: *Brecht on Theatre*, 71.

The poetry these writers produced was as different as could be from what Pearson regards, not only as the finest and most typically modern poetry, but almost as the supreme art. 'The romantic lyric,' he says, 'is superbly fitted for a fully authentic rendering of experience,' and he then dismisses in a few sentences the powers of the film, the play, the novel to do any such thing. Near the end he again links his touchstone of 'authenticity'–'Such an intensely personal, intimately autobiographical poetry is unimaginable before our century'–with his assertion that this is *the* modern literature, 'the really unique contribution of our century'. The poetry of MacDiarmid and Brecht is not at all intensely personal (in Pearson's sense), they don't offer us their intimate autobiographies, and both were Communists who found their way to a distinctively Communist poetry. In their work, if anywhere, should be the evidence that counters Pearson's claim for romanticism and his corresponding assertion that socialist realism has been, poetically, barren.

The vital factor common to Brecht and MacDiarmid may be approached in this way: Leavis has published several essays–which should be classics of critical theory–analysing poems for their 'reality', 'sincerity', and 'emotional quality', values closely akin to Pearson's 'authenticity'. In one of them, a prime example of a *sound* or genuine emotional quality is Scott's short lyric 'Proud Maisie'. Leavis argues that one excellence of it, in comparison with Tennyson's 'Break, break, break', is that it presents distinct particulars. These generate between them a strong effect, in which emotion plays a part. This emotion is not injected or larded-on from some unrealised inner feelings of the poet's–it belongs in and to the life that the poet has grasped and presented.[1] For my own argument it is significant that it should have been a poem in a folk mode that Leavis chose to exemplify this soundness. For MacDiarmid and Brecht were both masters of folk modes; they needed them in order to move beyond the post-Romantic impasse in poetry. The lyric in the hands of Tennyson, Rossetti, Dowson, the early Yeats had thinned down into the vehicle for a few dim moods. The folk modes, with their roots in an epoch before the rise of capitalism had brought about that split in the old 'unity of social and religious sanctions', not only offered a stylistic means of moving

---

[1] '"Thought" and Emotional Quality', in *Scrutiny*, XIII, 1 (Cambridge, spring 1945), 53.

out of the blurred emotions and crestfallen morale of the later Romantics; they also had the special function for Left writers that they could form a new link between literature and ordinary people with their still semi-oral culture.[1]

MacDiarmid came into his own as a poet by means of something close to pastiche. Folk songs, ballads, flytings (or stylised invective), the Burnsian domestic poem – all these he put to use in a lyric verse which is modern in that it is more idiosyncratic and more aware of concerns from abroad than the folk poetry yet is far less auto-biographical than the Keatsian type that Pearson has in mind. In a poem such as 'Focherty' (from *Penny Wheep*, 1926), which is about a brute of a farmer who steals the narrator's girl, we don't sense the least projection of some experience of the poet's. The stress is on the creation of outward character–

> His face is like a roarin' fire
> For love o' the barley-bree.
>
> . . . Blaefaced afore the throne o' God
> He'll get his fairin' yet–

> barley-bree, *whisky*: fairin', *desert*

and on satirical fantasy–

> He'll be like a bull in the sale-ring there,
> And I'll lauch lood to see,
> Till he looks up and canna mak' oot
> Whether it's God–or me![2]

After this first phase of short lyrics MacDiarmid began to use folk modes as the vehicle of themes that were large and public, objective, potentially progressive in their concern with Scotland as a 'distressed area', and certainly at the other pole from the autobiographical. His major theme from 1926 to 1930 was his growing sense during the years of deepening Slump that the Scottish community had become exhausted and second-rate, as in this lyric from his major long poem, *A Drunk Man Looks at the Thistle* (1926)–

> O Scotland is
> THE barren fig.
> Up, carles, up
> And roond it jig.

---

[1] See below, chaps. 12-14.
[2] Hugh MacDiarmid, *Selected Poems*, ed. David Craig and John Manson (1970), 24-5.

Auld Moses took
A dry stick and
Instantly it
Floo'ered in his hand.

Pu' Scotland up
And wha can say
It winna bud
And blossom tae.

A miracle's
Oor only chance.
Up, carles, up
And let us dance.[1]

Decidedly there is emotion here – a country-dance rhythm is used to suggest a frenzy of frustration, and the folk mode (drawing also on the abandon of American gospel singing) is indispensable to the effect because it leads the poet's own disillusion outwards to the experience of the beat-up community as a whole.

As MacDiarmid developed, this fusion of stylistic detachment and impassioned commitment to his own under-privileged people gave rise to the poetry of his creative peak, the years from 1930 to 1935 during which nationalism grew into the socialism of the two *Hymn to Lenin* volumes. In these, all kinds of backward-looking and undue inward-turning were left behind and the distinctive events and concerns of the twentieth century were at the centre of attention. For such work the poet needs a public manner, which he must manage without losing himself. Pearson is justifiably severe about the socialist-realist writing which is 'rhetorical in the bad sense, shouting for attention, behaving as though it had an audience at its feet, depending on some external doctrine that remains inert and unlived'. But a movement should not be judged by its grosser representatives. The following poem typifies MacDiarmid's use of the public mode commonly described as 'a hard-hitting speech' –

It is a God-damned lie to say that these
Saved, or knew, anything worth any man's pride.
They were professional murderers and they took
Their blood money and impious risks and died.
In spite of all their kind some elements of worth
With difficulty persist here and there on earth.[2]

[1] *Selected Poems*, 41-2.
[2] 'Another Epitaph for an Army of Mercenaries': *ibid.*, 100.

The rhythms of this poem are not attuned to the more delicate vibrations from the poet's inmost feelings. But they are distinctive; the poem is not at all characterless, not a blare from a loudspeaker. The completely sober tone, the way in which the phrases of that final sentence seem to measure themselves out scrupulously—such effects combine to suggest (with a precision no less real than the Keatsian sensitivity) an attitude of intentness, a rare dogged toughness, a refusal to evade the unpalatable. What comes over as a result is the *considered opinion* that war is both anti-human and avoidable, for, in that feeling of determination logically to state the case against war, we sense a grasp of the truth that war is explicable, the rational mind can grapple with it, and resistance is therefore possible.

Such poetry argues, it epitomises ideas[1], it is not mainly concerned to give us the feel of what it is 'like to be other people living in the world' (another formulation of Pearson's). MacDiarmid's passages on Lenin are usually in this best vein of his. They analyse, and hence (through that terse, deliberate movement) make us feel, those qualities of selflessness and complete concentration on the movement of the Russian people in history that gave Lenin his strategic mastery, his grasp of the need for revolution and of its processes—

> Lenin was like that wi' workin'-class life,
>   At hame wi't a'.
> His fause movements couldna' been fewer,
>   The best weaver earth ever saw.
> A' he'd to dae wi' moved intact,
>   Clean, clear, and exact.

So must the socialist poet be—

> But as for me in my fricative work
>   I ken fu' weel
> Sic an integrity's what I maun hae,
>   Indivisible, real,
> Woven owre close for the point o' a pin
>   Onywhere to win in.[2]

Unless one thinks nothing of such poetry, it cannot be denied that socialism here found a voice, one that was quite new in kind to a literature hitherto steeped in Romanticism and different also from the modernist reaction against it, which tended to be on exclusively literary grounds. It is true that MacDiarmid's poetry is

---

[1] The ideas in question are specified, with their sources, in the next chapter: see below, 239-40; the critical questions raised by MacDiarmid's tendency to opinionate in verse are discussed in my chapter in *Criticism in Action*, ed. Maurice Hussey (1969).   [2] 'The Seamless Garment': *Selected Poems*, 59, 61.

much stronger in giving the feel of militancy than in rendering its
content, for example the actual lives of the 'criminals of want, the
prisoners of starvation'. But this was a lack peculiar to MacDiarmid,
who is very much the pure intellectual; it is not at all inherent in
socialist realism. Brecht in his poetry caught more of the hard
and daily life of his time than any other poet one can think of,
and the new forms he needed drew on a still finer mastery than
MacDiarmid's of the folk modes.

Consider the poem 'Nannas Lied' from his adaptation of
Measure for Measure – Round Heads and Pointed Heads (1931-4). It is a
lyric, but not in the Keats/Pearson sense, for it is a song for the
stage. The emotion in it springs not from the personality of the
author but from the presentment of a distinct other character, with
her speech, her memories, given for themselves and not to project
the poet's ego. A prostitute is singing to the audience –

> Good Sirs, at seventeen summers
> I went to Lechery Fair
> And plenty of things it's taught me.
> Many a heartache,
> That's the chance you take.
> But I've wept many times in despair.
> (After all, I'm a human being, too.)
> Thank God it's all over with quickly,
> All the love and the grief we must bear.
> Where are the tears of yesterevening?
> Where are the snows of yesteryear?
>
> As the years pass by it gets easy,
> Easy in Lechery Fair.
> And you fill your arms with so many.
> But tenderness
> Grows strangely less
> When you spend with so little care.
> (For every stock runs out in the end.)
> Thank God, etc.
>
> And though you may learn your trade well,
> Learn it at Lechery Fair,
> Bartering lust for small change
> Is a hard thing to do.
> Well, it comes to you.
> But you don't grow younger there.
> (After all you can't stay seventeen forever.)
> Thank God, etc.[1]

[1] *Selected Poems*, 87.

The woman's life and attitude register themselves through a version of her own speech, with a supple modulation from one feeling or tone to another that demands speaking aloud. In its simplicity, naivety, and pathetic forced jauntiness the idiom scarcely departs from the clichés of casual speech and pop song, yet an extraordinarily wide range of feelings is conveyed: flickerings of desolate self-knowledge, suggested by checks and numbings of the rhythm, sighs of weariness, and then the aggressive emphasis of the old pro as she pulls herself together. It is an achievement precisely comparable with the Prologue to the *Wife of Bath's Tale* –

> But, lord Christ! whan that it remembreth me
> Up-on my yowthe, and on my jolitee,
> It tickleth me aboute myn herte rote.
> Unto this day it dooth myn herte bote
> That I have had my world as in my tyme.
> But age, allas! that al wol envenyme,
> Hath me biraft my beautee and my pith;
> Lat go, fare-wel, the devel go therwith!
> The flour is goon, ther is na-more to telle,
> The bren, as best I can, now moste I selle.[1]

Artless garrulity, seemingly untransmuted by literary art, is allowed to convey its own mixture of vivacity, homely advice, sudden bleak awareness of its own helplessness, all knit together by a stoicism that the poets have been able to respond to and fully to recreate because it so appeals to their own humanity.

The 'Nannas Lied' typifies the usual sort of recourse to a register (in the linguist's sense) from outside art poetry. 'Concerning the Infanticide, Marie Farrar' draws on quite another kind of register –

> Marie Farrar, born in April,
> No marks, a minor, rachitic, both parents dead,
> Allegedly, up to now without police record,
> Committed infanticide, it is said,
> As follows: in her second month, she says,
> With the aid of a barmaid she did her best
> To get rid of her child with two douches,
> Allegedly painful but without success . . .

If this were continued without variation, it would be only a satire on the law courts and police procedure. Brecht can also make this unemotional itemising mode plumb the agony of the woman –

> Between the latrine and her room, she says,
> Not earlier, the child began to cry until

[1] Lines 469-78.

It drove her mad so that she says
She did not cease to beat it with her fists
Blindly for sometime till it was still.
And then she took the body to her bed
And kept it with her there all through the night:
When morning came she hid it in the shed.
But you, I beg you, check your wrath and scorn
For man needs help from every creature born.[1]

It is not only the subject-matter that is socialist (concerned with the wretched of the earth), it is also the style, with its iron restraint that yet suggests no chilly aloofness on the poet's part (compare Eliot and the typist) and does not exclude an outright humanitarian appeal—separated into the refrain so as not to swamp or blur the 'case' itself. This style may be called scientific socialism made over into fully imaginative terms. The perfectly unbeautiful phrasing, conveying mainly facts, show that we have here gone beyond the old *charity*, which would 'relieve' distress but not abolish its causes. In *My Apprenticeship* Beatrice Webb tells us how the early scientific socialists detested Charity and all its works. They set themselves to find out, with objective precision, the facts of poverty, ill-health, bad housing, inequality in all its forms—facts that would serve both as scientific evidence of social injustice and as ammunition in the struggle for a better society. It is in this sense that so many of Brecht's poems are, in the very fibres of their style, supreme imaginative products of socialism.

In his range of modes Brecht makes the widest conceivable use of the popular. In the narratives of working life such as 'Song of the Railroad Gang of Fort Donald' and 'Coal for Mike,' the German intellectual was able to make himself at home in the tradition of American industrial folk poetry. In 'All of Us or None' and 'The United Front Song', he put his lyrics to practical use in the socialist workers' hand-to-hand fight with the stormtroopers of the S.A. The narrative ballad, with or without a tune, is used some-times for its traditional function of retailing a piece of life which bodies forth its meaning without comment ('Children's Crusade 1939'), sometimes to create satire of a militant kind on war-mongering and the high-minded views and institutions that condone, sanctify, and permit it ('Legend of the Dead Soldier', 'The Litany of Breath'). The common factor that must be stressed,

---

[1] *Selected Poems*, 23, 27.

over against Pearson's claims for the 'egocentric' and autobiographical, is that Brecht's own ego or self is only there in the sense
that without his mind and experience the poem could not have
come into existence. But, starting from what he knows, the socialist
poet, charged as he is by struggle and discussion of the most intensive kinds, is able to broaden out and lose the more self-regarding
emotions. Without any loss of 'authenticity' his poetry is opened to
the lives of individuals very different from himself, to whole classes
and peoples, and to ideas as such.

In these respects MacDiarmid and Brecht align themselves with
a distinct tradition. We can now say that what typifies the socialist
poet is his ready and fertile adaptation of popular styles quite as
much as his solidarity with exploited people. It is common for
Marxists today to deny this, presumably because the notion of a
socialist style has been all too liable, in the hands of a Zhdanov or
his Hungarian counterpart József Révai, to turn into a straitjacket.
Thus Ernst Fischer writes in *The Necessity of Art*:

> Against the definition of socialist realism as a method or
> style, the question immediately comes to mind: whose style,
> whose method? Gorky's or Brecht's? Mayakovsky's or Eluard's?
> Makarenko's or Aragon's? Sholokhov's or O'Casey's? The
> methods of these writers are as different as they can be, but
> a fundamental attitude is common to them all. This new
> Socialist attitude is the result of the writer's or artist's adopting
> the historical viewpoint of the working class . . .[1]

But surely such an adopting of an attitude would be no more than
a pouring of new wine into old bottles unless style, too, was transformed. Indeed, how could an artist of quality realign his deepest
human commitment without transforming his methods? To pick out
only those writers whom I know well, it is the case that Gorky,
Brecht, Mayakovsky, Sholokhov, and O'Casey have a main
quality in common: each has excelled at turning idioms and styles
from vernacular, popular, and public sources to new creative
effect. Gorky wrote his best work (the autobiographies) with the
oral improvisation of a folk storyteller. Brecht 'modernised' and
intensified a great range of modes from cabaret monologue to aria,
from peasant almanac to marching song. Mayakovsky went to the
slogan, advertisement, and street-corner speech (especially popular
in Russia around 1917) for his verse styles. Sholokhov is as ver-

[1] 1959; (Pelican ed., 1963), 110.

nacular-as trenchantly physical and at times as bawdy-as Burns. O'Casey makes a formal dramatic style out of the eloquence, exaggeration, and sharp-witted joking of Irish public-house and back-street talk. Alexander Blok in *The Twelve*, his poem on the October Revolution, draws on *chastushka* or factory rhyme, folk lament, revolutionary rhymes, and the 'bourgeois love song'.[1] It appears to be a law of literary development that the more a writer identifies himself with forces of radical change, the readier he is to go to the wellsprings of the oral tradition.

Pearson admits this only to disparage it as a self-deceiving effort to break out of the inescapable loneliness of the person. Mayakovsky, for example, is said to have suffered from a 'confusion between the impulse to communicate personal (which can of course include political) experience and to activate, authorise, or enthuse a movement which may have no true communal existence'. But Mayakovsky was writing in the thick of the Civil War and the first desperate years of Soviet life. His posters, articles, and poems went straight into the struggling communal life of the time and were immensely appreciated. He wrote verse-satires against bureaucracy for *Izvestia*, Army songs for the soldiers defending Leningrad against Yudenich in the Civil War. If this 'movement' which he was trying to 'enthuse' had 'no true communal existence', then the soviets, the Red Army, and the *subbotniks* must also have been figments. . . . And what of the open-air poetry readings in the Soviet Union, where large crowds come to hear the best poets speak their work? Pearson cannot deny their existence but an ingenious speculation helps him round the difficulty: 'Likely enough, Soviet auditors look to these poets to echo their own revolt against mass conformity, to escape the loneliness of modern industrial society, into a shared *solitude*.' This would be persuasive-clearly, huge industrial cities have much in common whatever the social system-were it not that the evidence of the poetry and of how it reaches people suggests that the give-and-take between poet and public in the Soviet Union is much more whole-hearted, more popular in every sense, than anything we could conceive of here.[2] The photo in the *Daily Worker* for May 12 1962 of Yevtushenko speaking his poems at University

[1] Helen Muchnic, *From Gorky to Pasternak* (1963), 168.
[2] At least until live readings began to flourish recently, led especially by a socialist poet, Adrian Mitchell, whose mastery of a range of popular modes challenges comparison with MacDiarmid's and Brecht's.

College, London, poised like a gymnast or a fencer, with his arms
flying, is the most telling evidence of how natural it is to a Soviet
poet to speak out loud to a community. In *The Observer* for May 27
of that year Yevtushenko wrote that on the National Day of Poetry,
in many Soviet cities, 'all the poets give readings of their verse in
the bookshops, and in Moscow in the evening they perform in the
Mayakovsky Square, where before an audience of 8,000-10,000
they read their verses for two to three hours, sometimes under
falling snow'. In the bookshops, 'They write remarks about the
books which it is proposed to publish and in this way the publishers
lay down the numbers of copies to be issued.' A few years ago in
London the editors of the *Soviet Literature* monthly were telling me
how poets like Tvardovsky were used to reciting their poetry at
length on the radio and in halls and lecture-rooms, and this tradition seems to foster a taste for the whole range of work, not only the
more public kinds. At Pasternak's readings the crowd would jump
to their feet after a poem and shout out gleefully the number of
the Shakespeare sonnet that they wanted to hear his version of
next.[1]

Does this sound as though those thousands come together to share
a solitude – to hear their most private emotions evoked for their
purely introspective response? Some of the poetry itself throws
doubt on this very Western suggestion of Pearson's. Yevtushenko
writes with effects as declamatory as we would expect from his
athletic gestures, for example exclamations and a repeated use of 'I'
which are impossible for most modern British poets in the printed
tradition. Yet Yevtushenko's 'Murder!', for example, is no hysterical
appeal for our self-righteous or sentimental horror at a killing. The
murder, a shooting for money, becomes as the poem goes on the
living death of a Party member hardened into an automaton by
the pressure to conform:

> Watching a senior comrade at his business
> it terrifies me to divine his death
> hardening over his face and his features.
> I am not strong enough,
> clench my teeth, stay silent.
> 'Murder!'
> I all but scream it out.[2]

---

[1] 'Impressions of Pasternak', in *New Reasoner*, 4 (Halifax, spring 1958), 90.
[2] *Selected Poems*, trans. Robin Milner-Gulland and Peter Levi (1962), 74-5.

Again and again Yevtushenko manages to point up seemingly 'obvious' styles, sometimes colloquial, sometimes rhetorical, to convey at once the energy and the hardness of Soviet life, in a spirit that fuses criticism with heartfelt admiration.[1] The blend of feelings is not unsubtle, yet the style is much closer to natural speaking, much less elaborately wrought, than most Western poetry. In short, he bears the marks of a writer supported by the knowledge that there is that body of people crowding to hear him not only to confirm their own intimate thoughts but also to experience the rehearsing of common events and habits of mind in a language that is not specialised but is a sharpening of customary idiom.

Yevtushenko will have been close to the oral wellsprings by means of his Siberian upbringing. In the Asiatic republics of the U.S.S.R., such as Kazakhstan, the ancient tradition of contests between minstrels has been kept up and transformed by the socialist government. On the initiative of the Union of Soviet Writers, national verse contests have been held at the Kazakh republican capital, Alma Ata. The songs chanted at the contests are taken down in shorthand, printed, broadcast, translated. The most famous of their minstrels, Jamboul, who died aged 99 in 1945, composed a great deal after 1917 in the form of long oral poems celebrating the new leaders and heroic radicals of previous generations. At his funeral the streets were packed and his oldest pupil sang a valedictory song which was taken up and chanted by other bards among the crowd.[2] This is the kind of culture that died out in Britain with the Victorian street singers.[3] Out on the fringes of industrialised production and marketing such work lives on—just. Fragments of the Gaelic epics are still known to some in the Outer Isles of Scotland; in the Lowlands singing families like the Robertsons, Higginses, and Stewarts pass on by word of mouth many pieces from that classic balladry which is a British equivalent of the ancient Greek cycles of tragedy. Capitalised industry, which drives cash-and-profit like an iron wedge between artist and community, cannot sustain such

---

[1] See esp. 'Birthday' and 'Party Card': *ibid.*, 71-3.

[2] George Thomson, *Marxism and Poetry* (1945), 57-8 and n. 72. Unfortunately Thomson goes on to claim that the bard's best work was post-Revolution. This is on the face of it unlikely and sounds like the wishful thinking of someone anxious to think well of Stalinism. Victor Serge quotes (from *Izvestia* and elsewhere) many samples of such panegyrics by poets from the Ukraine, Georgia, and elsewhere; without exception they are fulsome flattery couched in ornate doggerel: see *From Lenin to Stalin* (1937), 181-2.

[3] See above, ch. 3, 82-3.

H

a culture, although from time to time it stimulates, in resistance, a kind of vital backlash, like that of the pop groups who since the middle Sixties have made their own songs and toured with their own instruments and amplification.

The main Soviet literary tradition–and I deliberately call it that–is written off by Pearson in his essay in terms that differ little from the stock half-truths of the Sunday papers:

> The duty of Socialist writers begins to look absolute. Occasional dereliction looks like deliberate opposition. The responsible artists like Mayakovsky crack their voices with shouting. It is the sly ones like Ehrenburg, the utterly independent like Pasternak and Akhmatova, and the worst hacks who survive.

This kind of thing, the small-change of commentators who have scarcely opened a book of Soviet writing for themselves, is given the lie by the shelf-full of important literature that Soviet writers have produced: from Babel's *Red Cavalry*, hot from the Russo-Polish war of 1920, through the Twenties, which saw the first long works by Sholokhov and Fedin–the Thirties, when Gladkov, Sholokhov, and Leonov reached their prime–the Forties, which saw the award of Stalin Prizes to the first books of Fedin's trilogy, the nearest that the 'official' tradition could come to a classic, spanning the gamut of fictional modes from social comedy and intelligent debate to historical realism in the way of Tolstoy[1]–right up to the present phase during which the older masters have still produced fine work and new kinds of writer have come to the fore (as Pearson acknowledges in a footnote on Yevtushenko).

How inadequate that last sentence is! I am simply asserting my own judgement. But what is one to say? How can the Big Lie be dealt with in a few paragraphs? As yet there has been scarcely any literary criticism of the Soviet masterpieces. Novels and poems are thrown into the bear-pit of cold-war polemic and abuse. When Khrushchev expressed his blunt tastes, there was an outcry. When Dudintsev published *Not By Bread Alone*, there was a burst of applause. When *Doctor Zhivago* came out, even the angels seemed to join in the chorus of praise. But with a few honourable exceptions[2] scarcely one expert judge of literature has read, digested, and

---

[1] *Early Joys* (1948), *No Ordinary Summer* (1950), *The Conflagration* (? still unfinished: Part 1 pub. in trans., Moscow, 1968).

[2] For example, Ernest J. Simmons's book on Leonov, Sholokhov, and Fedin (Columbia University Press, 1958) and Helen Muchnic's book referred to already.

in due time done critical justice to Fedin's trilogy, for example, or the cream of the stories in *Winter's Tales*, No. 7 (Paustovsky's 'The Telegram' and Sholokhov's 'One Man's Life'), or Yevtushenko's poems (not his opinions or public appearances). With the rare exception of Pasternak's worthy but sadly uneven novel, which it has been possible for the exegetes to treat as a masterpiece of Christian symbolism, Soviet literature has no chance at all of getting the scrupulous attention bestowed on the latest works of the Bellows and Durrells.

Given this conditioning, most readers of this chapter will by now have decided that its author is a slavish partisan of the 'Communist line' on literature. I will not exonerate myself if it can only be done by accepting the Big Lie that a government, even when equipped with a secret police, is able utterly to squash the creative powers of a whole people with a classical tradition still potently alive in their culture as ours is not. Politically-motivated reactions, whether of adulation or of dismissal, are hopelessly crude as a response to the conflicting qualities of such a tradition under stress from a dictatorship which strives both to enlist the energies and faith of millions and to curb their initiative. What faces the critic and demands his most scrupulous thinking-over is that the typical *oeuvre* of a Soviet writer is an entity fraught with conflicts, from which three aspects (if limitations are at issue) stand out: The artist will have been in some way held back or deflected in mid-flow (Babel's taking to 'the genre of silence', the pauses of years as Sholokhov struggled to complete each of his three novels). He will have tended to hark back unduly to the heroic birth years of the Soviet Union, at the expense of more recent and ordinary experiences (*The Quiet Don*, *Zhivago*, Fedin's trilogy, which deals with the ominous lull between 1905 and 1917, the Civil War period, and the German invasion in 1941). And even in the best work there will be veins of unreality, stiffnesses, palpable surrogates for things that were crying out to be rendered (the thriller elements in *Virgin Soil Upturned*, the quite undue part played by coincidence in knitting together the many strands in *Zhivago* and *No Ordinary Summer*). That last example is especially significant for it takes us to the heart of the disability – like some pervasive nervous disease – which crept through the work of Soviet writers precisely as they tried to organise experience into a large continuum such as Western writers no longer had the spirit to attempt. The social forces that fired Soviet writers to make sense of life historically at the same time twisted their historical sense into a distorted form of itself. But already more has been said than can be made good in an essay of this scale. The last word must come from a writer, Victor Serge, who had lived with *good faith* through many of the worst situations in Europe from 1901 to 1947 – lived them so fully that the bones of his style were moulded by the effort to get his sentences out before a hand was clapped over his mouth.[1] In his essay 'The Writer's Conscience' he says, regarding Fedin's memoirs of Gorky:

> It is possible for me to verify the astonishing exactitude of the notes . . . the care which he has put into gathering the customary discourses of Gorky, whose gesture and voice I seem to find again. In each page, meanwhile, I discover the omission of ideas [*sc.* he] often expressed, of historical facts, of names. I admire the ability, the tenacity, the paralysed honesty of the writer who succeeds in tracing a truthful and powerfully living portrait while conforming without fault (but not without distress, I imagine) to the rule of obedience.[2]

To clinch the argument of this essay it has been necessary to move some way away from the centre of Pearson's attention, which is poetry: 'all worthwhile modern poetry is romantic', and the romantic poem can render experience more 'authentically' than any other medium. Seen now in the context of Pearson's distortion of socialist literary history, the fixation on poetry and especially its more ego-centred forms shows up all the more clearly as typical of most criticism which plays down fiction: it is backward-looking and it is eccentric. I had half wondered about bringing such names as Babel, Fedin, Sholokhov, Serge against that travesty of Soviet literature – it was so plain that Pearson had never even thought of the novelists as belonging in the same class of quintessential art as his chosen poets. But if he was not thinking of the novelists, he ought to have been. The title given his essay on the cover of the *New Left Review*, 'Poetry in the Ice-Age' – with its pun on the Cold War – and his sweeping references to 'The most reputable Socialist poetry' and

---

[1] I mean both the fierce pace of his novels and the speaking technique which he and other Soviet Oppositionists were forced to develop – short questions or factual statements between storms of heckling (*Memoirs of a Revolutionary*, 1963 ed., 216). This too is typical of socialist literature under stress: the poems Brecht wrote for the German Freedom Radio in the later Thirties had to be so condensed to get through despite jamming that each was a single verse, rhymeless, and untitled. (*Brecht on Theatre*, 120.)

[2] Published eight months before his death, in *Now*, No. 7 (March 1947), 55.

'The duty of Socialist writers' implicitly claim for the essay an extremely wide application. The evidence it offers is so scanty (conventional references to a few Soviet writers, the treating of Christopher Logue as the typical socialist poet of the West) that its general case collapses.

In one of his footnotes Pearson remarks that socialist realism might seem to be 'justified by the most reputable, humanly interesting and complex ideology'. It would be up to him, then, to search the heart of his beliefs and find how it could have been that so reputable, humane, and interesting a view of life had given rise to so little literature and then only as a by-product or by way of opposition, not from its core. When I look at socialism and its literature for myself, I find that it includes Brecht and MacDiarmid, the American Slump novelists (Dos Passos, Farrell, and Steinbeck at their peaks) along with Lewis Grassic Gibbon in Scotland, Anna Seghers in Germany, Malraux, Sartre, and Simone de Beauvoir in France, Lu Hsun in China, Silone in Italy, Neruda in Chile, the range of Soviet masters of fiction long and short, pioneers like Gorky and Robert Tressell, most of the new dramatists in Britain and Mitchell in our poetry—to say nothing of the new cultures of Hungary, Poland, Czechoslovakia, China and the rest, which will indeed have suffered seriously under the 'ice-age' but which must stand high on the agenda of anyone concerned with literature until he has honestly tried them for himself.

CHAPTER 11

MacDiarmid the Marxist Poet

HUGH MACDIARMID's poetry–to be precise, his work from 1923 to 1935–is so remarkable that it must be bracketed with Eliot's since 'The Hollow Men', Yeats's in *The Winding Stair* and *The Tower*, and Auden's between 1929 and the outbreak of the Second World War. I mean that these are the indispensable bodies of poetry from that time in Britain, although the *oeuvres* of the four poets vary greatly in scale and consistent quality. I suspect that most readers couldn't either confirm or give reasons for dissenting from such a judgement because MacDiarmid's work in general, for reasons of language, and the work of his second important phase, for quite different reasons, has remained closed, or visible only in patches, to most British readers. His stature is that of a grey headland, looming through a northern fog, with some of its impressive features standing out along with others that seem broken or crumbling.

Laziness will have played its part, the lordly laxity of a culture, the English, which is more fascinated by, say, the Paris models than by what is being created in the smaller member-countries of the 'United' Kingdom. Again, MacDiarmid's conversion to communism around the beginning of the Slump enabled readers, in Scotland as well as England, to avoid the exertion of making room in their minds for a new poet. He could be set aside as a 'lefty' and a propagandist, not really an artist. Again, the scanty publishing network outside London made it hard for an innovatory poet in the 'provinces' to get even a hearing, to reach the minds that might or might not have taken him in. By 1935 it took the most remarkable of critics still to be effectively in touch with his poetry and credit him with rare seriousness and disinterestedness, to the extent of nominating the 'Second Hymn to Lenin' for the 'very small ideal anthology of contemporary poetry'.[1] Altogether it has been as

---

[1] F. R. Leavis reviewing *Second Hymn to Lenin and Other Poems: Scrutiny*, IV, 3 (December 1935), 305.

though, say, Yeats's meditative poems on culture and art and on growing old, the vein that runs from 'Ancestral Houses' and 'Among School Children' to 'The Circus Animals' Desertion', had just not been there. Beside these supreme poems of Yeats's must be set MacDiarmid's counterparts—more flawed, less completely integrated, yet unmistakably from a creative nature of extraordinary depth: for example, his poems on the human struggle to rise to the full of our own nature and on the physical basis of that nature—'By Wauchopeside', 'Whuchulls', 'Water of Life', 'Harry Semen', and others.[1] Again, nearly all readers of recent poetry will at some stage have dwelt on those poems of Auden's with dates in their titles—'A Bride in the 30s', 'A Summer Night, 1933', 'Spain 1937', and the rest—which try to reach the marrow of their epoch by taking long historical and geographical perspectives on the immediate present in Europe. Beside these must be set MacDiarmid's ratiocinative poems—more abstract than Auden's best and not as subtle as 'Burnt Norton', yet unmistakably palpable—in which he tries to envisage what it might be and what it might take to break out of the viciously-circular waste of life and time that vitiates so much human effort. 'Supposing a bomb were put under the whole scheme of things, what would we be after? What feelings do we want to carry through into the next epoch? What feelings will carry us through?'[2] These radical questionings of Lawrence's give the spirit also of MacDiarmid's most concerned poetry—the vein that runs from the first part of *A Drunk Man Looks at the Thistle* to the 'Hymns to Lenin', 'The Seamless Garment', and 'Lo! A Child is Born':

> The beaten track is *beaten* frae the start. . . .
> No one but fritters half his time away. . . .

These assertions are in their contexts[3] felt to be charged with experience. They have nothing in common with the florid revolutionism of *The Magnetic Mountain* or *The Ascent of F6*. But you the reader will not get that charge from MacDiarmid's poems unless you make a new place in your mind. The received canon of poetry

---

[1] These are all in the *Selected Poems*, ed. Craig and Manson, 69, 71, 62, 88. Nearly all the references in this chapter will be to this edition since, obviously, it represents my view of what is the significant MacDiarmid and also because one-fifth of its contents are not in the so-called *Collected Poems* (New York, 1962, 1967).

[2] Lawrence, 'Surgery for the Novel—or a Bomb': *Phoenix*, 520.

[3] From *To Circumjack Cencrastus* (1930): *Sel. Poems*, 52; from 'Third Hymn to Lenin', *c.* 1935: *Sel. Poems*, 108.

has to be stretched. One's ears have to pick up sounds outside the customary range. It is not that MacDiarmid's poetry is so weird. He has a root in mundane experience which makes much of Auden sound like donnish stunts. But so much of our taste is, apparently, a kind of skimming off of whatever is or has been the metropolitan fashion that a special kind of persistent effort is needed if we are to make room for a whole, in effect new, and exacting kind of poetry.

This chapter doesn't aim to 'cover' MacDiarmid's poetry[1] but rather to trace what I take to be essential veins in it: their sources, their prime stretches, and their tragic petering out in the middle Thirties. Since the *Collected* volume confirms the usual fallacy that his first important work was done in 1925, here is a lyric called 'On an Ill-faur'd Star' (first published in a magazine of MacDiarmid's own, *Scottish Chapbook*) which must have been written in the year of *The Waste Land*:

> Far aff the bawsunt mount'ins jirk
> Their kaims o' ribie trees.
> Like howlets roostin' roon' aboot
> Are a' the seas.
>
> Ae rimpin i' the raich lan'
> Glowers at the lift revure;
> An' yont its muckle ringle-een
> Time scuds like stour.[2]

bawsunt, *white-striped*: ribie, *leafless like a plucked chicken*: howlets, *owls*: rimpin, *lean cow*: raich lan', *poor-coloured country*: lift revure, *lowering sky*: ringle-een, *eyes showing whites*: stour, *dust*

I hope that if I had been reading the little magazines in 1923, that poem would have stopped me in my tracks, taken root in my taste, and made me look for more by the same man. It *goes*, with the distinct ring and the muscular movement of achieved poetry. Thematically, it manages to image a sense of our whole planet by means of common-or-garden details; and though the foreboding on which it ends is undefined, the essence of it–the sense of all animal nature smitten by one shock of realisation–is caught with a natural-born poet's sense of how realised or how latent his symbols ought to be.

During the next five or six years MacDiarmid was to show that

---

[1] There is a factually useful survey: Kenneth Buthlay, *Hugh MacDiarmid* (*C. M. Grieve*), 1964.
[2] I owe a transcript of this poem to John Manson.

there was scarcely a lyric note that he couldn't strike. His percep-
tions seem to have been reincarnating themselves in metaphor and
rhythm as naturally as breathing. Yet, since we are concerned with
a remarkable poet whose powers seem to have failed when he was
in his middle forties, we also have to notice even in his best early
lyric poems signs that the sparks which fired him came rather often,
not from the stuff of his own experiences, but from literary origins—
dictionaries of Scots, old collections of poems and songs, transla-
tions that other people had made from European poems. Here, for
example, is a poem from his second important book, *Penny Wheep*
(1926), which suggests so finely the pure essence of compassion that
I can only liken it to the best work of Picasso in his Blue Period. It
is called 'Empty Vessel':

> I met ayont the cairney
> A lass wi' tousie hair
> Singin' till a bairnie
> That was nae langer there.
>
> Wunds wi' warlds tae swing
> Dinna sing sae sweet,
> The licht that bends ower a' thing
> Is less ta'en up wi't.[1]

ayont the cairney, *beyond the stone-heap*: tousie, *tousled*: till a bairnie, *to a child*:
dinna, *do not*: ower a' thing, *over everything*

MacDiarmid hadn't actually met the woman. He was adapting,
transforming, a brutally bawdy folk-song of the seventeenth or
eighteenth century that he had found in an old anthology:

> I met ayont the Kairney,
>   Jenny Nettles, Jenny Nettles,
> Singing till her bairny,
>   Robin Rattle's bastard. . . .[2]

The free ingesting and transmuting of all sorts of materials had of
course been usual among modernists since Pound's work with Sino-
Japanese, Latin, and Provençal materials and especially since *The
Waste Land*. It was also a sign of fine talent to pick that word 'bends',
which is right both scientifically and emotionally. Yet isn't one
bound to be chary about a poet who practises his technical mastery
on second-hand material more often than on his own concerns? In
those first two books, *Sangschaw* (1925) and *Penny Wheep*, there are

[1] *Sel. Poems*, 27.
[2] Buthlay, *MacDiarmid*, 33.

many poems in which MacDiarmid takes the doddering kinds of kitchen or farmyard poem that had been favourite in Victorian Scotland and makes them actual again. Thus the tearful cult of the old is made over into a poetry, as in 'The Widower', that concentrates the veritable situation into images of a fine physical distinctness which is also psychologically sensitive:

> Auld wife, on a nicht like this
> Pitmirk and snell
> It's hard for a man like me
> To believe in himsel'.
>
> A wheen nerves that hotch in the void,
> And a drappie bluid,
> And a buik that craves for the doonfa'
> Like a guisand cude.
>
> For Guid's sake, Jean, wauken up!
> A word frae your mou'
> Has knit my gantin' timbers
> Thegither or noo.[1]

Pitmirk and snell, *pitch dark and sharp*: wheen, *few*: hotch, *jerk*: guisand cude, *dry barrel*: gantin', *gaping*

Many other poems take the almost irretrievably hackneyed imagery of stars, moon, and universe and intensify them into unforgettable visions of what it is to be a mortal, for example 'The Eemis Stane' from *Sangschaw* (*Sel. Poems*, 21). But there is also this, from the sequence 'Au Clair de la Lune' in the same book:

> Her luchts o' yellow hair
> Flee oot ayont the storm,
> Wi' mony a bonny flaught
> The colour o' cairngorm.
>
> Oot owre the thunner-wa'
> She haiks her shinin' breists,
> While th' oceans to her heels
> Slink in like bidden beasts.
>
> So sall Earth's howlin' mobs
> Drap, lown, ahint the sang
> That frae the chaos o' Thocht
> In triumph braks or lang.[2]

luchts, *locks*: flee, *fly*: flaught, *gleam*: thunner-wa', '*thunder-mass*': haiks, *trails*: lown, *silent*: or lang, *before long*

[1] *Sel. Poems*, 25.
[2] 'The Huntress and her Dogs': *Sel. Poems*, 19-20.

Do we not feel that the idea of that last verse is hollow in its invoking of abstractions and at the same time unacceptable in its cursory contempt for life in the mass?

At all events, a remarkable poet had evolved in Scotland after a barren century and more.[1] His creative zest was enough to send him off next on a very long sequence or gallimaufry, *A Drunk Man Looks at the Thistle* (1926), which runs to a hundred pages and seems meant to be the poet's *Waste Land*. The stylistic range is marvellous. A couplet like

> And heard God passin' wi' a bobby's feet
> Ootby in the lang coffin o' the street[2]

is so weighty in its scornful wit you would think it had behind it a school of Scottish Drydens, yet MacDiarmid invented the manner for himself, and could keep it up for a 170-line meditation on the infinitude of organic life that dumbfounds human categories:

> First speir this bowzie bourach if't prefers
> The simmer or the winter, day or night,
> New or forhooied nests, rain's pelts or smirrs,
> Bare sticks or gorded fullyery; and syne invite
> My choice twixt good and evil, life and death.
> What hoar trunk girds at ivy or at fug
> Or what sleek bole complains it lacks them baith?
> Nae foliage hustle-farrant in windy light
> Is to the Muse a mair inspirin' sight
> Than fungus poxy as the mune; nae blight
> A meaner state than flourish at its height.[3]

speir, *ask*: bowzie bourach, *branchy cluster*: forhooied, *forsaken*: smirrs, *drizzles*: gorded fullyery, *fullblown foliage*: fug, *moss*: hustle-farrant, *tattered*

A Drunk Man finds a distinct vein of idiom and imagery for a hundred states of mind. It feels as though it represents an entire cultural gamut, from the starkly folk, whether sweet or trenchant, to the classically 'high'. Yet as a composition of feelings supposed to belong together beneath all their shifts – the emotions of hopeless frustration, creative energy and rage, and throwaway recklessness, all experienced in the environment of a Scottish intellectual's life – there is too little in the way of sustained meaning to give bone and

[1] See Craig, *Scottish Literature*, ch. 9, 'Emigration'.
[2] Second edition (Glasgow, 1953), 73.
[3] From the recently rediscovered 'Whuchulls' (1933), a poem about a wood near Langholm, MacDiarmid's birthplace: *Sel. Poems*, 72.

sinew to all those whirling words. The critics make great play with 'microcosm', 'the logic of dreams', 'dangerously balanced magnificence'[1] and other stand-bys of the academic faced with work he is not firm-minded enough to criticise adversely. But no-one has produced an account of what the latter two-thirds of the poem does in proportion to that blizzard of images of Man, thistle, and Eternity. For pages at a time, instead of development we have a mere running-on of the pen, the lack of grasped or focussed material showing particularly in the amount of verse spent on finding imagery for the working of the mind that is finding the imagery, rather than on anything 'out there':

> A black leaf owre a white leaf twirls,
> A grey leaf flauchters in atween,
> Sae ply my thochts aboot the stem
> O' loppert slime frae which they spring.
> The thistle like a snawstorm drives,
> Or like a flight o' swallows lifts,
> Or like a swarm o' midges hings,
> A plague o' moths, a starry sky,
> But's naething but a thistle yet,
> And still the puzzle stands unsolved. . . .[2]

flauchters, *flutters*: loppert, *coagulated*

I dwell on the shortcomings of a highly fertile long poem because its tendency to diffuse into verbiage, to lose its way, became common not only in individual poems of MacDiarmid's but in his long-term development. During the next four years, to 1930, he published no book of poetry, he became a founder member of the National Party of Scotland, and Great Britain sank into the Slump. He broke the short silence with another attempt at the sustained poem for which he was not (any more than any other modern poet) equipped – *To Circumjack Cencrastus*; but actually he was no longer doomed to flail around for a subject. His sense, now arrogant, now true, that his native culture was lacking in activities or people of a calibre to extend or match a mind as powerful as his own –

> Whiles
> I look at Scotland and dumfounded see't
> A muckle clod split off frae ither life,
> Shapeless, uncanny, unendurable clod. . . .[3]

[1] David Daiches, Introduction to *A Drunk Man*, xvi, xix; Buthlay, 51.
[2] *A Drunk Man*, 49.
[3] *To Circumjack Cencrastus*, 173.

was given a further, deeply historical justification by the paralysis of the Slump. For five years, until the breakdown of his talent in the middle Thirties, he was able to write intensely on two clusters of themes: the cultural and psychological evolution that had brought him to where he was, and the perspective on man caught up in momentous processes that came to him, or was clarified in him, as he grew into communism and Marxism.

It is the second, political aspect that will now be analysed: since there is less of it, it can be handled in one part of a single essay. But it would be wrong to offer any account whatsoever of MacDiarmid that didn't point out (it has never been distinctly noticed) that between 1930 and about 1935 he created a major sequence of poems which no one at that time, with the exception of the Yeats of 'Meditations in Time of Civil War' and the Eliot of the *Quartets*, could approach. They hang together thematically, since they all explore the organism of the human being, the particular form of it that is the poet himself, and the concerns (the relation between consciousness and the id, revolutionary politics, industrial work, rootedness in family and locality) that nourished or interfered with his deep processes. They also have enough in common stylistically for them nearly to make an integrated work. With few exceptions they are written in some form of six-line verse and in a long line, usually with four or five stresses, that has room for complex trains of thought. Rather than scramble an account of them here or attempt an interpretation which would need very lengthy quoting, I will put at the end of this chapter a schematic note suggesting the outlines of this wonderful family of poems.

Towards the end of this final creative run MacDiarmid wrote a poem, 'Harry Semen', which is both superbly created and yet painfully palpable as evidence that the integration necessary for creative work was failing him.[1] All through *Stony Limits* (1934), his second-last important book, from which 'Harry Semen' comes, there are signs of splits between lucid reason and his less conscious

[1] Only a well-informed and honest biographer could account satisfactorily for this breakdown. MacDiarmid is said to have said, 'I lost my rhythm', and to have mentioned a serious head injury. In his autobiography *Lucky Poet* (1943, 1972) he mentions an 'exceedingly bad state, psychologically and physically'–living on an island in the Shetlands, eating gulls' eggs, hardly able to afford stamps to send his work to be published (page 45). But in this essay it has been necessary to concentrate on the quakes that there were in MacDiarmid's life-sense from the start.

self, between his sensuous life and the intellect which tries to organise it and finally domineers over the unsatisfactory vulnerable and
wayward man of flesh. In 'Ode to all Rebels' and 'Harry Semen'
(both left out of *Stony Limits* by the godly Victor Gollancz when he
published it) there are signs of desperate disgust at sexual experience, not resolved by the rationalising and the fleering humour that
he brings in to handle the revulsion. Yet even this partial disinte-
gration between mind and whole self gives rise to a passage which
in its power of imagining into almost ineffable organic processes is
beyond any other poet I know:

> Particle frae particle'll brak asunder,
> Ilk ane o' them mair livid than the neist.
> A separate life?—incredible war o' equal lichts,
> Nane o' them wi' ocht in common in the least.
> Nae threid o' a' the fabric o' my thocht
> Is left alangside anither; a pack
> O leprous scuts o' weasels riddlin' a plaid
>   Sic thrums could never mak'.
> Hoo mony shades o' white gaed curvin' owre
> To yon blae centre o' her belly's flower?
> Milk-white, and dove-grey, wi' harebell veins.
> Ae scar in fair hair like the sun in sunlicht lay,
> And pelvic experience in a thin shadow line.
> Thocht canna mairry thocht as sic saft shadows dae.

    ilk ane, *each one*: sic thrums, *such threads*: blae, *grey-blue*

What deadened his later poetry was his intellectual will to force
theories onto this swarm of life-stuff—

> Enough human seed can be housed
> In a tooth-paste cap to father
> The world's 2,000,000,000 population. . . .
> After 48 complete divisions
> There are enough cells to constitute
> A fully developed baby—26 billion.
> My poems will drill the whole world of fact
> Precisely like that![1]

Presumably this drive to manage rather than understand experience
was intimately bound up with the revulsion from the flux of living
expressed in 'Harry Semen':

> Grey ghastly commentaries on my puir life,
> A' the sperm that's gane for naething rises up to damn
> In sick-white onanism the single seed
> Frae which in sheer irrelevance I cam.[2]

---

[1] *Lucky Poet*, 'The Kind of Poetry I Want', 128.   [2] *Sel. Poems*, 88-89.

During the previous four years, however, he had been able, in his maturity as a poet, to write work in which his Marxism or communism found a style, an imagery and rhythm, that drew on the very fibre of that movement. While the MacSpaundays were embedding the correctly ruthless and scientific imagery (pylons, aerodromes, scalpels, rifles) in an incongruous basis of the old Romantic or the new clever-clever styles, or forcing their verse to run with a jaunty popularness that remained embarrassingly *voulu* because it had at heart no fellow feeling for ordinary people, MacDiarmid rose to a Marxist intellectual content without losing his music or the vernacular of which he was a master.

In 'The Seamless Garment' he says:

> The mair we mak' natural as breathin', the mair
> Energy for ither things we'll can spare . . .

and in the 'Second Hymn to Lenin', catching perfectly the manner and thumping vehemence of the platform speaker, he says:

> Oh, it's nonsense, nonsense, nonsense,
> Nonsense at this time o' day
> That breid-and-butter problems
> S'ud be in ony man's way.[1]

This is the faith that human culture will expand immensely in an era of abundance and social ownership that has been an essential of communist thinking from Marx's *Critique of the Gotha Programme* (1875) and Engels's *Socialism: Utopian and Scientific* (1880) through to the programme which the Soviet C.P. adopted at their 22nd Congress in 1961. Again, when MacDiarmid writes in the 'First Hymn to Lenin':

> Christ said: 'Save ye become as bairns again.'
> Bairly eneuch the feck o' us hae been!
> Your work needs men; and its worst foes are juist
> The traitors wha through a' history ha' gi'en
> The dope that's gar'd the mass o' folk pay heed
>   And bide bairns indeed,[2]

feck, *majority*: gar'd, *made*

he directly recalls Marx's definition of religion as 'the *opium* of the people' and Lenin's expansion of this, both humanist and thoroughly militant: 'Religion is a sort of spiritual dope in which

---

[1] *Sel. Poems*, 60, 93.
[2] *Sel. Poems*, 54.

the slaves of capital drown the image of man, their demand for a
life more or less worthy of human beings.'[1] When MacDiarmid
writes in the second-last verse of the 'Hymn':

> . . . at last we are wise and wi' laughter tear
> The veil of being, and are face to face
> Wi' the human race,

he is putting into verse one of the deepest thoughts in *Capital*:

> The religious reflex of the real world can . . . only then finally
> vanish, when the practical relations of everyday life offer to
> man none but perfectly intelligible and reasonable relations
> with regard to his fellowmen and to nature. The life-process
> of society, which is based on material production, does not
> strip off its mystical veil until it is treated as production by
> freely associated men, and is consciously regulated by them in
> accordance with a settled plan.[2]

MacDiarmid had come onto this vein at the time when economic
depression was overtaking the Scottish Lowlands with their concentration on the heavy industry, the steelworking and engineering
and shipbuilding and mining, which was specially exposed to
falling orders and unemployment. Soon the lines of men queuing
for jobs and free meals stretched from Motherwell to Wishaw.
Socialism and nationalism, among the radically minded, began to
fuse. MacDiarmid had been a socialist since before the Great War,
as a member of the I.L.P. Before he was twenty he had served on
a Fabian Research Committee on Land Problems and Rural
Developing, contributing 'valuable memoranda' to the report
published in 1913. In the Thirties he was again doing practical
work for the country people, organising the cottars of Whalsay
where he was living to fight in the courts against the increased
assessments of their houses.[3] The first bibliographical list of his
writings, in the section on books and periodicals announced but
never published, consists mainly for the years from 1935 to the war
of work specifically on socialism, and there is also mention in *Lucky
Poet* (page 204) of a promised biography of John McLean, the outstanding Marxist thinker and speaker around the Clyde at the

---

[1] Marx, Introduction to *Contribution to the Critique of Hegel's Philosophy of Right*:
Marx and Engels, *On Religion* (Moscow, 1957), 42; Lenin, 'Socialism and
Religion', 1905: Moscow, 1954, 6.

[2] Part I, ch. 1, section 4, 'The Fetishism of Commodities', 91-2.

[3] W. R. Aitken, 'C. M. Grieve/Hugh MacDiarmid': *The Bibliotheck*, I, 4
(autumn 1958), 3; *Lucky Poet*, 87, 231.

Great War period. MacDiarmid's life-work thus takes its place as a key part of the social movement which included the Clydeside Shop Stewards' Movement, political leaders such as Keir Hardie, Willie Gallacher, and John McLean, and the contribution made by Red Clydeside to the founding of the Communist Party of Great Britain.

It would be misleading to draw a hard and fast line at the point where one supposes his pre-Marxist poetry ended and his Marxist began. With one exception there is no expressed awareness of communism in his poetry before the hymns to Lenin. But his coming to Scots as the indispensable literary medium for people living and working in Scotland contains the germ of a progressive trend. In writing the sort of lyric he did in the Twenties he was acting as a nationalist as surely as when he helped found the National Party of Scotland. In recent years, as the developing countries—India, Cuba, Ghana, Kenya, Algeria, Vietnam, and many more—have struggled for their independence from imperialist political or economic rule, we have become familiar with the truth that nationalism is often a first stage to socialism. Mao Tse-tung and Chiang Kai Shek could collaborate to defeat the Japanese, but the Communists had to fight and defeat the Kuomintang to establish socialism. Castro's rising in Cuba against native and American tyranny found itself, once it had to start construction, turning into a Marxist-Leninist revolution. Such are the reasons why MacDiarmid's singling out of the language of a small, exploited, non-imperial nation as a vital medium for modern poetry seems to me, in a potential way, progressive.

This trend in his thinking soon found, with the fertility of genius, its own style. There is a note in MacDiarmid's poetry of 1930-35 that can be heard nowhere else, and it is the very sound of his Marxism finding its voice. It occurs, along with other timbres, in 'Lo! A Child is Born' from the *Second Hymn to Lenin* volume.[1] The poem is an allegory in nineteen lines of the birth-pangs of history and here is its close:

. . . Then I thought of the whole world. Who cares for its
         travail
And seeks to encompass it in like loving-kindness and peace?
There is a monstrous din of the sterile who contribute nothing.
To the great end in view, and the future fumbles,

[1] The poem was long ago picked out as outstanding by John Speirs in *The Scots Literary Tradition* (1940), 187.

A bad birth, not like the child in that gracious home
Heard in the quietness turning in its mother's womb,
A strategic mind already, seeking the best way
To present himself to life, and at last, resolved,
Springing into history quivering like a fish,
Dropping into the world like a ripe fruit in due time. -
But where is the Past to which Time, smiling through her tears
At her new-born son, can turn crying: 'I love you'?[1]

The peak of intensity is reached in the splendid double simile of
fish and fruit. Here feelings are wonderfully united: the measured,
nearly Biblical gravity of the repeated participles, 'Springing. . . .
Dropping', allied to the richness of the images, creates a feeling
both springy and solid. The momentum at this point seems both to
flow onwards and yet gather itself monumentally. With unerring
touch the poet has evoked sheer vitality in nature and at the same
time the experience of dwelling on it with steady intellectual intent.
The lines recall Yeats's consummate passage from 'Sailing to
Byzantium':

             . . . The young
In one another's arms, birds in the trees
- Those dying generations - at their song,
The salmon-falls, the mackerel-crowded seas,
Fish, flesh, or fowl, commend all summer long
Whatever is begotten, born, and dies.

Both poets can make us feel how even as they experience nature in
its teeming power, their analytic intellects permeate their responses.
But Yeats comes, deliberately, to the verge of an almost luxurious
surrender to ripeness. MacDiarmid, characteristically, has less free
Romantic flow of emotion; his impulses are subordinate to his
long-range concerns.

'Lo! A Child' is less clearly socialist than other outstanding
poems of that time; it could be purely humanist. But the sense it
gives of looking out over the whole of man's struggle to develop can
be seen to draw on his Marxism. 'Strategic mind' is clue enough:
Lenin's concern with strategy - the finding and co-operating with
main trends of progress - has a special fascination for MacDiarmid:

Lenin was like that wi' workin' class life,
    At hame wi't a'.
His fause movements couldna been fewer,
    The best weaver Earth ever saw.

[1] *Selected Poems*, 99-100.

A' he'd to dae wi' moved intact,
    Clean, clear, and exact.

On days of revolutionary turning points you literally
        flourished,
    Became clairvoyant, foresaw the movement of classes,
    And the probable zig-zags of the revolution
    As if on your palm. . . .[1]

Lenin's mastery has evidently typified for MacDiarmid the kind of
clarity he has desperately wanted since 1930 or before.

At the start of the Thirties when he came onto his most serious
and distinctive poetry, the note I have mentioned can be heard
time and again. There is one forerunner, in *Penny Wheep*, a poem
adapted from the German called 'The Dead Liebknecht'.
MacDiarmid had nothing to do with revolutionary socialism in
those days, yet he comes onto his most serious vein in a poem on
the German Communist leader who was murdered during the
suppression of the short-lived revolution in Germany just after the
Great War. It ends:

> The factory horn begins to blaw
> Thro' a' the city, blare on blare,
> The lowsin' time o' workers a',
> Like emmits skailin' everywhere.
>
> And wi' his white teeth shinin' yet
> The corpse lies smilin' underfit.[2]

> lowsin', *unyoking*: skailing, *scattering*

We bring up with a shock at the final image – saved from the merely
creepy (the *Cabinet of Dr Caligari* touch in German art of the
Twenties) by its setting in a lifelike contemporary environment.
Closing on such an image makes us feel a potent force biding
unshaken just under the surface of society. This is the gist of the
finest touch from 'John McLean (1879-1923)' (another of the
poems kept out of *Stony Limits* by Gollancz):

> . . . 'justice' may well do its filthy work
>   Behind walls as filthy as these
> And congratulate itself blindly and never know
> The prisoner takes the light with him as he goes below.[3]

The words in the last line fall on to the page in monosyllable after
monosyllable, enacting the slow steps of the sentenced man. This

[1] *Sel. Poems*, 59, 103.   [2] *Sel. Poems*, 26.   [3] *Sel. Poems*, 85.

is also the movement of 'Another Epitaph for an Army of Mercenaries', one of the best poems that speak out for socialism's traditional belief in peace:

> It is a God-damned lie to say that these
> Saved, or knew, anything worth any man's pride.
> They were professional murderers and they took
> Their blood money and impious risks and died.
> In spite of all their kind some elements of worth
> With difficulty persist here and there on earth.[1]

Who else has written with quite that dogged insistence, every phrase doing its terse bit to establish an unanswerable logic, without the least concession to the honey-flowing or beautiful? We can feel in this poetry that grips so hard on experience and measures itself out so sparingly a rare mental stamina, the quality that could sustain, as Yeats did, a complex train of thought down many long lines, but with fewer flourishes than Yeats and greater earnestness:

> Christ's cited no' by chance or juist because
> You mark the greatest turnin'-point since him. . . .
>
> Certes nae ither, if no' you's dune this.
> It maitters little. What you've dune's the thing,
> No' hoo't compares, corrects, or complements
> The work o' Christ that's taen ower lang to bring
> Sic a successor to keep the reference back
>   Natural to mak'.[2]

This extraordinarily intent, intellectually concentrated vein is the perfect style for his main progressive ideas on culture:

> Gin I canna win through to the man in the street,
>   The wife by the hearth,
> A' the cleverness on earth'll no' mak' up
>   For the damnable earth.
>
> 'Haud on, haud on; what poet's dune that?
>   Is Shakespeare read,
> Or Dante of Milton or Goethe or Burns?
>   –You heard what I said.[3]

It is also the right style for his core idea of what he himself has had it in him to give to the progressive struggle:

> And as for me in my fricative work
>   I ken fu' weel

---

[1] *Sel. Poems*, 100.   [2] *Sel. Poems*, 53.   [3] *Sel. Poems*, 91-2.

> Sic an integrity's what I maun hae,
>   Indivisible, real,
> Woven owre close for the point o' a pin
> Onywhere to win in.[1]

maun hae, must have

Again the words bind together with rare density, in a way that enacts their content ('the seamless garment'). Finally there is the little poem called 'The Skeleton of the Future', subtitled 'At Lenin's Tomb':

> Red granite and black diorite, with the blue
> Of the labradorite crystals gleaming like precious stones
> In the light reflected from the snow; and behind them
> The eternal lightning of Lenin's bones.[2]

Reading this, we realise that no other British poet has cared enough for politics to exalt a political leader as high as that, and not through empty rhetoric–'eternal lightning' is an image full of meaning.

These examples have almost all been militant and revolutionary in their content. But that is not why they picked themselves. As poetry what they have in common is that utter intentness, the whole being focussed on its object, all self-regarding feelings burned away by the intensity of the concern for the large objective purpose. The most comparable thing in British literature is the cluster of poems by Englishmen of the Civil War period in which we can feel the gallantry of the gentleman steadied and hardened into a new gravity by the dire epoch through which his class was passing: Marvell's 'Horatian Ode Upon Cromwel's Return from Ireland', Shirley's 'The glories of our blood and state', Roger Lestrange's 'Loyalty Confin'd' (which can be found in the *Oxford Book of Seventeenth Century Verse*), and (a late case) the finest of the choruses from *Samson Agonistes*, in which Milton turns the Commonwealth cause and its defeat at the Restoration into Christian allegory. Like MacDiarmid's poems they typify what he calls in the 'Second Hymn' 'Disinterestedness,/Oor profoundest word yet'.

In 'The Seamless Garment' he had been able to create what the left-wing poetry of the Thirties painfully lacked, a manner in which the socialist who was in effect setting himself up as a spokesman for

---

[1] *Sel. Poems*, 61.   [2] *Sel. Poems*, 81.

'the masses' could address the working class with no trace of *de haut en bas*, with a natural man-to-man directness that political poetry needs if it is not to be a new kind of sermonising or the bullying of the cheer-leader:

> The haill shop's dumfounderin'
>   To a stranger like me.
> Second nature to you; you're perfectly able
>   To think, speak, and see
> Apairt frae the looms, tho' to some
> That doesna sae easily come. . . .
>
> Are you equal to life as to the loom?
>   Turnin' oot shoddy or what?
> Claith better than man? D'ye live to the full,
>   Your poo'ers a' deliverly taught?
> Or scamp a'thing else? Border claith's famous.
> Shall things o' mair consequence shame us?
>
> Lenin and Rilke baith gied still mair skill,
>   Coopers o' Stobo, to a greater concern
> Than you devote to claith in the mill.
>   Wad it be ill to learn
> To keep a bit eye on their looms as weel
> And no' be hailly ta'en up wi' your tweel?[1]

deliverly, consistently: tweel, cloth

That was at the start of his Marxist vein. It runs out in the 'Third Hymn to Lenin' about four years later, which wasn't even published in full till 1957. It rises to a vehement rhetoric of honest anger such as had not been heard (apart from the Trench poets) since Shelley's *Mask of Anarchy*:

> Our frantic efforts go all ways and go none;
> Incontinent with vain hopes, tireless Micawbers,
> Banking on what Gladstone said in 1890
> Or Christ a few centuries earlier,–there's
> No lack of counsellors, of *die List der Vernunft*.
> The way to Hell is paved with plenty of talk,
> But nothing ever happens–nothing ever will;
> The future's always rosy, the present no less black.
>
> Clever–and yet we cannot solve this problem even;
> Civilised–and flaunting such a monstrous sore;
> Christian–in flat defiance of all Christ taught;
> Proud of our country with this open sewer at our door,

[1] Sel. Poems, 59-60.

Come, let us shed all this transparent bluff,
Acknowledge our impotence, the prize eunuchs of Europe,
Battening on our shame, and with voices weak as bats'
Proclaiming in ghoulish kirks our base immortal hope. . . .

Lenin, lover of music, who dare not listen to it,
Teach us to eschew all the siren voices too
And get due *Diessitigkeit.* Countless petty indulgences
–We give them fine names, like Culture, it is true–
Lure us up this enchanting side-line and up that
When we should stay in stinking vennel and wynd,
Not masturbating our immortal souls,
But simply doing some honest service to mankind.[1]

die List der Vernunft, *betrayal by reason*: Diessitigkeit, *situatedness*

There the vein ends. And nothing else takes its place. The poets'
work runs out in a vast graveyard of ideas–the 'Cornish Heroic
Song' (1939), *In Memoriam James Joyce* (1955), *The Kind of Poetry
I Want* (1961)–monuments to his failure to fulfil a text from Lenin
that is quoted twice in *Lucky Poet*:

> It would be a serious mistake to suppose that one can become
> a Communist without *making one's own* the treasures of human
> knowledge. . . . Communism becomes an empty phrase, a mere
> façade, and the Communist a mere bluffer, if he has not *worked
> over in his consciousness* the whole inheritance of human know-
> ledge. . . .[2] (my italics)

The examples necessary to back this judgement are in the nature
of the case so huge that they would use up more space than they
deserve. Perhaps it will be enough, and fair to the poet, if I quote
the end of 'On a Raised Beach', written at a time when creative
rhythms were still moving in him–the preceding section, beginning
'if only one of these stones would move', is very fine.

> Diallage of the world's debate, end of the long auxesis,
> Although no ébrillade of Pegasus can here avail,
> I prefer your enchorial characters–the futhorc of the future–
> To the hieroglyphics of all the other forms of Nature.
> Song, your apprentice encrinite, seems to sweep

[1] *Sel. Poems,* 107.
[2] *Lucky Poet,* xxxii, 152-3. MacDiarmid ascribes the passage to Lenin's last
speech, to the Fourth Comintern Congress in November 1922. In fact it occurs,
differently translated, in the speech to the Third Congress of the Russian Young
Communist League on 2.10.1920: see Lenin, *Selected Works* (Moscow, 1952), II,
pt. 2, 477, 479.

The Heavens with a last entrochal movement,
And, with the same word that you began it, closes
Earth's vast epanadiplosis.[1]

Can such forced and limping rhythms and musty poetic-diction
encourage us even to look up in a dictionary 'auxesis', 'futhorc',
and the rest? The Communist poet (he joined the party the year
that book came out) is lapsing into the kind of confusion that was
diagnosed by one of the profoundest English Marxist critics:

> Only when the bourgeois passes to the anarchistic stage where
> he negates all bourgeois society and deliberately chooses words
> with only personal associations, can rhythm vanish, for the
> poet now dreads even the social bond of having instincts
> common with other men, and therefore chooses just those
> words which will have a *cerebral* peculiarity. If he chooses
> words with too strong an emotional association, this, coupled
> with the hypnosis of a strong rhythm, will sink him into the
> common lair of the human instincts.[2]

The reasons for this drive to get up into the thin air of pure
intellect can't have been exclusively psychological. This most
poignant occurrence, the drying up of a creative flow, must make
us look back at the flow itself, and if we consider MacDiarmid as a
Communist and a Communist poet, some odd things come to light
even in the hymns to Lenin. In the second one MacDiarmid con-
fides to Lenin that 'politics is bairns' play' compared with what
poetry must be—a claim difficult to reconcile with sseriou communism. Babette Deutsch in *This Modern Poetry* (1936) interprets
'poetry' in the 'Hymn' to mean the whole distinctively human
imaginative faculty.[3] Of course if you stretch terms far enough you
can prove anything, and if 'politics' were so treated it could easily
be made to mean the whole of human social activity, in which case
to exalt 'poetry' above it, or *vice versa*, could lead only to the most
inane metaphysical speculations. Again in the vehement lyric from
the 'Hymn', 'Oh, it's nonsense', the argument runs into this:

> Sport, love, and parentage,
> Trade, politics, and law
> S'ud be nae mair to us than braith
> We hardly ken we draw.[4]

[1] *Stony Limits and Scots Unbound* (Edinburgh, 1956 ed.), 56; the poem is also in
Longer Contemporary Poems, ed. David Wright (1956).
[2] Christopher Caudwell, *Illusion and Reality* (1946 ed.), 125.
[3] Quoted in *Lucky Poet*, 68.
[4] *Sel. Poems*, 94.

This simple assertion deserves a simple reply: how could love and parentage, vital physical-emotional links between us as human beings, ever dwindle to mere reflexes, in any conceivable stage of mankind's evolution?

Surely the poet here is no Marxist, no historical materialist. He is using Marxism's concern with the future to license a maddened desire to escape from the necessities of existence as we know it. In the 'Third Hymn' the dialectical materialist is found writing that

> only one or two in every million men today
> Know that thought is reality–and thought alone![1]

This is the purest idealism–treating the mental processes that well up from material existence as somehow higher than it, more 'real'. It is what the leading exponents of Marxism-Leninism have specifically argued against time after time.[2] They have done so because they know that idealism tends to go along with reactionary tendencies when it comes to social issues. And sure enough we find MacDiarmid writing in 'Reflections in a Scottish Slum', published in an anthology just three years after he rejoined the Communist Party:

> . . . It is good that the voice of the indigent,
> Too long stifled, should manage
> To make itself heard.
> But I cannot consent to listen
> To nothing but that voice.[3]

Who asked him to listen to nothing else? The Aunt Sally he is knocking down is the merest figment from the bogey version of socialism, 'levelling down instead of levelling up', etc. Its occurrence suggests a quake in the foundations of his communism, for every communist should have forever in his mind the words of Gene Debs, pioneer of the railwaymen's union in America: 'While there is a lower class I am of it, while there is a criminal class I am of it, while there is a soul in prison I am not free.'[4]

If we consider MacDiarmid's communism as a body of thought, his tendency to lapse into mere ideas takes its toll there too. Although fellow feeling with the workers has been strong in him, pure nationalism has been even stronger. He is for workers'

---

[1] *Sel. Poems*, 108.

[2] See esp. Engels, *Ludwig Feuerbach and the Outcome of Classical German Philosophy* (1888), and Lenin, *Materialism and Empirio-Criticism* (1908).

[3] *Honour'd Shade*, ed. Norman MacCaig (Edinburgh, 1959), 49.

[4] Quoted by John Dos Passos in *The 42nd Parallel: U.S.A.* (New York, 1937), 28.

republics. But this turns out to mean a 'Celtic Union of Socialist Soviet Republics' embracing Scotland, Ireland, Wales, and Cornwall![1] How could such a fantasy, usually unsupported by any evidence of the economic viability of such a union or the desire of the peoples for it, ever have been put forward seriously?

The objective reason for this must be that MacDiarmid was a victim of the confusions that have made unity of the Left so hard to achieve in Britain for generations now. Communists are banned from participation in institutions such as the Trades Union Congress and the Labour Party. Nationalism, even when it refuses to commit itself to any economic or class policy for the period after its precious independence has been won, can still attract political support and even win constituencies. The one long-standing Communist Member of Parliament had had a struggle before he understood why the Scottish Communists should go in with a British C.P. rather than form their own party.[2]

Perhaps the most constructive way of making the point is to put MacDiarmid's work side by side with Brecht's, as he too was a poet with that fine disinterestedness permeating his verse. He too was a communist and a man formed by the Great War and its aftermath, he too came to communism as the European crisis deepened in the late Twenties. He too can base a spare stating (rather than evoking) poetry on a straight, terse vernacular: this verse from 'A worker Reads History' could almost have come from the 'Second Hymn to Lenin':

> Every page a victory,
> At whose expense the victory ball?
> Every ten years a great man,
> Who paid the piper?

Brecht too makes breathtaking transitions from 'low' language to a lofty style from classic literature–disparate manners fused by his sense of history and his position as an intellectual aligned with the workers. The passage from *A Drunk Man* that begins in the old ballad way–

> O wha's the bride that cairries the bunch
> O' thistles blinterin' white?

blinterin', *shining*

---

[1] E.g. *Lucky Poet*, 26; *Francis George Scott* (Edinburgh, 1955), 37–here Ireland has been dropped for some reason.

[2] William Gallacher, *Revolt on the Clyde* (1949 ed.), 253-4.

–and works up through proverb-like couplets, coarse colloquial asides, and gnomic folk rhymes to the sardonically desperate 'song' –

> O Scotland is
> THE barren fig[1]

–has many a counterpart in Brecht, the entire *Threepenny Opera* for example, or (in a condensed way) the 'Nannas Lied' from *Round Heads and Pointed Heads* (discussed in the previous chapter) that gets its effect by modulating from jaunty folk song to flat speech and heightened refrain.[2]

But differences are equally marked. MacDiarmid wanted his poems to be 'spoken in the factories and fields'. Brecht's actually were sung in the Army, on United Front marches, in the workers' theatres. Brecht can bring poetry to the verge of prose–factual, barely rhythmical–but it never sounds like broken-down verse, it doesn't run out of control into ranting verbiage. 'The Rug-weavers of Kajan-Bulak Honour Lenin', for example,[3] could be prose and is plainly close to a newspaper or magazine original. But it is so controlled by its intentness upon social conditions outside the poet's imagination that it becomes a finished, lucid fifty lines such as we fail to find anywhere in MacDiarmid's *colossi*. Brecht could dare to break up the poetic forms because he had lost neither his own rhythm nor his trust in 'the people's mouth'–the styles of utterance naturally current in society.[4]

No doubt temperament plays its part in the difference, but weight must also be given to the political situations of the two men. Brecht was forced to a deadly point of responsibility and a pitch of urgency by the most savage of all reactionary antagonists, the Nazi Fascists. The duties of a Marxist poet in such a society are at least painfully obvious. By contrast it is small wonder that MacDiarmid's talents should have been allowed to splairge all over the place in the un-urgent, fumbling, amateurish milieu of Scottish Nationalism.

At the time when MacDiarmid's poetry was coming to grief he was expelled from the Communist Party because he had advocated nationalist policies incompatible with the main purposes of the workers' movement. But there has also been continuity in his

[1] *Sel. Poems*, 40-41.
[2] See above, ch. 10, 219-20.
[3] All the Brecht examples are from the *Selected Poems*, 109, 87, 135-7.
[4] In the essay 'On Rhymeless Verse with Irregular Rhythms' Brecht remarks that Luther had 'watched the people's mouth': *Brecht on Theatre*, 117.

position. In the article he wrote for the *Daily Worker* of March 28 1957 on 'Why I Rejoined', he used points that he had first made in the 'First Hymn to Lenin':

> Even if the figures of the enemies of Communism were accurate, the killings, starvings, frame-ups, unjust judgements and all the rest of it are a mere bagatelle to the utterly mercenary and unjustifiable wars, the ruthless exploitation, the preventable deaths due to slums, and other damnable consequences of the profit motive, which must be laid to the account of the so-called 'free nations of the West'.

This is the same overriding of the facts of Stalinism that accounts for a rare uncreated patch, a piece of bluster, in verse 9 of the 'Hymn':

> As necessary, and insignificant, as death
> Wi' a' its agonies in the cosmos still
> The Cheka's horrors are in their degree;
> And'll end suner! What maitters't wha we kill
> To lessen that foulest murder that deprives
> Maist men o' real lives?[1]

So MacDiarmid's convictions and the poetry that has depended so much on them have gone in and out, now clear, now muddied, often losing themselves or failing to achieve wholeness. Setting that vein of concentrated intentness from the first half of the Thirties in the perspective of his life's work, we can see that it was too much an evocation of the *attitude* of militancy–the daily life of work and struggle that should have been dealt with in the light of this attitude or view never quite appeared. The poems singled out in the second part of this chapter are like a foretaste of what a successful progressive poet might achieve; the substantial doing of it doesn't materialise, except in 'The Seamless Garment'. Yet even to have evoked the idea of such a poetry, to have brought it at least to the verge of realisation, is an achievement unique (for obvious reasons) in the 'English-speaking' world.

NOTE ON THE MAJOR POEM SEQUENCE OF THE EARLY THIRTIES

The following 'table' sets out this work in the order in which it appeared. The left-hand list names the poems that deal more autobiographically with MacDiarmid's thinking about his life to

---

[1] *Sel. Poems*, 54. For a discussion of this aspect of the 'Hymn', see my chapter in *Criticism in Action*, 41-4.

date and the right-hand list names the ones that deal more objectively and philosophically with his intellectual concerns. Of course
this distinction is not rigid. No such 'table' can suggest even the
lines of an adequate interpretation of the poetry. The aim is purely
to draw attention to a body of work, 820 lines long, which would
have to be compared with one of the key books of Wordsworth's
Prelude if one were to suggest its range of insights and fluent lucidity
of versification.

	First Hymn to Lenin
	Prayer for a Second Flood
Charisma and My Relatives	
	The Seamless Garment
Water of Life	
Work in Progress	
By Wauchopeside	
	Whuchulls
	Milk-wort and Bog-cotton
Lynch-pin	
From 'The War with England'	
	Harry Semen
Bracken Hills in Autumn	

(These poems are all in *Selected Poems*.)

Section Four

THE NEW WAVE

CHAPTER 12

Hear Them Talking To You

FIFTEEN years ago it was understandable that people should be wondering if the arts in Britain had run dry. In Cambridge we used to ask, dispiritedly, but with a certain covert pessimistic gratification, 'What *is* there?' Which meant: had *any* good plays or novels or books of poetry been published–apart from work by artists established before 1939–in the post-War decade? Since then, however, we have had a flowering–wildly mixed in quality but unmistakably fertile–in the theatre, in fiction, in songs and popular music, in new arts of radio and television.

The artists concerned form a real movement, although many of them, being individualists, have disowned this grouping. The Angry Young Men catch-phrase never did justice to all they had in common. They included: Brendan Behan, playwright and songster, a house-painter from Dublin; Alan Sillitoe, novelist, who began his working life in the Raleigh factory at Nottingham; Arnold Wesker, playwright, who did various manual jobs after leaving London's East End; Shelagh Delaney, playwright, a shop assistant from Salford; Keith Waterhouse, playwright, novelist, and scriptwriter, son of a corner shopkeeper in Hunslet, Leeds; David Storey, novelist and playwright, a miner's son from the West Riding; John Braine, novelist, a West Riding public-librarian; Raymond Williams, novelist and critic, son of a Welsh railway signalman. . . . The list could go on: what matters is that almost without exception these artists–unlike the poets and novelists of the Thirties–had not had further education or at least came from a home, and a class, where it was exceptional, and that in their writing they stayed close to their own culture, by which I mean the speech and the habits and experiences among which they were brought up. The new work is also mainly provincial, and especially Northern: to the above could be added the Lancashire playwright Henry Livings, the Yorkshire playwright John Arden, in criticism Richard Hoggart from Leeds, in the folk song revival Ewan MacColl from Salford, and in the most popular arts the Merseyside beat groups and the best of the television serials (especially 'Z Cars' and 'Coronation Street'). An artist, or an artiste, no longer needs to *disown his background* in order to succeed. One actor, a regular on 'Z Cars' and its sequel 'Softly Softly', summed it up when he said that when he first went on the stage he had to train the Midland accent out of his voice; now, for television work, he has had to rediscover it.

What matters about this many-sided cultural movement is not only that it redeems the creativity of regions often written off as a wilderness (apart from the brass bands and *The Messiah* at Christmas) but also that it has come as a refreshment to the whole national culture. This should not surprise us, if we have any sense of history, for time and again a break-through has come from sources close to the provincial working-class, after a phase when the polite arts had elaborated themselves into a dead-end. After gentlemanly poetry's long ascendancy in the sixteenth and seventeenth centuries and the final running dry of a poetry of personal experience came the demotic novel of Defoe and Fielding. After the formal Augustan poetry (based on London) and a shift of the novel into the drawing-room came a rediscovery of 'the real language of men' as a poetic medium, done 'naturally' by Burns, synthetically by Wordsworth and Coleridge. After the Thirty Years' Peace (1815-1848) and the corresponding literary lull there came, in the Hungry Forties, a wave of fiction rooted in common life or the life of outcasts from the propertied classes.[1] A shift back to the drawing-room and the elaborate analytic method natural to a leisured culture (the later Victorian novel) was followed again–during the socially militant period called the Great Unrest (1885-1914)–by a wave of writers from the working-class, very different in their natures (Shaw, Wells, Lawrence) but alike in the usual directness of their attack on social issues. And now the present wave follows three decades in which literature of some significance was written almost exclusively by metropolitan intellectuals.

This simple history should by itself check the patronising line of opinion which treats a 'vernacular' break-through as fruitful merely in that it supplies a medium in which writers can create lifelike images of working people with their mundane experiences. My view is that the re-opening of vernacular sources vivifies the main-

[1] See above, ch. 5, p. 111.

stream of expression by making possible effects, by bringing into focus experiences, of a kind which a 'received standard' language tends to miss out. This is a matter of moral quality or essential attitude, rather than of suitability to this or that regional or class setting. Standard or educated style has usually tended–and markedly so in the period of Eliot, Auden, and Greene–to stand back aloof from the human subject, sometimes neutrally, sometimes in fastidious revulsion, whereas a vernacular can hardly help embodying some kind of fellow-feeling between author and other people. For example, consider a pair of stories on roughly the same theme, one of them vernacular, the other standard. They are Brendan Behan's 'A Woman of No Standing' (*Brendan Behan's Island*, 1962) and Angus Wilson's 'A Story of Historical Interest' (*The Wrong Set*, 1949; Penguin, 1959). In each story an old man is dying and the family are scandalised by the presence of a woman, not the wife, whom the old man is attracted to. Behan's style has the unbuttoned ease of the oral medium–it was spoken onto tape; but although it is next door to a comedian's monologue, it is never facetious. It can move from satire on the priesthood, to an effortless physical vitality which precludes morbidity ('the grave diggers [were] well away to it'), to the stricken atmosphere of the ending. It is an extraverted style, based on people's speaking aloud to each other, yet (one should not need to say 'yet') this does not at all preclude nuances of feeling and tone:

> The sods were thrown in and all, and the grave diggers well away to it when Máire spotted her.
> 'Mother, get the full of your eyes of that one.'
> 'Where, alanna?' asks Ria.
> 'There,' said Máire, pointing towards a tree behind us. I looked towards it.
> All I could see was a poor middle-aged woman, bent in haggard prayers, dressed in the cast-off hat and coat of some *flahool* [generous] old one she'd be doing a day's work for (maybe not so *flahool* either, for sometimes they'll stop a day's pay on the head of some old rag, rejected from a jumble sale).
> 'But I thought,' says I to Ria, 'that she'd be like–like–that she'd be dolled up to the nines–paint and powder and a fur coat maybe.'
> 'Fur coat, how are you,' said Ria scornfully, 'and she out scrubbing halls for me dear departed this last four years–since he took bad.'
> She went off from behind her tree before we left the cemetery.

When Ria, Máire and myself got into the Brian Boru, there
she was at the end of the counter.

I called two drinks and a mineral for Máire, and as soon as
she heard my voice, she looked up, finished her gill of plain
porter and went off.

She passed quite near us and she going out of the door—her
head down and a pale hunted look in her eyes.

This ending catches perfectly the inglorious feelings of the
characters: just as they are too chastened to speak, so the story
avoids any impressive flourish to end with. It is the kind of effect
that plain-spoken prose finds natural.

Wilson's story contrasts with Behan's straightaway in the description of the illness. Where Behan writes simply, 'His face all caved
in, and his hair that was once so brown and curly was matted in
sweat, and God knows what colour', Wilson dwells wincingly on
detail:

> His face looked so strange, almost blue grey, and at intervals
> he was sick into the little white bowl which she or Harold held
> up to him . . . just a thin, watery fluid with globules of green
> phlegm floating in it. . . . The thick hairs had got coated to-
> gether and stuck to the body with sweat and urine, and she
> had pulled at them in her efforts to sponge him.

'She' is Lois, the old man's unmarried, unattractive daughter,
bitterly disapproving, secretly envious, of the boldly sexy Irish
nurse who attracts the old man's attentions. To pick a sure path
through this queasy ground it would be essential for the writer to
make it plain that the story was done through Lois's *persona*, that the
style and attitude were hers. Yet this is just what fails to emerge:
for one thing, the style has the same nagging pettiness in the noting
of little repulsive details, little unworthiness or spots of 'bad taste',
when description is coming straight from the author as it does when
the awareness is Lois's; and secondly, this same style is indistin-
guishable from the author's in his other stories where there is no
persona and where we still find that same disproportionate insistence
on the unpleasant (an old woman getting blind drunk and obscene,
a little boy torturing a bird).

There is, then, no simple scale by which one could place Behan
as too obvious or 'simple' and Wilson as satisfactorily complex or
subtle. For Wilson's is a sensitivity that is off-balance, a studied
fullness of realisation which goes against the grain of the morally
acceptable, which *feels* so much that it winces and shudders with

revulsion. And even that mis-states the matter: Wilson feels, not *so much*, but *in such a way* that he cannot bear physical humanity, for there is a fullness of physical experience and an extreme of awareness (e.g. D. H. Lawrence's) which does not entail a neurotic distaste for what is experienced. (This point has to be made in the teeth of a prevalent literary opinion that if you plumb humanity to the depths, you discover horror, with the converse that it is superficial to consider humanity not irredeemably twisted.)

This is by no means a demand for the elevating, cheering, or 'positive', nor an equally doctrinaire argument that the educated literary medium today is bound to express neurosis. Wilson is an extreme case – the middle-class sensibility in caricature form. Other writers have been able to work in the same stratum of social experience with quite different results. An example most relevant to this matter of vernacular idiom is the story 'To Room Nineteen' from Doris Lessing's collection *A Man and Two Women* (1963). In it a well-to-do woman, at the end of her tether, moves steadily towards suicide. The milieu is Wilson country: parties in Richmond, converted cottages in the Home Counties, professional people in an uneasy world of status, self-conscious taste, standards to be lived up to. Yet the final effect is not one of pettiness so remorselessly concentrated on that it extinguishes all sense of life being at least in some way valuable. The difference lies in the style – in the quality of attitude that it embodies.

> And so they lived with their four children in their gardened house in Richmond and were happy. They had everything they had wanted and had planned for.
> *And yet . . .*
> Well, even this was expected, that there must be a certain flatness . . .
> Yes, yes, of course, it was natural they sometimes felt like this. Like what?
> Their life seemed to be like a snake biting its tail. Matthew's job for the sake of Susan, children, house, and garden – which caravanserai needed a well-paid job to maintain it. And Susan's practical intelligence for the sake of Matthew, the children, the house and the garden – which unit would have collapsed in a week without her.
> But there was no point about which either could say: 'For the sake of *this* is all the rest.'
> . . . Both Susan and Matthew had moments of . . . looking in secret disbelief at this thing they had created: marriage,

four children, big house, garden, charwomen, friends, cars . . .
and this *thing*, this entity, all of it had come into existence,
been blown into being out of nowhere, because Susan loved
Matthew and Matthew loved Susan. Extraordinary. So that
was the central point, the well-spring.

The mobile colloquial style plays freely on and around the subject,
evoking a flickering sense of various possibilities which the author
explores (however ironically) with the characters. She is not standing back and eyeing them without feeling, like specimens pinned
out for dissection; they are allowed to speak out their own drama,
for the narrative style is the English they would use in life. Thus the
play of emotion that is there in any life, however seized-up, is
caught as it cannot be in Wilson's frigid demonstrations, and for
the reader a richer, less predictable experience results. The key
linguistic difference is that where Wilson is writing standard
English, basically a printed medium, Doris Lessing is using a
vernacular, which can follow thoughts and feelings as they spring
to the lips.

Thus the vernacular is not only working-class, provincial, or
dialect (although these are indeed the areas least influenced by the
centralised media). The fresh impulse that has come into fiction,
drama, and song is that ordinary life is being allowed to speak out
and dramatise itself in its own medium. 'Ordinary life' is often
thought a question-begging term—is not everyone 'ordinary'? The
fact is that most of the classic literature in our tradition is from the
viewpoint, in the idiom, of people who, partly by temperament but
mainly by their place in society, are able to stand back from
immediate experience and inspect it, analyse and define it, by
introspection, generalisation, by applying the techniques fostered
by higher education. A working man, typically, does something
material, he gets a finite result which he sees before his eyes: he
chamfers steel cylinders at a lathe (Arthur Seaton in *Saturday Night
and Sunday Morning*), he kicks a football (Arthur Machin in *This
Sporting Life*), he plants seed-potatoes (the characters in Arnold
Wesker's *Roots*), he sells over a counter or hauls a net. The professional or employing-class person, typically, works at a point of
indirect relationship with material existence: a business-man deals
in steel or fruit or money, not with his own fingers but *via* signs on
paper, *via* the physical actions of someone else. The immediate
object of his activity—a document, a book, a set of figures—is not

complete in itself, it signifies only as an equivalent of something else. His activity is thus secondary; not less real, but different. We have to think of social classes, therefore, as having distinctive cultures, or in literary terms distinctive styles, which are intelligible mutually, and shade into each other, but are distinct at their extremes.

Criticism, therefore, must not assume that leisured analysis, and the elaboration of style that it gives rise to, is the ideal to which all literature must tend, with the converse that the simpler a style is, the cruder it is and the less adequate to the complexities of experience. The verbal counterpart of the workman's life (as sketched above) is *directness*, bluntness. He typically speaks short and sharp and is less likely than someone from the middle-class to filter his meaning through euphemism, elaborate forms of address, or qualifications arising from personal feelings and consciousness of self. The best New Wave work has shown how a medium of seeming bluntness can be rich, unobvious, and morally searching in its total effect. For example, 'ordinary life' (as used above) means life at the kitchen sink, clocking-in at work, being an order-taker rather than an employer or a free-lance, having just enough to live on and no extra resources behind you. This is commonly considered 'limited', as when critics and headmistresses are surprised that someone of sensitive talent should have come from a manual worker's home.[1] Consider, however, the ending of Wesker's story 'Pools' (in *Modern Jewish Stories*, ed. Gerda Charles, 1963). An old widow woman in the East End of London has a summer holiday unexpectedly paid for by neighbours grateful for all she has done for them. She goes off to a seaside village in East Anglia. But the peace and quiet of Sunday in the country seems very blank to the Londoner. She can't even get a paper to check her pools. She beats a retreat to London and, overcome by nerves and excitement, begins to think that she must have won the £75,000. A soiled sports page is fluttering about the station floor and she goes off to check her results in the one private place, the women's toilet:

> Carefully she folded the newspaper leaving in sight in the smallest space possible all the results she wanted. Then, with-

---

[1] E.g. John Russell Taylor, *Anger and After* (1963 ed., 131): Wesker 'seemed in the first place a highly unlikely candidate for literary distinction: his father was a tailor and after leaving school his first jobs were as plumber's mate and kitchen porter.'

drawing a yellow pencil from her handbag she checked, one by one, her entries on her coupon.

Now that the excitement was over she could not recollect why it had ever been. Her feelings were bruised, but she and the world were quite normal now. 'Why,' she said to herself, 'should Mrs. Hyams win £75,000 anyway?' She walked out of the toilet into the huge dome of the station. 'Who is Mrs. Hyams?' she asked, walking towards the luggage office. Idly she bumped into someone and said: 'I beg your pardon,' then continued among the crowds and answered herself: 'She's no one. She's nothing. So? Nu?'

It is a perfect ending, almost a non-ending, with no climax or unexpected twist. The stream of incident melts quietly back into everyday normality again. Ordinariness is, indeed, almost affirmed as a value. And what this ending, like the whole style, is based on is the carrying-on, the making-do, the staunchness and lack of self-importance that are typical of unprivileged people. This is not to say that sheer ordinariness has some self-justifying value. Its significance cannot be brought out without creative skill in the rendering, as when Wesker chooses to *end* precisely at that moment of realisation for Mrs Hyams. The unmemorable, deadpan art that results from rendering the ordinary or usual with no particular sense of value or direction can be seen in Stan Barstow's West Riding novel *A Kind of Loving* (1960): for example, contrast its breakfast scene (chap. 3) with the exactly similar scene in another West Riding novel, Keith Waterhouse's *Billy Liar* (1959, chap. 1). The one is nothing but a neutral image of the average, which quite fails to sharpen or deepen our sense of things we know perfectly well already, whereas Waterhouse's scene is permeated by a fresh sensuous feel for that kind of moment in the day and further sharpened by his exact noting of the incongruities of ordinary conversation.

Can the vernacular manage longer flights? Can it suggest thought? Consider a dialogue from Colin MacInnes's *Absolute Beginners* (1959). The book is written in a version of London teenage slang. Like much of MacInnes's fiction it is half-imagined, half-documentary; he aims to 'cover' the life of coloured people, or teenagers, or prostitutes and policemen, to cover the Notting Hill race riots much as a first-rate reporter might have done. So his novels are up-to-date, and presently will become out-of-date and lose part of their interest. But in places he is more closely engaged

with people, as in this dialogue (from the first chapter) between a
youth who scoots about on his Vespa, taking photographs for smart
magazines, and a Lesbian ponce who lives in the same block of flats:

'I mean, anyone can have a bash, that's obvious, there's
nothing to it, but is there any pleasure?'

'Well, isn't there, big boy?' she asked me, giving a great, fat
smile.

'Oh, of course there is, in that way, yes, but there isn't
really, because you can't have it just like that without messing
something else that matters up, and this brings you badly
down.'

'Even if you like the party of the second part, it brings you
down?' said Jill, getting interested, as I could see.

'If you *like* the other number, I mean like the looks of them,
really dig them sexually – and I mean really – then it isn't quite
so bad, because at least you're only acting like a pair of
animals, which isn't a bad thing to do. . . . But even then,
you're still wrought badly down.'

'Wrought down because you might lose them?'

'No, no, not that. Because you've not really got them,
because they aren't the person.'

'What person?'

'The person you really dig, with all of yourself, your other
half you'd give your life to.'

'You're not referring to marriage, are you?'

'No, no, no, no, no, Big Jill.'

'To *love*?'

'Yep. That's it. To it.'

Big J's eyes were pale, so that she seemed to be staring into
herself, and not out into the room at me.

'You ever had that combo?' she enquired.

'No.'

'Not even with Suzette?'

'No. Me, yes, I was ready for that everything stage of it but
for Suze it was only a head, bodies and legs thing, when it
happened.'

One is absorbed here by the drama of two people trying to winnow
out the truth. Their slang (scrupulously kept to) cannot go deep,
it can't suggest nuances of inmost feelings or come out with a classic
statement of what 'love' is. It creates significance in a different way:
the lad's reluctance to bring out the easy, hallowed word 'love', his
embarrassed circling round it and finally having to accept it, shows
us, with idiomatic precision, sincerity in action.

MacInnes's novels, it is true, do not follow through a life;
characters are used to set moving some events which will enable the

novelist to rove among topical scenes, which he renders because
they matter socially at present. In David Storey's *This Sporting Life*
(1960) there is a full and strong sense of following through a life—
that of a man slowly coming to realise that there will never be
anything very exhilarating for him. It is done in a style as close
as possible to what we can imagine coming from someone with
no special language, no extraordinary sensitivity, with which to
register experience. The style seems, phrase by phrase, blunt,
coarse, abrupt; yet the effect is of a lot being explored, of complex
personalities being plumbed. Arthur Machin is employed at a big
engineering works in the West Riding and plays rugby in the
League for the money and the kudos:

> He [a workmate, already a League star] was admired and he
> was detested. It wasn't difficult to decide who felt what. He'd
> given up using the works' canteen and went to a nearby
> transport cafe with a couple of pals. He looked pretty special
> I thought. And he was only my age.
> By playing Rugby League he kept his head above the
> general level of crap, and that to me was the main thing.
>
> (Part 1, ch. 2)

If the main figure, the 'I', so echoes an attitude of heedless, brutal
cynicism, can he be an adequate medium for the novel? won't he
sink it in a limiting coarseness of feeling? or if this is criticised, can
it be done without a sheer rejection of *la vie moyenne sensuelle*, a
turning-away which would fail to substantially register the object
of its revulsion? In practice the effect is not crude at all. Consider
the scene in which Arthur, newly signed on by the Club, is given
a lift home by the director who is also owner of the factory:

> Standing under the lamp was the Bentley. It had a blue
> gleam. I could smell it twenty yards away. I walked round the
> other side and waited for him to open the door. A pale hand
> reached out to release the catch. 'Jump in, lad,' he invited.
> 'I've got the heater on.' It was warm, soft, and scented: a
> cinema armchair.
> We slid down the lane and turned into the road. 'Fairfax
> Street, you said?'
> It sounded a new place, maybe a dirtier, scruffier place,
> now that it was coated with his voice. 'Yes,' I replied.
> I didn't say anything for a while, then I told him, 'I thought
> I saw you at the "A" team match this afternoon'. I looked at
> his rubber outline and felt hat. It seemed he was concentrating
> on the road.

'This afternoon,' he said with faint interest. 'Yes, I came to watch.' He smiled with quiet reproval. 'You didn't play too well.'

'Did anybody?'

'That's a point.'

He moved the wheel a bit, flashed a few lights, changed a gear, switched the dashboard glow on a second, squinted at the dials: everything as if I wasn't there.

'What do you think of Wade's bargaining powers?' he asked, 'Did you find him "tough opposition"?'

'I don't think I found him anything. I just kept saying five hundred and hoping the result'd turn out right.'

He shot round a couple of cars, dimmed his lights, and said, 'Has it?'

'Turned out right? I think so. I hadn't expected it to be done so quickly.' He must have thought, with the five hundred now in my pocket, I was trying to be naive. He glanced across. 'I don't really know what to think,' I said.

'What's it feel like to be five hundred up in one day?'

How much of me did he want? I could feel him polishing me and putting me on the shelf as his latest exhibit. He came and breathed over me and gave a gentle rub of his cuff.

'I don't feel anything yet.'

'It's all a bit quick,' he suggested vaguely.

'Yes.'

. . . We passed Highfield and he said, 'Riley–he looked a bit sick, I thought. What do you think? He likes to manage these affairs rather smartly, you know. Make them look like big business. These crumby accountants, I find they always like to do that. Dress the money up to disguise the filth it is. What do you think?'

'Maybe it's filth I like.'

He was laughing again. It was like turning a little knob. He wanted me to feel a good chap, so he laughed. I laughed with him. I couldn't say I disliked him. He was giving me all these confidences, if they were that. 'One of the family' business. I just felt a bit shy, being the newest member.

(Part 1, ch. 1)

The moral slant and general texture of this are typical of the novel and they strike me as perfectly done. There must be no too-righteous prompting to disapproval of Weaver: that would be out of character for a worker narrator, the working-class being less prone to moralise and disapprove than the middle-class. Yet Weaver's insidiousness and manipulation of people must be placed somehow. It is done by the brief but intense physical touches– 'coated', 'rubber outline'–and by the half-admiring, half-scornful attitude to the Bentley, which is more of a presence than Weaver himself. In sum it is of course a fuller, more searching narrative of the experience than a worker-footballer would be likely to come out with, yet from point to point it does not go beyond the immediate, rather than deliberately analytical, insight natural to such a man. The key is the style, staccato and full of humdrum details in the manner of the kind of book that Arthur would read—Peter Cheyney and debased Hemingway generally. Yet each detail is so placed and sharpened by the novelist that interest and significance are created even while character is being kept to.

The special interest of the scene is that it shows us the middle-class man repeatedly inviting the working-man to feel, judge, introspect, define, and generally detach himself intellectually from his experience in a way that is precisely foreign to his culture. This is also the trend of Beatie Bryant's arguments with her family in Wesker's *Roots*, when, having been converted to Culture by her literary boy-friend Ronnie, she goes home for a visit in the spirit of a missionary sent by the intelligentsia into darkest Norfolk. The wisdom of the play is in the fact that the advantage at the end lies neither with Ronnie's self-conscious intellectualism nor the family's stubborn refusal to extend their minds and tastes; it lies with Beatie in her triumphant discovery of how to express her cultural deprivation *in her own words*:

> The writers don't write thinkin' we can understand, nor the painters don't paint expectin' us to be interested—that they don't nor don't the composers give out music thinkin' we can appreciate it. 'Blust,' they say, 'the masses is too stupid for us to come down to them. . . . If they want slop songs and film idols we'll give 'em that then. If they want words of one syllable, we'll give 'em that then. If they want the third rate, BLUST! we'll give 'em THAT then . . .' We want the third-rate—we got it! We got it! We got it! We . . .
> (*Suddenly* BEATIE *stops as if listening to herself. She pauses, turns with an ecstatic smile on her face—*)
> D'you hear that? D'you hear it? Did you listen to me? I'm talking. Jenny, Frankie, mother—I'm not quotin' no more.
> MRS. BRYANT (*getting up to sit at table*): Oh hell, I had enough of her—let her talk awhile she'll soon get fed up . . .
> (*The murmur of the family sitting down to eat grows as* BEATIE'S *last cry is heard. Whatever she will do they will continue to live as before and the* CURTAIN FALLS *as* BEATIE *stands alone—articulate at last.*)

Critics have objected, 'But what is Beatie to do with her articulacy?'[1] I can't see that we are entitled to reach beyond the play (any more than we need be assured that Malcolm will rule well after the end of *Macbeth*). But one thing that Beatie's *generation* have done with their articulacy is to give an image and a voice to the life of the majority in a way that has been too rare in art.

[1] John Mander, *The Writer and Commitment* (1961), 190.

CHAPTER 13

Sillitoe and the Roots of Anger

THE paperback of *Saturday Night and Sunday Morning* used to show the hero (as played by Albert Finney in the film which Sillitoe himself scripted) standing with legs astride, in a draped jacket, the whole posture and expression like something from a gangster film, with a quotation at the side: 'Makes *Room at the Top* look like a vicarage tea-party'. And *Room at the Top*, as a film, had itself been advertised (in Leeds) under the caption: 'Savage Tale of Lust and Ambition in Bradford'. My own copy of Brendan Behan's auto-biography *Borstal Boy* (1958), which is a prose masterpiece, was bought at the stall on Darlington Station platform, in a cover that showed a brown-clad borstal boy, evidently at bay, in a boxer's stance, with fingers hooked – although the book has little savagery or bloodshed in it. There is no excuse for marketing work under false pretences. But what is wholly good is that our writers should now be able to write in a style – to transmit on a wavelength – that has something in common with what *most people read*. Ever since the time of Dickens, a split has been opening wider and wider between the popular and the 'quality' – between lowbrow and highbrow, to use the suitably pernicious terms. But now, since the 1950s, many of the best writers have rediscovered the approach of Frank Norris, the Chicago novelist from early this century: 'A litera-ture that cannot be vulgarised is no literature at all and will perish'.[1]

This movement has been more concerned than any other in literary history with the experience of youth. In *Saturday Night* Arthur knows that he is having a last fling (several last flings) before the responsibilities of manhood close in. The hero of Sillitoe's next work, a long story, 'The Loneliness of the Long-distance Runner' (1959: film 1962), is still in his teens and is lashing out at the system of law and respectability. The heroine of Shelagh

---

[1] Used by Farrell as one of the epigraphs to *Studs Lonigan*.

Delaney's play *A Taste of Honey* (1958: film 1961) is also in her teens and is struggling to form her first independent relationship. Colin MacInnes made the life of the coffee-bars and the Notting Hill back-streets, at the time when the mods were starting to vie with the rockers, the subject of *Absolute Beginners*. Keith Waterhouse has written two novels which in a seemingly light, and very funny, style recreate to perfection late childhood and early and late youth in the West Riding cities (*There Is a Happy Land*, 1957; *Billy Liar*, 1959)–exactly as Sid Chaplin has done, with a Tyneside setting, in *The Day of the Sardine* (1961; Panther 1965).

What is more, these writers have been so close to the way most people live, so interested in everyday experience, that they have allowed such life to unfold in its own language, the speech of the characters themselves, rather than the standard English of a detached observer as in most literature hitherto. Not only the dialogue but the whole narrative of *Absolute Beginners* is in the speech of a smart young mod, giving his elders flip nicknames ('serf', 'conscript', 'squalid') and lacing his speech with short-lived slang from the latest trends in showbiz and pop. Brendan Behan wrote as he spoke, in the quick-witted Irish English that can pass from a joke to a scalding protest inside one sentence. In *There is a Happy Land* Waterhouse catches the child's absorption in the present moment by writing the whole novel in the child's own mixture of daft nonsense-talk, violent slanging matches, and the like.

This faithfulness to speech may well stem partly from television, which ruthlessly shows up any touch of the high-flown or false and therefore makes writers develop an acute ear for natural language. A slavish or hurried use of this approach can reduce the literary artist to a tape-recorder, able only to catch what life offers him at the moment, lacking in long-range themes of his own. The reader of *Saturday Night* has to decide whether it is solidly created through and through or whether, in places, it too easily takes for granted certain attitudes and images (e.g. the 'I'm-all-right-Jack' working man) which were already in the headlines and on the screen.

We can come nearer to Sillitoe's art by listening to his style:

> Who loses on a wage-snatch–the workers? Of course not. It's the company–and they can usually stand it. It's the same with banks–if I have a few thousand from a bank, theoretically it's their customers' money I've taken. But you never hear of a bank apportioning the losses round their customers, do you?

'We're so sorry, Major Bloodworthy, somebody blew our
safe last night and took ten thousand quid—and it was your
ten thousand quid that was in there!' Mind you, I'm not
saying they shouldn't; to me it's quite an attractive idea.

This in fact comes from a book tape-recorded by a prison visitor
from the spontaneous talk of a professional thief.[1] In its eloquence,
its aggressive self-justification, its quick shifts of viewpoint, and its
broad popular caricaturing, it is 'pure Sillitoe': the likeness shows
how close and strong is Sillitoe's feeling for the *culture* of the rebellious, the ill-used, the unskilled. Here is the long-distance runner
recalling, in borstal, the theft that got him caught:

> . . . how good it was that blokes like that poor baker didn't
> stash all his cash in one of the big marble-fronted banks that
> take up every corner of the town, how lucky for us that he
> didn't trust them no matter how many millions of tons of
> concrete or how many iron bars and boxes they were made of,
> or how many coppers kept their blue pop-eyed peepers glued
> on to them, how smashing it was that he believed in money-
> boxes when so many shop keepers thought it old-fashioned
> and tried to be modern by using a bank, which wouldn't give
> a couple of sincere, honest, hard-working, conscientious blokes
> like Mike and me a chance.'[2]

The long-distance runner is bitterly soured against a society which
he has harmed and which has harmed him. Yet his reactions to the
world are still lively: we feel it in the vigour of the very words,
'coppers kept their blue pop-eyed peepers glued'. This appetite for
experience, this facing up to its details however raw or gritty, is
what gives Sillitoe's writing its characteristic onward drive and its
repeated explosion into metaphors and militant asides. *Saturday
Night* is not told in the first person but it feels as though it were,
especially in the informal, sometimes headlong movement of the
style and the closeness to Arthur's trains of thought as he sums up
his life or stops short to justify himself. Of course it is not the same as
actual spoken reminiscence: the language is often heightened by
deliberate art, as when a trolley-bus is seen as 'a lighted greenhouse
growing people'. But the whole thing is so flexible that the joins
never show: a fine balance is struck between straight imitation of
rough speech and a style which is rooted in such speech but makes
it express more than it would in life.

[1] Tony Parker, *The Courage of his Convictions* (1969 ed.), 92.
[2] *The Loneliness of the Long-distance Runner* (1959), 29.

The style registers vividly all sorts of particulars from the noisy, busy, congested life of an old industrial town. We are made to see, hear, feel, smell, and sense in our muscles Arthur Seaton's Nottingham. Any writer must do that with his chosen environment. But we particularly need writers who can do it for the towns and cities that grew fast after 1800, where most people live. Ever since industrialism took over, writers in the vein of Ruskin and William Morris, Lawrence and Eliot, have either argued from the physical ugliness, the blight of spoiled ground and the sprawl of unplanned jerry-building, to the feelings of people themselves, not seeing that human beings have extraordinary inborn powers of resistance and enjoyment; or else they have taken a disgusted line about modern human nature itself and supposed that our actual capacity for experience has been weakened ever since the good old days (whenever they were).

Sillitoe's way of writing in *Saturday Night* shows that he knows these arguments very well. He emphasises the ugliness, dirt and noise of the environment and presents this side of the Midland city as being indeed what Lewis Mumford has called the 'insensate industrial town' from the age of 'palaeotechnic disorder'–the unplanned, coal-powered phase of the Industrial Revolution.[1] Sillitoe also emphasises the rote nature of the work which Arthur has to do to earn his living. But instead of turning these things into a one-track account which would in effect write off the possibilities of satisfying experience under modern conditions–as Eliot does throughout *The Waste Land* or Lawrence in the colliery passages of *The Rainbow*, *Women in Love*, and *Lady Chatterley's Lover*–Sillitoe is able to show us convincingly, again and again, the openings for satisfaction and enjoyment, and the ability to seize them, which are there not only in the teeth of the insensate industrial town but partly through its very busyness and closeness. In that image quoted already, the trolley-bus 'like a lighted greenhouse growing people', the grubby clanking vehicle is seen afresh, enhanced. But it isn't prettified or gilded. The image is visually very exact, and it also has the extra lift given by that imaginative touch, 'growing people', which in a flash puts us in touch with all the back gardens and allotments where tomatoes and chrysanthemums hold up their coloured heads amongst a waste of rubbish tips, condemned

[1] See *The Culture of Cities*, ch. 3 and plates 11-12, or *The City in History*, ch. 15 and plates 39-40.

buildings, and dirty canals. As for Arthur's way of life, he does indeed spend many hours at his lathe binding and grinding at the way the work ties him down. But anyone who thinks this is unrelieved–that the job crushes the least opening for freedom, initiative, or pride in skill and strength–should ponder the paragraphs from chapter 2 beginning 'The bright Monday-morning ring of the clocking-in machine' and ending 'ran in the drill to a neat chamfer. Monday morning had lost its terror'. The total effect of those paragraphs is a blend of many feelings and suggestions, and they must all be allowed to count.

Sillitoe, then, brings to the writing of his novel a many-sided feeling for life, without which a writer simply cannot keep his head amidst the swarm and shock of urban life as it is now. This feeling of his he seems to owe to his origins. He had come from the thick of city life and been in no way sheltered from it. His father had been active on the Left wing before the War; this comes through in the novel as those stinging vernacular wisecracks that make a monkey of the Establishment (government and trade-union leadership alike). The passage at the start of chapter 15, 'Once a rebel, always a rebel', goes so perfectly with the rhythms of a man laying down the law in the public bar that it always kindles laughter when read aloud to a crowd. What matters is not the agin-the-government point of the cracks, which is ordinary enough, but rather the relish as the words land smack on target. In this way Arthur's militancy is not political–his anti-political bias will be touched on later–but rather the aggressive side of a general relish for life that we might call 'heartiness' if that word hadn't been ruined. The Christmas merry-making in chapter 14, the horse-play as the wage-packet is divided out on Friday evening (chapter 4)–that kind of zest in handling basic things like drink and food and money, along with the rebelliousness, is extraordinarily like Burns's poetry. Burns too finds choice abusive phrases for his bugbears in the Establishment– the businessman

> purse-proud, big wi' cent. per cent.
> An' muckle wame.

Burns too revels in drinking and spending and makes his words describing them run with a kind of dance of enjoyment:

> . . . ilka melder wi' the miller,
> Thou sat as lang as thou had siller;

That ev'ry naig was ca'd a shoe on
The smith and thee gat roarin' fou on. . . .
Fast by an ingle, bleezing finely,
Wi' reaming swats that drank divinely. . . .

melder, *load of grain*: siller, *money*: swats, *mugs*

They both spend their most vehement sarcasm on moral restraint, whether it is cankered puritanism and self-righteousness or sober good-sense. They are even alike in their sudden, momentarily surprising but absolutely natural delight in wild nature: Burns looking with a friendly eye at the hare scudding down the furrows on a fresh summer morning, Sillitoe's hero beside the 'willow-sleeved' canal sensing the likeness between the landed fish and himself about to be married. In one thing after another the eighteenth-century Scottish poet and the English novelist of our own time are closely alike. They embody, in a word, the mixed feelings and experiences *of their class*.

That generalisation is disputable, especially at a time when it is often suggested (e.g. by the *Sun* in its first editorial, in 1965) that class has disappeared in Britain. It is true that it is hard to form an acceptable definition of any one class, in its typical behaviour and outlook, and equally hard for a reader to decide whether a character represents a group of any kind or is purely himself (if that is possible). First, we must know what the author himself is trying to do. Sillitoe surely does mean Arthur to stand as in many ways a typical working man. The title of the novel plants it firmly in the life, the routine, of the wage (and not the salary) earner. Passage after passage, especially those which establish Arthur's sense of where he belongs in England and his view of other groups and ways of life, present him as a type of worker from an old centre of manufacture, hard-drinking, free-spending, instinctively against the boss. A type but not the type. A type, especially in literature, need not mean an average, or one of a majority; it need mean only that enough traits have been picked and rendered to bring out the factors common to many members of a group whatever their other differences. Working-men rightly resent the sort of argument which seems to suppose that twenty million people can be covered by one label. A West Riding garment worker at a class of mine was making this point when he objected that Arthur had only himself to blame for his discontents – 'he could easily have become a charge-hand if he'd wanted to'. This perhaps overlooks the rebelliousness rooted in Arthur's temperament which no promotion could do away with. But at least it reminds us that not all who live a life something like Arthur's would necessarily accept him as their spokesman.

Arthur's particular temperament, then, takes away from his typicality to some degree. At point after point the reader has to decide for himself whether a reaction that is shown comes from Arthur's innate habit of aggressive self-justification, always looking for trouble, or whether it has been wished on him by the conditions of his life. Is his resentment at Robboe the foreman an inevitable reaction to the dour factory discipline? or is it envy of the comfort which Robboe has truly earned? If the fiction is solidly-created through and through, it should be possible to answer such a question. In particular readers will want to dwell on all those instances where Arthur experiences a sudden flare-up of rebelliousness or plain aggression, when he wants to blow Nottingham Castle sky-high or to get some of Them in the sights of his Bren-gun. When (near the end of chapter 2) Arthur thinks how he would like to blow up the factory and says to himself, 'Not that I've owt against 'em, but that's just how I feel now and again,' have we been shown enough in the way of motive for this impulse? or has it been sprung on us? When (at the end of chapter 14) Arthur secretly exults at the crack of the beer glass on Jim's forehead, do we know where his emotion is coming from? has it been led up to? The more socially-directed Arthur's destructive anger is supposed to be, the wider the grounds it must be given, if we are not to suspect that a personal chip on the shoulder has been smuggled in in the guise of objective militancy, and at some points the writing makes it hard to be sure which it is. Arthur's spite against the castle (e.g. near the start of chapter 5) is tinged with anti-Establishment feelings, and the castle was indeed burned by Radicals in the 1830s; but the fact remains that it is now a perfectly worthwhile art-gallery and museum (admission free), and that Arthur's feelings have been touched off by personal pique. Above all, when Arthur is leading up to his grand finale about 'fighting every day until I die . . . Fighting with mothers and wives, landlords and gaffers, coppers, army, government', the reader will want to think back and consider which of these famous bugbears Arthur has actually grappled with.

Perhaps the most fruitful way of rounding off one's thinking about this aspect of *Saturday Night* is to compare it with David

Storey's *This Sporting Life*. Storey's hero, Arthur Machin, is like Arthur Seaton in that he simmers with frustration at his way of life. Towards the end he too breaks into one of those scalding outbursts against conventional life that have been familiar since John Osborne's *Look Back in Anger*: 'Mothers, mothers. Always mothers. Women are never anything but mothers. . . . Mothers or prostitutes –that's women.'[1] What makes this ring so validly in its context in the novel is that Machin has only been driven to this denunciation by a long series of cruel stresses. There is no danger of his being a ready-made mouthpiece for the author. This is confirmed by the style of the novel. Although it is in the first person, it is so terse, each phrase so biting, that it never threatens to run away with the novel – to lead the author to identify himself too much, and unwittingly, with his hero.

It still has to be explained why writers with these characteristics should have appeared when they did: 'The period has seen, almost for the first time in Britain, the appearance of a quite sizable body of fiction that can fairly be called working-class'.[2] This matter is so large, and new, that it must be thought over and worked out by us all, as our reading goes on, rather than guessed at before we know enough; but the causes must surely reach into the heart of our society. People had come out of the War with a new confidence. The old dependence was waning fast as the social causes of it grew less – fear of unemployment, dictatorial bosses able to do what they liked and treat workers as mere 'hands', a wage only just high enough for survival, and the rest of the crushing social conditions shared by millions until 1939. During the War the trade unions were consulted by government, treated as partners, as never before. The armed forces had become much more egalitarian than in the Great War: officers lived and dressed plainly, at least at the Front, and took the rank and file into their confidence. The 1944 Education Act held out the promise that schooling till 18 and college training after that could become as possible for a clerk's or a docker's child as for a bank manager's or a doctor's. Somewhere amongst these liberating forces must lie the source of that surge of outspoken confidence and initiative which, since the summer of 1945, has shown itself everywhere in our society, in politics, industry, and schooling, in songs and television and literature. The

[1] 1962 ed., 209.
[2] Walter Allen, *Tradition and Dream*, xxii.

matter can be taken further by raising three specific points that are bound up with it: Why are Sillitoe and his fellow writers radical-minded yet mistrustful of politics? deeply interested in violence and crime? and much more interested in daily working life than any other group of writers before them?

Sillitoe is certainly close (through his father) to the labour movement, and he ends his longest novel, *Key to the Door* (1961), with the hero ready to live out his adult life as a trade-unionist with communist leanings. Yet Sillitoe himself goes with no party (although he has written for the Anarchist paper) and he repeatedly gives his characters anti-political views to utter. Nearly all the new artists and artistes have lent their weight to the peace movement; but with the exception of Wesker, who has done his campaigning for a non-profit-making culture in co-operation with the trade unions, they seem to have felt that the more organised bodies (unions, parties) can only thwart or corrupt individual initiatives. Writers with radical views have usually been free-lance rebels, like Sillitoe or Arden or Osborne or Behan (after he left the Irish Republican Army), or else they have in the end given up their radicalism, like Kingsley Amis and John Braine, who in 1967 sent their famous letter to *The Times* approving British support for the American warfare in Vietnam.

This trend contrasts with the Thirties, when writers were willing to channel their protest through Left-wing political groups and to accept a Left-wing ideology. What are the roots of this mixture of protest at the existing state of affairs and dislike of outright commitment? The protest carries on from 1945 when resistance to the old ruling-class at last mustered itself enough to rout its adversary.

> When 'Bomber' Harris told Churchill that eighty per cent of the Royal Air Force would vote against him, and (as the unkindest cut) that the other twenty per cent wouldn't bother to vote at all, he was not speaking of a necessarily vindictive attitude. He was simply describing a reflex attitude to national reverence.[1]

This reflex attitude persists powerfully in, for example, *Look Back in Anger*—in Jimmy Porter's attitude to his Indian Army father-in-law—and in the anti-Establishment feelings of all Sillitoe's heroes. Yet, in the new literature, the rebel makes common cause with

---

[1] Anthony Howard, 'We are the Masters Now', in Michael Sissons and Philip French (eds.), *Age of Austerity, 1945-51* (1964 ed.), 18.

no-one: his anger at bosses of all kinds does not drive him into the arms of any other group. So far as can be traced in literature, the great collective swing in the General Election of 1945 left only a short-lived residue of collective feeling and thinking throughout the country. One train of causes leading to this may be traced back to the use Labour made of its power after 1945. Hopes of social reconstruction were pinned to it that could hardly be realised. By 1949, when Labour was backing down from the policy of 'socialising whole industries' (*Age of Austerity*, 328-9), we had got a limited Welfare scheme, not 'free' but paid for partly by insurance contributions, and state ownership of the utilities plus coal and (for a few months) steel. What Aneurin Bevan was to call the 'commanding heights' of the economy, the big manufacturing industries, were still privately owned. One Labour Chancellor of the Exchequer, Dalton, was to regret that land had not been taken into social ownership; and another, Callaghan, was to say that between 1945 and 1951 Labour had 'hardly touched' the distribution of wealth in Britain. Finally the Prime Minister, Attlee, at the bidding of President Truman, decided on a 'defence' budget of £4,700 million for the following three years:

> ... the British economy now had to bear the strain of devoting 14 per cent of its national income, and almost the whole of its increased wealth for the next three years, to the needs of defence ... probably, in the long run, in excess both of the country's needs and its capacity.[1]

The more idealistic hopes for thorough social reconstruction and secure peace were dashed. Wesker makes the characters of his trilogy (which covers the years from 1936 to 1959) sum the matter up like this:

DAVE. A useless, useless bloody war because Hitler still made it, didn't he, eh? And out went six million Jews in little puffs of smoke. Am I expected to live in the glory of the nineteen thirties all my life?

SARAH. Sick. ... You're all sick or something. We won the last war didn't we? You forgotten that? We put a Labour Party in power and ...

RONNIE (*with irony*). Oh, yes, that's right! We put a Labour Party in power. Glory! Hurrah! It wasn't such a useless war after all, was it, Mother? But what did the bleeders do, eh? They sang the Red Flag in

[1] L. C. B. Seaman, *Post-Victorian Britain, 1902-1951* (1967 ed.), 494.

Parliament and then started building atom bombs.
Lunatics! Raving lunatics! And a whole generation
of us laid down our arms and retreated into ourselves,
a whole generation![1]

Our writers do not have a particularly vicious society to protest
about. It is rather that, while being naturally disinclined to accept
things as they are, they have found themselves left high and dry by
their 'own' movement. They are also unlikely to have faith in more
drastic kinds of politics after the Thirties and the War, with their
aftermath of revulsion against extremism, and then, in the Fifties
themselves, the exposure of Stalin's atrocities at the 20th Congress
of the Soviet Communist Party and the Soviet crushing of the
Hungarian workers' and students' rising in 1956. In such conditions
it is all too easy for someone with a strong sense of man's inhumanity
to man to find his conscience sparking off into a void like electricity
without a circuit. Hence, in part, the literally aimless rebelliousness
that Sillitoe reads into the Arthur Seaton type with his motto of
'No one's telling *me* what to do'.

As the Fifties wore on, another factor entered in: the end of
austerity, the sharp rise in real wages for large sections of people.
This took the worry out of millions of homes and made possible a
new comfort that people had dreamed of for ages. The mothers I
remember in my childhood in a Scottish city, aged twenty but
looking thirty-five, yellow-faced, drably dressed, carrying a baby
up the steep steps with two more young ones trailing behind, have
been replaced by brightly dressed young women pushing new
prams along the pavements of new-built estates. But the writers do
not seem glad. Sillitoe concentrates on whatever is still frowsy,
sordid, or life-denying.

Most of my mates wanted an easier job, less hours, more pay,
naturally. But it wasn't really work they hated, don't think
that. They didn't all want to be doctors or clerks, either.
Maybe they just didn't like working in oil and noise, and then
going home at night to a plate of sawdust sausages and cardboard beans, and two hours at the flicker-box with advertise-
ments telling them that those sausages and beans burning their
guts are the best food in the country. I don't suppose they
knew what they wanted in most cases – except maybe not to be
treated like cretins.[2]

[1] *I'm Talking About Jerusalem* (1960): Act III, Scene 2.
[2] *The Death of William Posters* (1965), 44.

Similarly Wesker has summed up average life as 'chips with every-thing' and Osborne has scourged us for having mini-lives – mini-cars and mini-thoughts.[1]

This protest is often expressed as a criticism of affluence. The 'private affluence' of large wage-packet and easy credit has gone along with what J. K. Galbraith has called 'public squalor': housing sinking into slums faster than old slums are cleared, one and a quarter million children in overcrowded homes, families totalling seven million living on incomes less than the National Assistance level. Our affluence has been reached by a road – the mixed economy – which allows deep inequalities, the patchiest kind of improvements, and a flourishing of rackets (Rachman-type land-lords, clubs run by crooks on American lines) which almost advertise the attractions of getting rich quick by the most anti-social methods. This climate affects the labour movement like everything else. The union organiser may find the ground taken from under his feet when the minimum wage he has won for his members is easily beaten by a go-ahead contractor. An organisation like the Lump, hiring building workers at good money but with no regard for union membership, insurance, redundancy pay, or any of the other safeguards, makes a monkey of the old labour solidarity and reduces the tie between men and job to cash and cash alone.

We can see that such a set-up might well produce men like Arthur; but where does his fascination with violence come from (in so far as it is typical)? Arthur is not of course a convict. He is not a borstal boy, unlike the heroes of 'The Long-distance Runner' or Behan's autobiography or the title-story of Sillitoe's *The Ragman's Daughter* (1963). He doesn't do time in prison, unlike the hero of David Storey's latest novel *Radcliffe* (1963) or the characters of Behan's best play *The Quare Fellow* (1956). Nor does he actually get round to using a Bren-gun on a living target, unlike the hero of *The Death of William Posters* who ends up with the freedom fighters in Algeria. Yet at one time or another Arthur gets away with adultery, criminal assault, and being drunk and disorderly, and his thoughts seethe with images of violence. This is true of nearly all the new work, from the most documentary and topical (e.g. Colin MacInnes's *Mr. Love and Justice*, 1960, a study of sex-racketeers and plain-clothes men) to the most sophisticated (e.g. William Golding's allegories of civilisation breaking down).

[1] *A Subject of Scandal and Concern* (1961), 47.

This outbreak of concern with violence has made it impossible to
believe any longer that, as social reconstruction goes ahead, crime
dies down along with poverty. In fact the Fifties were a time of
mounting crime, especially among young people, and as much in
Moscow, Milan, Vienna, and Berlin as in Birmingham and London.
Typical figures for crimes of violence against the person are: in
1938, by offenders aged seventeen to twenty-one, 163; in 1956,
1248; in 1958, 2084; in 1961, 3066.[1] Sociologists have shown that
these figures are misleadingly high in so far as people are now
probably readier to notify offences, the police to arrest, and
magistrates to convict (see *New Society*, May 16 1963, 16-17). But
the figures cannot be made to disappear, and in any case there are
so many other, perfectly uncriminal signs of ferment among young
people that it cannot be denied that it exists. Is not the sane way
of taking the matter to see it as, for better and for worse, the freeing
of young people from traditional bonds? All wages have risen but
the wages of workers aged fifteen to twenty-one have risen twice as
fast as those of any other section: by 1960 they were in real terms
half again as high as pre-War (Fyvel, 132). The better off you are,
the less dependent you are on your parents for board, transport,
recreation, clothes, for most of the ingredients of your life. This
freedom may hang heavy on your hands if you live in a place like
those described by Fyvel (71-2) in which six cafés, five of them
pretty dim, cater for 200,000 people. But the freedom is delightful
if you can get away with your girl on your own transport, well-
dressed and well-set-up. It is worth analysing the means by which
Sillitoe in *Saturday Night* and *The Ragman's Daughter*, and MacInnes
in *Absolute Beginners*, suggest a gaiety, style, and free-ranging capacity for experience in their youthful characters while not at all
blinking the ugliness and destructiveness of much that goes on.

The crime and the joy-rides are what go on in people's leisure
time. The new writers have been equally good at presenting people
in their working lives. Before the late Fifties it would have been
impossible to find an actor who had made his name in Shakespeare
productions speaking like this about his work (Albert Finney on
filming *Saturday Night*):

> What was marvellous for me at that stage, very exciting, was
> to work in the Raleigh factory, where certain scenes were shot.
> The reality of working the lathe, as an actor who'd just worked

[1] T. R. Fyvel, *The Insecure Offenders*, 1961 (1963 ed.), 17.

in the theatre for two years before these four, I found very exciting. When I was being photographed working at that lathe, then I could absolutely concentrate on what the character was supposed to do. There was no cheating involved, you know. On the stage it would have been made of cardboard and part of my job as an actor would have been convincing the audience that that cardboard lathe was an iron one.[1]

What fascinates Finney is not the industrial setting as such but the very style of art it imposes. He likes the authenticity of it. Since 1956 our playwrights, scriptwriters, actors, and directors have done away with the old conventional settings – the drawing-rooms full of gilt-backed chairs, the country houses with terraces and french windows – and replaced them with factory work-benches and washrooms, bed-sitters, boiler rooms, café kitchens, building sites. The human being at work is no longer written off as just a drudge, part of the blank or repulsive underside of life, unfit to be material for art.

That doesn't mean to say that daily toil is made to seem all very rich and fascinating. Here we return to the mixed suggestions in that sequence of Arthur at his capstan lathe. Much of what Sillitoe has written has been concerned with whether life is satisfying enough for those who work 'in oil and noise', 'earning your living in spite of the firm', going through routines 'without thought so that all through the day you filled your mind with vivid and more agreeable pictures than those round about'. This concern with the human effects of machine work and mass production is absolutely central to our way of life. Nothing could be more important to think out and get right. The problem is the one defined by Thomas Hodgskin in 1825 –

> There is no longer anything which we can call the natural reward of individual labour. Each labourer produces only some part of a whole, and each part, having no value or utility in itself, there is nothing on which the labourer can seize, and say: It is my product, this I will keep to myself –

and by Karl Marx in 1867:

> [Manufacture] seizes labour-power by its very roots. It converts the labourer into a crippled monstrosity, by forcing his detail dexterity at the expense of a world of productive capabilities and instincts. . . . Not only is the detail work distributed to different individuals, but the individual himself

[1] *The Listener*, August 24 1967, 239.

is made the automatic motor of a fractional operation. . . .
The knowledge, the judgement, and the will, which, though
in ever so small a degree, are practised by the independent
peasant or handicraftsman . . . these faculties are now required
only for the workshop as a whole . . . the detail-worker of today
[is] crippled by lifelong repetition of one and the same trivial
operation, and thus reduced to the mere fragment of a man.[1]

It is a restatement of these classic insights, brought up to date, that
we have in the arguments between the characters in Wesker's *The
Kitchen* and *I'm Talking About Jerusalem*, in Arthur's thoughts on the
job throughout *Saturday Night*, and (the most famous instance)
Charlie Chaplin in *Modern Times* desperately tightening nuts at the
assembly line.

In the new literature this theme merges with the theme of youthful discontent and violence because it is the young worker's sense of
being condemned to rote-work, work that *does not extend him*, in the
organisation of which he has little say, that arouses much of the
discontent. Here the work of Sillitoe (and Wesker, and Henry
Livings) is topical in the best sense: it dramatises a social need
which is always there and every now and again becomes urgent.
In the big labour dispute at Fords, Dagenham, early in the Sixties,
it turned out that what Chaplin had mimed in *Modern Times* was
still as true as ever:

> The incidents began on the Classic Trim section where our
> members were assembling the complete doorglass, channels,
> regulators and quarter vents at the rate of 35 to a shift.
> The last time the work load increased from 32 to 35 the
> members were told that if they did the 35 no further increases
> would be asked for. Then the company sought to increase the
> number of doors by four per man per shift.
> It was proposed to do this by cutting the gang on the opera-
> tion from nine men to eight without cutting the line speed.
> The gang agreed under protest to try this and a man was taken
> off on Monday, October 15.
> As eight men could not do the work previously done by nine
> they were pulled out of position down the line. . . .[2]

We can see that an understanding of exactly how people have to
work is one of the insights which our society most needs. How unfree
is the mass-production worker? could he be more free, more fulfilled
in his work, while maintaining the flow of goods that we all want?

[1] *Labour Defended Against the Claims of Capital*, 25; Marx, *Capital*, 396, 534.
[2] *What's Wrong at Fords* (Joint Ford Shop Stewards Committee, 1962), 8-9.

can the flow be maintained unless he is more free? This last is the question now being asked by experts in operational research, under the term 'work enlargement'. They are studying whether someone works better when he has more say in the conditions of employment (e.g. piece rates, speed and quality of output) and in the detailed arrangement of tools and materials. It seems that if it can be proved to managements that output falls when the worker's inner frustration is too keen, and rises when he has more personal scope in his job, it may even come about that the worker's area of freedom will be enlarged, for the sake of higher productivity.

Lacking this satisfaction, Arthur Seaton is left at the end with 'nothing but money to drag you back there every Monday morning. Well, it's a good life and a good world, all said and done, if you don't weaken'. Again Sillitoe renders mixed feelings. It is worth tracing to its source the new vein of fresh and exultant emotion which enters the novel towards its end; and it is also worth comparing the ending of the novel with the different ending which Sillitoe and the director, Karel Reisz, gave to the film. In the film Arthur is walking with Doreen in a field at the edge of town, looking down at the new housing estate where they will go to live. Doreen delights in its spruce neatness, Arthur shares her pleasure; then, after she has walked in front of him a few paces down the field, he takes a stone from the dyke and throws it towards the houses – a little gesture to himself. This is the art of a writer and director who do not want to lay down in a fixed, artificial way the perspective which they see opening out ahead. It is a mark of the modern artist that he can return us to life, at the end of his work, with a renewed sense of the mixed, contradictory, and 'unfinished' elements in our common experiences.

CHAPTER 14

Growing Points of Literature

'Literature is news that stays news.' – Ezra Pound

THE general disrespect for art, the feeling that it is an unnecessary self-indulgence on the part of a slightly deranged minority, has its good side in that it stops us from taking it for granted that art has some supreme and unquestionable right to attention or that it should blossom in privileged aloofness from daily life. In a healthy culture art should be fed by reality as a whole and feed back into it. The question is, how does this work? What sort of art is close to reality and what is debilitated by its existing at a remove from it? What is the organic chain connecting the incidents and utterances that occur naturally with the seemingly self-contained works of art that we regard as the best?

Lu Hsun, one of the master writers of this century, was able as a Chinese, living in a backward country struggling to get a footing on the threshold of the modern world, to see our age nakedly revealed, and in the teeth of the worst that Japanese fascism and native tyranny could do to his homeland, his wit and sanity held firm. In a talk on August 12 1931 he said:

> Revolutionary writing is being suppressed, and the magazines sponsored by those doing the suppressing contain no literature either. Do the oppressors really have no literature then? They have, but not here. It is contained in telegrams, decrees, news items, nationalist 'literature', court sentences and the like. A few days ago, for instance, the *Shun Pao* carried a story of a woman who accused her husband of buggering her and beating her black and blue. The court replied that there was no law forbidding a husband to bugger his wife, and although she was bruised from her beating that did not count as a physical injury, so her charge could not be accepted. Now the man is suing his wife for making a 'false charge'. I know nothing of law, but I have studied a little physiology. When the skin is black and blue, though the lungs, liver and kidneys are not necessarily impaired, physical injury is done to the place bruised. This is common enough in China

286

today—nothing out of the ordinary—yet I think this gives us a better picture of society than the average novel or long poem.[1]

This is provocatively extreme, but I think it is true. Great literature is not a sport, in the biologist's sense of a species that springs up freakishly apart from the main line of evolution. Literature evolves in society as do, say, houses, tools and political parties. Hence literature has close relatives in non-imaginative writing, and by considering them, especially where they start to evolve into literature proper, we can grasp literature more fully, just as we can understand man better by considering apes and ape-men.

Consider that any piece of literature, however fantastic, has been made in a certain time and place. It may start from a situation and get little beyond it, like 'Potatoes', a poem by James Thomson, a weaver near Edinburgh, written in 1796 (a good year for potatoes) on the subject of abundance and hoarding.[2] It may start from a situation, keep close to the facts of it, yet create from it images and types so striking that their interest is undying, as Dryden does with the disputed succession to the throne in his 'Absalom and Achitophel' or Tressell with the poorly organised state of the house-painters in his *Ragged Trousered Philanthropists*. It may re-create the situation as a 'myth' that leads out to the broadest aspects of human nature, as Shakespeare does with the divine right of kings in *Macbeth* and *King Lear*. But in every case there is a kind of intermediate work, which *has* re-created the real situation through language—e.g. the pamphlets and primitive polemics of the 1640s, which were Dryden's forerunners[3]—but has not yet 'taken off' and become a work which can inspire people even when the situation has passed away. By looking at such work, or finding the traces of it in literature proper, we can see how the writer is related to society through the agency of those media which exist simply to do a job—the news report, speech, sermon, pamphlet, money-raising turn or song, and plain commercial pop of all sorts.

This approach is dialectical in that it treats forms as they change, as they come into being or turn into something else, and it is

---

[1] 'A Glance at Shanghai Literature': *Selected Works*, III (Peking, 1959), 127-8.
[2] See Craig, *Scottish Literature and the Scottish People*, 88.
[3] With Dryden's 'The Medall', ll. 173-88, 248-301, compare polemics quoted in R. H. Tawney, *Religion and the Rise of Capitalism* (1938 ed.), 203, and in D. W. Petegorsky, *Left-wing Democracy in the English Civil War* (1940), 66 and n. 2, 67 n. 1.

materialist in that it sees art as dealing, not with eternal essences or ideal forms of life, but with the life lived in particular conditions, as all life is. Two sets of examples will show the range of the two things, the changeability of literary forms and their particularity.

Many of the best pieces of 'New Wave' drama borrow so freely from outside the theatre that they can hardly be called 'straight plays'. John Osborne is close to music-hall in *The Entertainer*. Scenes are numbered in lights at the proscenium side, like turns, and are introduced by corny patter from the comedian hero, Archie Rice, who is used both to project deflating humour at the expense of Britain's 'Great Power' complex and also to act out his own crack-up as a person. In *Luther* Osborne makes Friar Tetzel, as he sells indulgences, talk direct to the theatre audience in the vein of a hard-selling salesman today: 'There is something, and that something I have here with me now up here, letters, letters of indulgence. . . . Look at them, all properly sealed, an indulgence in every envelope, and one of them can be yours today, now, before it's too late! . . . There isn't any one sin so big that one of these letters can't remit it.'[1] The whole effect is to break the conventional pretence that the stage encloses a piece of real life on which the people in their seats are somehow eavesdropping, and by this means it comes home to us that sixteenth-century Germany was once real and alive, in its own place and time. In *The Caretaker* (Act II) Harold Pinter suggests that average talk is aimless by casting some dialogue as the patter of the radio or vaudeville comic–one can almost sense the sly sideways looks, the pauses, the appeals for laughter:

> My uncle's brother had a marvellous stop watch. Picked it up in Hong Kong. The day after they chucked him out of the Salvation Army . . . Had a funny habit of carrying his fiddle on his back. Like a papoose. I think there was a bit of the Red Indian in him. To be honest, I've never made out how he came to be my uncle's brother.[2]

In practice Pinter seems too heartless, too much the manipulator, to do more than exercise techniques for their own sakes. The point is that he is one of the many playwrights today who find as many fertile leads in the pop as in the classical forms. A whole scene of Wesker's *Chips with Everything* (scene 10) consists of a bunch of R.A.F. recruits, in perfect silence, pinching coal from a wired-up dump by

---

[1] John Osborne, *Luther* (1961), 49.
[2] Act 2 (1960 ed., 33).

some ingenious business with a pair of chairs, a pair of stools, and a pair of buckets. The effect owes much to circus clowning, yet the effect is to show people learning to combine and rebel. It also works with the unemotional exactness of a technical demonstration in a documentary, without declaiming, posturing, or explanation. Much of the action throughout the play is in fact drill or other straight military business. The effect is to remind us that this kind of workaday routine is more typical of human action than swopping epigrams over a tray of cocktails. Average and working life is seen to be as inherently dramatic as the introspective, self-analytic ways of a leisured class such as had monopolised the stage for many generations.

Those examples don't altogether transform the straight play. This has been done recently in a series of works which yet strike one as keeping in the mainstream of realism, however unlifelike their style is on the surface. In Brendan Behan's *The Hostage*, the characters explicitly stop the action for a song from time to time, and the minor characters dance or run on and off like a revue chorus. Yet this is all the vehicle for a deeply-felt moral to the effect that violence can be self-defeating politically, that (in Brecht's words)

> Hatred, even of degradation,
> Distorts the features,
> Anger, even against injustice,
> Makes the voice harsh.

At the end the English private, held by the I.R.A. in Dublin against a hostage in Belfast, gets shot–by accident. The company shrinks back horrified into the wings and a ghostly green spotlight falls on the dead soldier, who then gets up, walks down to the footlights, and sings straight to us:

> The bells of hell
> Go ting-a-ling-a-ling,
> For you but not for me.
> Oh death, where is thy sting-a-ling-a-ling?
> Or grave, thy victory?
> If you meet the undertaker
> Or the young man from the Pru,
> Get a pint with what's left over,
> Now I'll say goodbye to you,[1]

[1] 1962 ed., 108-9.

and the play ends with the whole company singing this in reprise. Behan has only taken a rough troops' song from the Great War (which itself had used a bit from *The Pilgrim's Progress*) and mixed in with it an advertising slogan and a drinker's cheerio. Yet one feels that nothing could have better summed up the play's whole-hearted sanity. Death is not negated. But life prevails.

In *The Hostage* a kind a rackety good-humour loosens up the formal drama until it falls apart, and this is precisely fitting because the aim is to mock to pieces a muscle-bound political fanaticism. (I have known an adjudicator in an amateur drama competition refuse to judge the company that did *The Hostage* on the grounds that the piece was 'not a play'.) In the Joan Littlewood-Charles Chilton *Oh What a Lovely War*, story-line, realistic sets, and charac-ters are dropped altogether, in order not to distract us from facts so dire that they almost dramatise themselves—any fictional style would have boggled at the scale and manner of the Great War slaughter. So the facts themselves, e.g. mounting casualty figures, are screened at the back, while in front a troupe of pierrots represent the combatants. Fictional individuals with names would have been too puny to stand for the millions involved. Stylised characters can seem more representative. The clash between the clown's costume (which can be adapted with a few additions to look either British or French, officer or ranker) and the terrible happenings enables the producer to swing the audience freely from irony to hilarity to horror. And the comic style gives full scope to the punchy humour which the troops did in fact use so as to cope psychologically, in the most hellish conditions—

> Phosgene and mustard gas
> Are much too much for me . . .

The parodied hymn—

> Forward Joe Soap's Army
> Marching without fear,
> With our own commander
> Safely in the rear . . .

The brilliant and typically *popular* trick of lampooning Haig's tactics (throwing unlimited forces into the attack) by seeing them as a child's game—

> The first staff officer jumped right over
> The second staff officer's back,

> The second staff officer jumped right over
> The third staff officer's back, etc.

I would say that such willingness to make free with the conventional forms is, and has constantly been, a condition not only of growth in the arts but of cultural health itself. It is a way of renewing and re-popularising the arts, which forever threaten to become bound by the culture (the language, styles, types, and assumptions) of the class in power.

This willingness to disrupt classic style is peculiarly popular in that it is always happening among performers who wouldn't count themselves as artists, who do it as they go along, for some social purpose. A. L. Lloyd has spoken of the *singing organisers* who gave American folk song a new lease of life during the desperate, militant years of American trade-unionism between the wars.[1] A man like Joe Hill (actually pre-Great War) used his banjo and his talent for rhyming as a way of getting a crowd together at a corner, as a way of drowning out the Moody and Sankey hymns that were competing for the minds of American working men, and to give them something better to think about, in a form that comes naturally to everyone–the song. No doubt he broke off singing to speak his message, argue with a heckler, and then weld the meeting together again with a song whose humour was aggressive:

> Holy Rollers and Jumpers come out
> And they jump and they holler and shout,
> But when eating time comes round they say,
> You will eat on that glorious day.

> (Chorus)
> You will eat
> By and by
> In that glorious land in the sky
> Way up high.
> Work and pray,
> Live on hay,
> You'll get pie in the sky when you die.
> (That's a lie.)[2]

In short, the mixing of forms–from argument to comedy to song– is *natural* amidst the fluctuating rhythms of a crowd, whose pulse-beat the performer must go with and control. Preaching shows this particularly well, for it was the forerunner of political agitation, the

[1] 'The Folk-song Revival': *Marxism Today* (June 1961), 170-1.
[2] 'The Preacher and the Slave': *Songs of the Wobblies* (Labor Arts LP, Detroit), side 2, band 3.

main inspirer in the days before the proletariat came of age. Consider this *strike sermon* from Loray, North Carolina, in 1929; the preacher was kneeling on an old store counter salvaged from the strikers' headquarters, which had been broken up by the boss's thugs:

> I call to God to witness who has been the violent man in this strike. But we must bear it. Paul and Silas had to go through with it, and today they sit a-singing around the great white throne. In a few days you'll be a-singing through the streets of Loray with good wages. God's a poor man's God. Jesus Christ himself was born in an old ox-barn in Bethlehem. He was kicked about, speared about and finally nailed on a cross. And for what? For sin. It's sin that's causing this trouble. Sin of the rich man, the man who thinks he's rich . . .
>
> All the wealthy men in this here crowd hold up their hands. I'll hold up mine for one. My father owns this whole world. He owns every hill in this world and every tater in them hills.[1]

Every touch is lively. The colloquial idiom makes the legend from Palestine at home in the American farming country. Confident assertions mix with snap questions, direct give-and-take with the crowd, and unexpected wisecracks in the best American vein, the tradition of Mark Twain. Compare a sermon from western Texas, which modulates into a semi-chant:

> O Lord, once more again, mm-hmm, I want to thank you, for looking after me as I slumbered 'n' slept, mm-hmm, last night, and lifted me from my bed an set me on my feet this mornin, flashin the sunlight over this broad wide land 'n' walkin' me out into it. But Lord, now I'm comin to you t'day talkin 'bout all your children down here. Somehow another sum done gone wrong. The aeroplanes is a-flyin' over the earth, a-droppin them big ole bombs down, mm-hmm. . . . Hush down the cannons from a-blowin' around earth. A-quiet the children's cryin in the morning of the world, Lord. Bring laughter again into this here world. *Lord*, a long time ago you created just one world, mm-hmm. You created just one world and it's us that's divided it up, Lord . . .[2]

This must be heard to get it fully, but each 'mm-hmm' represents a short pair of musical syllables, hummed on a note to which each sentence returns. It gives a light lilt, a buoyancy, suggesting a momentum that cannot be stopped. The whole style is beautifully

---

[1] Sermon by H. J. Crabtree, quoted from Hobsbawm, *Primitive Rebels*, 190.

[2] Sermon of Old Cooper, transcribed from 'Magnoliaville, U.S.A.', a programme on Pacifica Radio.

confident and natural, modulating from pleading to hortatory to lyrical.

The whole gamut, including comedy, can be heard in that elastic medium, the talking blues. The original seems to have started as a parody of the revivalist sermon, spoken rhythmically, dead-pan, to the jaunty picking of banjo or guitar:

> If you want to go to heaven let me tell you what to do,
> You gotta grease your feet in a little mutton stew,
> Slide out of the devil's hand
> And ooze over to the Promised Land.
> Take it easy, boy, but go greasy . . .

The performer can add verses about whatever he likes, whatever is topical–prohibition, a pit disaster, a union recruiting drive.[1] The form is just right in that it is entertaining enough to carry an audience along yet pointed and trenchant enough to heighten *morale* and consciousness. British culture seems to have been too stiffened up for some generations now to evolve any such flexible in-between form; perhaps the nearest counterpart is the vernacular 'patter' of the street singers, described by Mayhew, and still used by song-makers of Tyneside at the end of last century.[2]

That kind of thing is not deep, or even very remarkable. It is just a natural enhancing of common experiences or beliefs and common usages to a point where they verge on art–the kind of thing any thriving culture should be able to give out plentifully. We have considered various things which hover between song and poetry, speech and chant, drama and show, reportage and the imaginary, the directly useful and the artistic. Very often this changeability of the forms is related to their particularity, their closeness to a certain time and place. Brecht's theatre style hovers between unemotional demonstration and drama that involves us more personally. This means that it can absorb straight facts where necessary, e.g. Helene Weigel's playing of Mother Courage when she hears that her son Swiss-Cheese is dead:

> Her dropped jaw, mouth agape with head thrown back and eyes closed, shoulders shrugged and hands lying in the lap, is a purely physical posture that can be adopted without trace

[1] *Folk Blues*, ed. Jerry Silverman (New York, 1958), 277-8; Jack Elliott on Collector JEA 5 (1961), side 2, band 2; Pete Seeger on *Hootenanny N.Y.C.* (Topic TOP 37, 1958), side 1, band 2; *Folk Blues*, 283.

[2] *Mayhew's London*, 148-9; *Tommy Armstrong of Tyneside*, esp. 'The Skeul Board Man'.

of emotion–it is pure 'showing' and said to have been copied from a newsreel photograph–but it gripped the mind of the spectator firmly enough for sympathy to be an inevitable outcome.[1]

This is indeed the true art of an age in which (to adapt Lu Hsun) a news-cameraman's photo, if he is a Capa or a McCullin, may 'give us a better picture of society than the average novel or long poem'. The fact is so intense that it projects itself as an art image, with little further stylising. In *Sergeant Musgrave's Dance*, when Attercliffe wants to stop his sergeant staging a kind of mock reign of terror in the north-country town, he leaves his Gatling gun and squats on the ground.[2] It is a sit-down, it is what hundreds of thousands of non-violent demonstrators have done all over the world. The political act hardly needs changing to become a stage device. When the Oxford Experimental Theatre Club applied the revue technique to the subject of hanging, in *Hang Down Your Head and Die*, a key moment was the piece of absolute inaction which lasted as long as the electric shock took to kill Julius Rosenberg. The crowning instance is the scene in *Oh What a Lovely War* in which the pierrots, with *poilus'* caps on, first refuse to advance to certain massacre, then do advance with the slogan 'like lambs to the slaughter', bleating like sheep, alternating the raucous bleats with lofty slogans–'*Pour la gloire*', '*La France*'–until the staccato of the machine-guns drowns them out. On seeing or hearing this, one thinks: 'What a devastating extreme of dramatic caricature.' It turns out that it was *actually done*, by a French regiment at Craonne in May 1917.[3]

Clearly the direct resort to fact will always be only one of the many realistic devices. But it has been so recurrent in the best post-war theatre that it seems to be typical of realism in its prime, when artists are confident of their stance in the world and determined to see things as they are.

Particularity, however simple or rough, is an essential of art, for it is a sign that the artist wants his style to be a medium for experience of the world, not an end in itself or a mirror for Narcissus. It comes time after time in songs.[4] Perhaps the hallmark

[1] Ronald Gray, *Brecht* (1961), 100.
[2] John Arden, *Sergeant Musgrave's Dance* (1960), 93.
[3] See Leon Wolff, *In Flanders Field* (1961 ed.), 85.
[4] Some of the following examples may not seem much on the printed page. They were all made up for singing and are mere skeletons without their tunes.

of them, whether industrial or country, recent or early, is the way they find what seems the quintessential image for a feeling or situation. They make us say: 'That's just it.' The love-songs, for example, have no fear that a humdrum detail will let the wind out of a grand passion. The part of 'The Butcher o' Crieff' which Jeannie Robertson of Aberdeen sings as 'My Plaidie's Awa' begins:

> There wis a bonny lassie
> And she wis gaun tae Crieff.
> She met in wi a butcher laddie
> And he wis sellin beef . . .

Naming the meat doesn't at all take away from the exhilaration that seems to blow through the song, with its melody that floats up high:

> O I canna say the wind blew
> My plaidie awa.[1]

In fact the homely actual detail intensifies the passion because it presents it as it is, in the conditions in which it has to be lived out. A Cumberland song, collected from a Workington miner in 1951, has this perfect detail for the collier's sweetheart who loses her lover to the recruiting sergeant:

> As I walked over the stubble field,
> Below it runs the seam.
> I though of Jimmy hewin there
> But it was all a dream.
> He hewed the very coals we burn,
> And when the fire I'se leetin,
> To think the lumps was in his hands,
> It sets my heart to beatin.[2]

The nearer the song gets to the workaday and supposedly 'un-poetic', the intenser is the feeling in the poetry; a complete image of a life, its routine shot through with emotions, has been created. And the style is the opposite of either romantic art-poem or pop song, which depend on whipping up a heady illusion of strong feeling in an atmosphere emptied of the circumstances in which we necessarily have our experiences.[3]

[1] *Jeannie Robertson* (Topic 10T52, 1959), side 1, band 3.
[2] 'Jimmy's Enlisted or the Recruited Collier': *Come All Ye Bold Miners*, 43; sung on *The Iron Muse*, side 1, band 3. The song is by Robert Anderson and was written on April 19 1803; first published as 'Jenny's Complaint' in his *Ballads in the Cumberland Dialect* (1805). The words have changed over the years: originally Jimmy was a farm worker who had ploughed the field and carted the coals.
[3] See above, ch. 1, 35.

The songs made by people for themselves constantly hit upon such detail because they express a way of life in which conditions bear down so hard or press so close that they must come out. A song collected in High Heworth, Co. Durham, in 1920:

> When I was young I used to sport and play,
> But now I'm married and the cradle's in the way . . .

A song got recently from an east coast barge skipper:

> When I was single I wore a black shawl.
> Now that I'm married I've nothing at all . . .

A song brought back by the Irish navvies from America in the railway age and collected since the war in Hellifield, Yorkshire, and Birkenhead:

> In Eighteen hundred and forty-one
> Me cord'roy breeches I put on,
> Me cord'roy breeches I put on,
> To work upon the railway . . .[1]

Such details are so quick that one doesn't normally ponder them; but one can work out that what makes the corduroy breeches so 'right' an image is the quick shift from the date, a whole year, to the plain personal item. In a flash it gives us a whole generation of workers or the whole experience of signing on for a new job, just as some lines from 'Muleskinners' epitomise the take-it-or-leave-it attitude with which the unskilled worker is given a job:

> Hey, little water-boy, won't you bring that water around?
> Hey, little water-boy, bring that water around.
> If you don't like your job, lay that water-bucket down.[2]

The bucket, the breeches, the shawl, the cradle, ordinary though they are, manage to become symbols. They seem, not single objects, but foci of whole areas of experience. That is one reason why folk songs are so good at bringing to mind the life of generation after generation.

Comparison with art-poems makes this still clearer (of course there are things classic poetry can do that folk-songs can't, but the reverse is true too and is more often played down). Between 1792 and 1805 or so, Wordsworth repeatedly wrote poems, in ballad

---

[1] *The Penguin Book of English Folk Songs*, ed. R. Vaughan Williams and A. L. Lloyd (1959), 102; *Still I Love Him* (Topic 10T50, 1958), side 2, band 4; *Shuttle and Cage*, side 2, band 5.

[2] Sung by Jack Elliott, Collector JEA 5, side 1, band 1.

style and blank verse, about hard cases–deserted village girls, destitute war veterans, shepherds whose sons had gone to the bad in town, and so on. It is an important body of work in that new vein of concern for the human condition which emerged in the Radical era. Unfortunately Wordsworth is forever watering down the effect, and letting an enfeebling piteousness creep in, by being too vague about the causes of the suffering. By 1800 or so his sufferers just are like that, crippled or deserted, for no given cause, as though the aim were almost to create an opening for surplus compassion. It has been noticed that the habit grew as Wordsworth became less inclined to admit injustice in the social system and even came to *justify* poverty–as a stimulus to benevolence.[1] With that compare the Cumberland song already quoted (a product of Wordsworth's own time and region), which glosses over neither the causes nor the pain of the distress and does not play down the passions involved, as Wordsworth does to keep his moral lessons unexceptionable, or, again, the following song from Arkansas in the 1850s, which was sung by an actual vagrant, to get money:

> I lost my eyes in the blacksmith's shop
> In the year of fifty-six,
> While dusting out a T-planch
> Which was out of fix.
> It bounded from the tongs
> And there concealed my doom.
> I am a blind fiddler
> And far from my home.[2]

No conventional fear of the 'unpoetic' or 'inartistic' deters the singer from going into the technical details, just as no fear of naivety deters the Scottish singer from naming individuals in a pit disaster ballad collected at Markinch, Fife, in 1951:

On the twenty-sixth of August, our fatal moss gave way.
Although we tried our level best its course we could not stay.
Ten precious lives there were at stake. 'Who'll save them?' was
the cry.
'We'll bring them to the surface or along with them we'll die.'

There was Rattery, McDonald, Hynd and Paterson.
Too well they knew the danger and the risk they had to
run . . .[3]

[1] See F. M. Todd, *Politics and the Poet* (1957), 78, 89, 131, 148, 164, 173, etc.
[2] Pete Seeger, *American Industrial Ballads*, side 1, band 2.
[3] *Come All Ye Bold Miners*, 79; sung on *The Iron Muse*, side 1, band 6.

The four men are named again in the last verse, and one feels that there could scarcely be a more poignant elegiac touch than this literal, plodding repetition.

This down-to-earth quality, flinching from nothing, is the opposite of the usual art-poetry, of which two very general things can be said: it tends to idealise; and it is written by and for the middle and upper classes. *Euphemism* is forever threatening to congeal the language of literature, and one of the worst types, the Augustan poetic diction by whose standards Shakespeare was faulted for mentioning lowly things like a knife and a blanket at a high moment in *Macbeth*, can be shown to have originated in the desire of the new middle class, after the Restoration in 1660, to gild the sources of their wealth.[1] Since the simultaneous rise of the novel and of the town reading-public, the middle class has been the dominant section of readers, and they are specially prone to shy away from life rendered as it is, having neither the unworried lordliness of the upper class nor the bluntness of the working man.[2]

The principle implicit here is that class position determines the idiom or style of art. Class position itself, as Marxism defines it, varies according to people's relation to the means of production, whether they live only on the sale of their labour-power or partly on the surplus-value made by the work of others. There is great variety, of course, inside the class of wage-workers, but the majority tend to be close to production itself. The worker has to cope with the stubbornness of materials. He cannot escape into the less solid realm of words, concepts, figures, or any of the other *renderings* of reality, at one or more removes, in which the intellectual, the politician, and the business director, for example, spend much of their time. A cheque or a balance-sheet are, of course, realities too, of paper and ink, but they are *dependent* on the original productive activity, they are *secondary*. If the wheel will not turn or the edge not cut, it cannot be made to, the result cannot be got, by any merely logical device. As reality is material, the worker in materials is close to reality. Here is a source of the particularity, the 'facty' quality, typical of the songs. This doesn't at all mean that a workman has only to open his mouth to utter a vernacular masterpiece.

---

[1] Clearly this needs detailed argument; the line I have in mind runs from Dryden's 'Annus Mirabilis' through Addison's *Spectator*, esp. No. 69, to such poems as James Thomson's immensely fashionable *The Seasons* (1726-30) and John Dyer's *The Fleece* (1757). [2] See above, ch. 1, 34.

It does mean that there is a key quality of art–particularity–which is inherent or potential in work itself.

It is not only the facts about working processes and conditions that can be particularised; it is also class position and the values that grow from it. Again and again a working-class singer uses the details of his trade, the simple naming of it, the materials, the work-place, as a kind of declaration of where he stands, as in a recent Dundee jute-mill song:

> Ma mither died when I was young, ma feyther fell in France.
> I'd like tae been a teacher but I never got the chance.
> I'll soon be gettin married tae a lad they ca Tam Hill,
> And he is an iler intae Halley's Mill.[1]

A middle-class lyric (or a commercial one) would be quite different: the bourgeois would not demean himself by speaking as though he could be summed up by where he worked or what he did, it would infringe too much on his individuality, whereas that song, by naming the work-place and the job, impressively suggests a solid hold on reality. This is common in the colliers' songs, where the marks of the trade are even flaunted to affront the genteel:

> The collier has a dochter,
> I vow she's wondrous pretty;
> The collier has a dochter,
> She's black, but, O, she's witty!
> He shawed her gowd in gowpins
> But she answered him fu' ready:
> 'The lad I love works underground,
> The colour o my daddie.'[2]

gowpins, *handfuls*

Dickens, the great adapter of popular styles, made precisely that clash between euphemism and particularity the hinge of one of his finest comic scenes–the interview between Dombey and Toodle in *Dombey and Son* (ch. 2). The wealthy business man is trying to find out if the labourer is decent enough for his wife to be chosen as little Dombey's wet-nurse:

> 'Can you read?' asked Mr. Dombey.
> 'Why, not partick'ler, sir.'

[1] *The Iron Muse*, side 2, band 7.
[2] 'The Collier's Bonnie Lassie': *The Shuttle and Cage*, ed. Ewan MacColl, 24. In the version first printed for the reading public in 1724, the details of work were censored and euphemisms substituted: see Robert Chambers, *The Scottish Songs*, 530-1 and n.

'Write?'

'With chalk, sir?'

'With anything?'

'I could make shift to chalk a little bit, I think, if I was put to it,' said Toodle, after some reflection . . .

'Where have you worked all your life?'

'Mostly underground, sir, till I got married. I come to the level then. I'm a-going on one of these here railroads when they comes into full play.'

The advantage should have been all with Dombey. In fact Toodle has routed him, by the simplest factual replies regarding his own abilities and place of work. Satire and pure comedy blend here: the comic vision of Toodle, impelled by the mysterious power of marriage to pop up on to the surface, also makes of him a moral hero, too simple (in a good sense) to be overfaced by matters of status.

This example has taken us from folk song to 'real literature'. A remarkable number of the master writers for some generations past have excelled in a sheer cleaving to fact. Much of Tolstoy's method is simply to present life in full detail, so that, quite implicitly, the falsifying conventions and assumptions melt away. This is as true of his 'pure' realism—as in *Anna Karénina*—as in his work with a vein of social criticism, for example *The Death of Iván Ilých* and *Resurrection*. In Gorky's autobiographies, the work in which he found his own style amidst the various florid and tendentious ones that so often spoiled him, we seem to be following not so much words as life itself, jagged, unexpected, motley, natural—fruitful and wasteful at once. *Childhood*, *My Apprenticeship*, and *My Universities* bring home to us the amazing range of life that covers the earth and bring home with a minimum of loading or pleading, with little but straight presentation, that it matters. People, we are made to feel, jolt against each other, injure or inspire each other, *like that*. Again, to take another work from the heyday of naturalism, much of Robert Tressell's *Ragged Trousered Philanthropists* seems at first 'unimaginative'—so much sober documentary; yet from this a most original and mordant irony arises:

. . . when the workers arrived in the morning they wished it was breakfast-time. When they resumed work after breakfast they wished it was dinner-time. After dinner they wished it was one o'clock on Saturday.

So they went on, day after day, year after year, wishing their time was over and, without realising it, really wishing they were dead.[1]

Each sentence by itself seems just matter-of-fact yet taken together their effect is piercing, and so weighted that it is more than satirical.

Even the great oddities of modern writing–Pound's *Cantos*, Joyce's *Ulysses* and *Finnegans Wake*–show the overweening modern regard for facts turned to artistic ends. Altogether it is as though various essentials of life today–physical science, accurate observation of many kinds, the social survey, the peculiarly wide-awake attitude of the town working-man–have come together to form what may be called the style of our culture. In literature it can be illustrated by two quite different and perfectly original works both of which take the standard question as put in the social survey, or the stock response to a 'sales' offer on the street, and transmute it into the mainspring of a new style. In 'Leaflets' Adrian Mitchell presents a series of acutely observed reactions in a seemingly unshaped list:

> Outside the plasma supermarket
> I stretch out my arm to the shoppers and say:
> 'Can I give you one of these?' . . .
> The first shopper thanks me.
> The second puts the leaf in his mack pocket where his wife
>   won't see. . . .
> The fourth says: 'Is it art?' I say that it is a leaf. . . .
> The eighth complains that it is an oak leaf and says he would
>   be on my side if I were also handing out birch leaves, apple
>   leaves, privet leaves and larch leaves. I say that it is a
>   leaf. . . .

After listing ten typical responses, the documentary idiom unexpectedly blossoms into a luxuriant image that ends the poem on a breath of pure naturalness:

> But you took your leaf like a kiss.

> They tell me that, on Saturdays,
> You can be seen in your own city centre,
> Giving away forests, orchards, jungles.[2]

Again in the radio ballad *Song of a Road* by Charles Parker (producer), Ewan MacColl (songs), and Peggy Seeger (musical arrangement), it is the interviewer's question that makes the backbone of the fine six- or seven-minute sequence in which workers on the

---

[1] Ch. 7 (1955 ed., 97).   [2] *Out Loud* (1968), poem 51.

London-Yorkshire motorway say what brought them to the work and how they find it. The musical part, written out, would look like a song with a verse made up of a line twice repeated, on a rising note, plus a refrain line. As we hear it, the repeated line, which is sung, takes the form of an interviewer's question: 'What made you come into this game?' Each time there comes an actual reply, recorded on the motorway site with the throb and rattle of bulldozers and Euclid dumpers audible behind the voices. A man with an accent from Belfast or Glasgow or Newcastle or the south-east tells us why he took the work: 'To get outside, to get mud on me boots.' 'What made you come into this game?'–'Change of faces, change of places!' 'Conditions of work–not sufficient work in the London area, not for builders.' 'There's no work in Peter-head. I used to be travellin' the fishin', workin' among the herrin'. Then the steam drifters went out, diesel came in–they didn't need half the men.' Then the refrain: 'And take to the open road.' The singer's voice lilts its enquiry, deep and casual: 'How long you bin doin' this, mate?'–'I've been married twenty-one year an' I've been away from home twenty-one year, workin' . . .' 'How do you like the job, mate?'–'I like it fine.' 'Nothing to shout about.' 'What are the beds like, matey?'–'Humps an' hollas. Bejabers, it was like a camel's back. Me arse was all blisthers an' carribuncles.' The quiet twang of the guitar, the deep voice sounding, knits it all into musical shape. Yet the song seems to be reaching us out of the hubbub and coming and going of the work site. It is as though we had at the same time the raw material and the finished art. The interviewer with his portable tape-recorder must have put his question to dozens of men: 'What started you on this work?' Back in the studio with the tapes (up to eighty hours of sound for a single radio ballad) the composers, MacColl and Seeger, have picked out actual sentences and made them over into song-lines. The result is a form that gets closer than anything before into the experiences, feelings, conditions of people at work.

Such a form results from trusting the material of life to have in it not only the data but the style needed for creative use.[1] It is the same respect for working life and the articulacy of people involved

[1] Parker says in 'The Radio Ballad' (*New Society* 14.11.1963) that this realisa-tion of the quality of actual speech came to them as they made the first ballad, *John Axon*. They were going to script it, but the language of the railwaymen at the Newton Heath loco shed in Manchester was so good that they scrapped the written prose entirely.

in it that Brecht felt strongly and made use of in all those productions which forsook complete stage-illusion and insisted on the
actuality of the themes, the actors, and the very props, without
emptying the dramatic experience of its richness. As Brecht puts it
in his poem on his wife's acting:

> Impossible to mistake
> The working-woman's much-used bag
> Crammed with her son's leaflets
> For the one that is filled with the change. . . .
> Everything is chosen
> According to age
> Uses
> And beauty
> By knowing eyes and her
> Net-making bread-baking
> Soup-cooking hands
> At home with reality.[1]

The last phrase has a special value for me because it coincides,
fittingly, with a sentence of Engels's that gives the heart of materialism. Discussing working people's attitude to religion in Manchester
in the early 1840s, he writes: 'Practically he lives for this world, and
strives to make himself at home in it.'[2] Here is the motto for
mankind today.

Clearly my emphasis on the 'facty' and closely lifelike is at odds
with a great deal of what is now most in favour. 'Appearance and
reality' (implying that it is hard to tell which is which), Yeats's
theory of masks, 'the unknowable', 'the problem of identity',
dreams, the absurd, the meaningless, the serious content of
nonsense—here is a predominant body of notions in the literary
culture just now. Clearly it is right to acknowledge how potent the
sub-rational is, what havoc it can wreak in a society or a personality,
for ours is the only age in which a group of psychopaths have
geared a whole nation to their obsessions and so dragged the entire
world into war. But attending mainly to the sub-rational is like
ignoring the decisive political and economic causes which, in
Germany from the 1870s onwards, brought about the situation in
which psychopaths could come to power.[3]

[1] Weigel's Props': Brecht, *Poems on the Theatre*, trans. John Berger and Anna
Bostock (1961), 22.

[2] Marx and Engels, *On Britain*, 158-9.

[3] This side-tracking onto the unduly psychological explaining of social events
can be seen in W. H. Auden's changing attitude to the European smash-up, from
'A Summer Night, 1933' to 'Spain, 1937' to 'September 1, 1939'.

This cult of the sub-rational is always close at hand, threatening to twist our view of art. A revealing example is the section on the art of early man in a recent popular book on anthropology–edited, written, and produced in that stronghold of religion, the Federal Republic of Germany. The author is bent on exalting the sub-rational as the main creative part of man and on blurring the links between actual objects and the subject-matter of art. One caption to plates of drawings on bone from the Dordogne reads: 'Representations of dreams, zone of the unreal'. Yet the drawings seem plainly to be likenesses of people in animal masks and pelts doing totemistic dances, which very likely were the origin of mime, dance, and song, and therefore a key subject for art. Another caption says: 'Representations of the imaginary and dreamlike'. Yet the bone drawing looks very like a series of doodles of real objects–a bison's head, spine, and forelegs and some simplified human figures. We know that early man could draw animals with great skill but rarely troubled to draw people or else produced something rough and sketchy. Schenk knows this but he cannot explain it. He can only rhapsodise: 'Behind the ambience of late Palaeolithic men a thousand invisible forces acted in which a long departed past formed an indissoluble entity with the present and expected future', soon to be withered by 'The cold overpowering of nature'.[1] Yet sixty years ago Plekhanov was able to explain the excellence at art of hunting peoples and the feebleness at it of grain-growers, with a wealth of evidence from many cultures, in terms of the different skills each needed to produce the means of life. In order to raise their morale and enhance their powers for the hunt, men took imaginative possession of the animals by drawing (and occasionally modelling) them. To be efficient in marksmanship, skinning, and dismembering, they needed to know the bodies of the animals very well. And the skills of co-ordination and manual dexterity vital to a spear-thrower or a bowman were precisely those of the draughtsman and sculptor.[2]

It is in keeping that Schenk should rejoice in the 'wonderful symbols and abstractions' done by Cromagnon man without being able to produce more than one possible abstraction amidst a wealth of primitive realism, and in the teeth of the proofs of Plekhanov and others that 'designs which have the appearance of geometrical

[1] Gustav Schenk, *The History of Man* (1961), 140-1, 154, 157.
[2] *Unaddressed Letters and Art and Social Life* (Moscow, 1957 ed.), 136-46.

figures are actually abbreviated or stylised representations of quite definite objects, mostly animals'.[1] The obscurantist bias of Schenk is plain; earlier he says that the discovery of the Old Stone Age cave paintings 'shattered the overweening self-assurance of the people of our times', shut out as we are from the rich inner world by our 'rational, logical line of thought in a technical-mechanical civilisation' (p. 135). This is very like the ex-Bishop of Woolwich quoting Paul Tillich to the effect that for atheists life is bound to seem shallow, devoid of depths,[2] as though the material and especially the organic world, of which we are part, were not so rich that we can plumb it endlessly, with no need of supernatural fantasies to eke out the 'limitations' of materiality.

This pointer to the obscurantist notions that hover round abstract art completes my argument. At present there is little sign that abstraction has begun to retreat out of its dead-end. The jet-black and plain-white 'pictures' go on exciting the critics in London, New York, Venice, variegated by the arbitrary novelties of pop art. In an essay called 'Beyond Bond Street', suggested by a local amateur art exhibition, John Berger sets out the range of ideas that we need as a standard in our culture, where the highbrow and the pop have both run to such destructive extremes:

> Some enjoy the abstraction of stereotyped glamour: others the glamour of abstraction. You can daydream with pin-ups or–to use Malevich's phrase–you can daydream in 'the desert of non-objective feeling'.[3]

That last phrase is a key one, and applies as well to literature–e.g. Beckett's monotonous later experiments–as to the abstract painters. I am not suggesting that the sort of work indicated by my stress on the vernacular, local, factual, and closely lifelike is the only way out of the desert of non-objective feeling. But it does serve to show how literature is rooted in this world in which we strive to make ourselves at home.

[1] The reader who doubts this point should search through the illustrations of Old Stone Age art in such books as Herbert Kühn's *Rock Pictures of Europe* (1956, 1966) or Ucko and Rosenfeld's *Palaeolithic Cave Art* (1967) and see how many abstract designs they can find from that age.
[2] John A. T. Robinson, *Honest to God* (1963), 22.
[3] John Berger, *Permanent Red* (1960), 57.

Index

307